Carol McKinney
H-1

MOZAMBIQUE

PROFILES • NATIONS OF CONTEMPORARY AFRICA
Larry Bowman, Series Editor

Also of Interest

MOZAMBIQUE

From Colonialism to Revolution, 1900–1982

Allen Isaacman and Barbara Isaacman

Westview Press • Boulder, Colorado

Gower • Hampshire, England

Profiles / Nations of Contemporary Africa

Published in 1983 in the United States of America by
  Westview Press, Inc.
  5500 Central Avenue
  Boulder, Colorado 80301
  Frederick A. Praeger, President and Publisher

Published in 1983 in Great Britain by
  Gower Publishing Company Limited
  Gower House, Croft Road
  Aldershot, Hampshire GU11 3HR, England

Library of Congress Cataloging in Publication Data
Isaacman, Allen F.
  Mozambique: from colonialism to revolution, 1900–1982.
  (Profiles. Nations of contemporary Africa)
  Bibliography: p.
  Includes index.
  1. Mozambique—History—1891–1975. 2. Mozambique—1975– . I. Isaacman, Barbara. II. Title. III. Series.
DT463.I82 1983   967′.903   83-14683
ISBN 0-86531-210-9
ISBN 0-86531-211-7 (pbk.)

British Library Cataloguing in Publication Data
Isaacman, Allen
  Mozambique: from colonialism to revolution 1900–1982.
  1. Mozambique—History
  I. Title II. Isaacman, Barbara
  967′.9   DT459
ISBN 0-566-00548-4

Printed and bound in the United States of America

For our children, Geoffrey and Erik,
and for all Mozambican children, the nation's *continuadores*

Contents

Illustrations

Figures

Acknowledgments

Many friends and colleagues devoted a great deal of time and effort to reading initial drafts of this book. We would like to express our gratitude to Edward Alpers, Gerald Bender, Harry Boyte, Larry Bowman, Iain Christie, Alves Gomes, Steven Feiermen, William Minter, Adam Schesch, Charles Pike, Tony Rosenthal, and John Stuart for their penetrating criticisms. We also want to thank Aquino de Bragança, Joseph Hanlon, Barry Munslow, John Saul, and Roberta Washington, from whom we have learned a great deal about contemporary Mozambique, and Ricardo Rangel, whose photographs grace this book. To our many informants and interpreters, who shared with us their experiences, both past and present, our profound thanks. We hope that this book in some small measure will capture the suffering they and their ancestors endured, as well as their struggle for social justice and dignity, and be useful for future generations of Mozambicans. It is to them, the *continuadores*, as well as to our sons, Geoffrey and Erik, who have understandingly accepted our long absences, that we dedicate this book.

This study was funded in part by the Graduate School and the Office of International Programs at the University of Minnesota and was subsidized by Susan Isaacman and Jens Beck, who served as surrogate parents during our research trips to Mozambique.

A final thanks to Sue Cave and Carley Murray, who patiently typed the many versions of our manuscript.

Allen Isaacman
Barbara Isaacman
Minneapolis, Minnesota
November 10, 1982

The capital, Maputo—formerly known as Lourenço Marques (Credit: *Notícias*)

1

Introduction

Straddling the Indian Ocean and the volatile world of racially divided Southern Africa, Mozambique has assumed an increasingly strategic international position. Its 2,000-mile (3,200-kilometer) coastline and three major ports of Maputo, Beira, and Nacala—all ideally suited for naval bases—have long been coveted by the superpowers (see Figure 1.1). These ports, from which a great power could interdict, or at least disrupt, Indian Ocean commerce and alter the balance of power in Southern Africa, also offer international gateways to the landlocked countries of the region. Through them Zimbabwe, Zambia, Botswana, Swaziland, and Malawi can reduce their economic dependence on South Africa.

No less important is Mozambique's proximity to South Africa and Zimbabwe (formerly Rhodesia), which gained its independence in 1980 with substantial military and strategic assistance from Mozambique. A progressive regime in Mozambique provides inspiration to the 20 million oppressed South Africans as well as support to the African National Congress (ANC), which is leading the liberation struggle. As the spirit of insurgency spreads within South Africa, the region may well become a zone of international conflict in which Mozambique would figure prominently.

The young nation's strategic importance, however, transcends its geographic position. Mozambique, according to Western analysts, has enormous mineral potential.[1] The world's largest reserve of columbotantalite—used to make nuclear reactors and aircraft and missile parts—is located in Zambezia Province, and the country is the second most important producer of beryl, another highly desired strategic mineral. The country's coal—10 million tons will be produced annually by 1987—has also attracted the attention of such energy-starved countries as Italy, France, Japan, and East Germany. The Cahora Bassa Dam,[2] the largest in Africa, has the potential to meet much of the energy needs of Central and Southern Africa. Large natural gas deposits and the increasing likelihood of offshore oil enhance Mozambique's role as an energy producer.

The goal of the Front for the Liberation of Mozambique (FRELIMO), the country's liberation movement and governing party, to create "Socialism with a Mozambican Face" and to break out of the spiral of impoverishment and underdevelopment carries important ideological implications for the continent as a whole. Whereas most African nationalist movements were

1

FIGURE 1.1 Mozambique, 1982

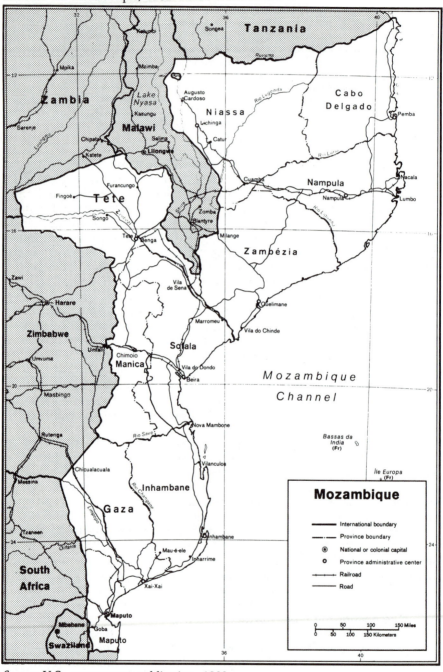

Source: U.S. government publication, 1982.

content to capture the colonial state, FRELIMO's ten-year armed struggle radicalized it. Political independence became only the first step in the larger struggle to transform basic economic and social relations.

"Socialism with a Mozambican Face," as expressed by FRELIMO, is not a variant of the vaguely defined form of African socialism that was in vogue in the late 1960s. Nor is it an Eastern European model transplanted onto Mozambican soil. To Mozambican leaders it means a synthesis of the concrete experiences and lessons of the armed struggle—experimentation, self-criticism, self-reliance, peasant mobilization, and the development of popularly based political institutions—and the contemporary Mozambican reality with the broad organizing principles of Marxism-Leninism. Listen to Mozambique's President Samora Machel:

> Marxism-Leninism did not appear in our country as an imported product. Mark this well, we want to combat this idea. Is it a policy foreign to our country? Is it an imported product or merely the result of reading the classics? No. Our party is not a study group of scientists specializing in the reading and interpretation of Marx, Engels and Lenin.
>
> Our struggle, the class struggle of our working people, their experiences of suffering enabled them to assume and internalize the fundamentals of scientific socialism. . . . In the process of the struggle we synthesized our experiences and heightened our theoretical knowledge. . . . We think that, in the final analysis, this has been the experience of every socialist revolution.[3]

Mozambique's social experiment also merits critical attention because of its highly visible campaign against tribalism and racism. In a continent marred by ethnic, religious, and regional conflict, the intensity with which the Mozambican government is combating these divisive tendencies is unprecedented. It is no easy task. Mozambique's population—12 million in 1980[4]—is divided into more than a dozen distinct ethnic groups (see Figure 1.2 and Table 1.1). Although they have some common cultural and historical experiences, each has its own language, material conditions, identity, and heritage. The patrilineal, polytheist Shona of central Mozambique have little in common either with the matrilineal, Islamized Yao and Makua to the north or with the Shangaan to the south, whose ancestors migrated from South Africa only a century ago. Historical rivalries, fanned by the Portuguese colonial strategy of divide-and-rule, heightened particularistic tendencies. FRELIMO is also committed to the creation of a nonracial society in which the 20,000 whites and somewhat larger number of Asians enjoy the full rights of Mozambican citizenship. Although impressed with the government's vigor in attacking racism, skeptics, both black and white, question whether Machel's policies are not naively attempting to jump over history.

Despite its uniqueness, Mozambique shares with other African nations the host of problems associated with underdevelopment. These include the lack of transforming industries and skilled workers, a staggering level of illiteracy—more than 95 percent at the time of independence[5]—the widespread incidence of debilitating diseases, a high infant mortality rate, and the absence of internal transportation and communications networks.

4

FIGURE 1.2 Ethnic Groups in Mozambique

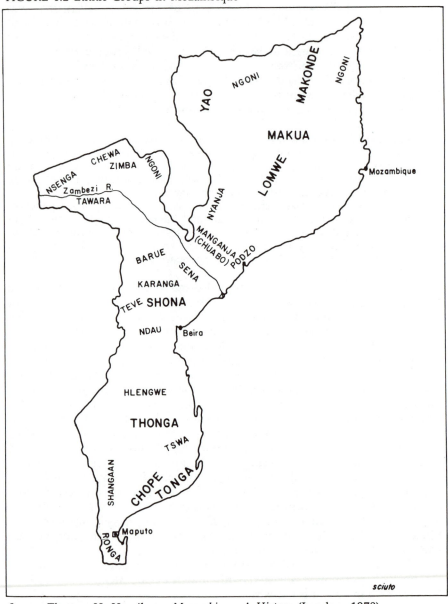

Source: Thomas H. Henriksen, *Mozambique: A History* (London, 1978).

TABLE 1.1
Population, 1980 and 1981

Province	Area (sq km)	August 1, 1980			December 31, 1981 (estimated)			Population Density (per sq km)
		Men	Women	Total	Men	Women	Total	
Niassa	129,056	246,300	267,800	514,100	256,152	278,512	534,664	4.1
Cabo Delgado	82,625	445,300	494,700	940,000	463,112	514,488	977,600	11.8
Nampula	81,606	1,189,200	1,213,500	2,402,700	1,236,768	1,262,040	2,498,808	30.6
Zambezia	105,008	1,224,600	1,275,600	2,500,200	1,273,584	1,326,624	2,600,208	24.8
Tete	100,724	393,100	437,400	831,000	408,824	454,896	864,240	8.6
Manica	61,661	307,200	334,000	641,200	319,488	347,360	666,848	10.8
Sofala	68,018	535,200	530,000	1,065,200	556,608	551,200	1,107,808	16.3
Inhambane	68,615	458,100	539,500	997,600	476,424	561,080	1,037,504	15.1
Gaza	75,709	469,300	521,600	990,900	488,072	524,464	1,030,536	13.6
Province of Maputo	25,756	235,700	256,100	491,800	245,128	266,344	511,472	19.6
City of Maputo	602	404,000	351,300	755,300	420,160	365,352	785,512	1,304.8
Total	799,380	5,908,500	6,221,500	12,130,000	6,144,480	6,470,360	13,615,200	15.8

Source: Comissão Nacional do Plano, Moçambique: Informação Estatística 1980/81 (Maputo, 1982), p. 290.

Faces (Credits: Ricardo Rangel; Mozambique Ministry of Information)

In 1978 the per capita gross national product (GNP) was estimated at $140, the lowest in all of Southern Africa.[6] And although the terrain is fertile, only 10 percent of the land is under cultivation and food shortages pose a recurring problem.

To understand the enormous economic, social, and political difficulties the young nation faces requires an examination of the precolonial and colonial periods. Impoverishment and inequality, rooted at least as far back as the sixteenth century, dramatically increased as a direct consequence of the imposition of colonial-capitalism during the early years of this century. Yet if underdevelopment, oppression, and mass deprivation constitute recurring themes in Mozambican history, so, too, does the long tradition of resistance—a tradition that dates back to the arrival of Portuguese merchants, settlers, and missionaries in the sixteenth century.

We have attempted to focus our study on the changing and complex Mozambican reality and to avoid depicting the colonized people as passive victims. Nevertheless, it must be emphasized that events outside Mozambique increasingly narrowed the range of local choices; and as the country became progressively incorporated in the world capitalist economy and the Portuguese imperial network, all ethnic groups and indigenous social classes correspondingly lost their autonomy. Their future became inextricably bound to shifting international realities. The demand for slaves, the discovery of gold in South Africa and the need for migrant Mozambican labor, changing commodity prices on the world market, and North Atlantic Treaty Organization (NATO) military support for the Portuguese colonial regime in its war against FRELIMO all helped to shape the course of Mozambican history.

Throughout the book we have sought to weave these external factors into our broader discussion of the changing Mozambican reality. Chapter 2 focuses on the patterns of interaction among different social groups, the process by which Mozambique became incorporated into the world economy, and the efforts of various Mozambican societies and social classes within them to maintain their autonomy in the face of Portuguese imperialism. It is followed by a discussion in Chapter 3 of Portuguese rule, which highlights the various, and at times contradictory, strategies the colonial state used to extract Mozambique's human and natural resources and the social cost the Mozambicans paid. But the people of Mozambique—peasants and workers, old and young, women and men—were more than merely victims of oppression and objects of derision. In a variety of ways, discussed in Chapter 4, they asserted their dignity and struggled to limit colonial exploitation. Ultimately, this spirit of insurgency, coupled with Portugal's intransigence, convinced a number of dissidents that only through armed struggle could independence be gained. Chapter 5 examines this struggle, the radicalization of FRELIMO, and the attempts of Lisbon and its NATO allies to maintain Portuguese hegemony. Having captured the colonial state, FRELIMO faced the more difficult task of creating a nation and a new socialist political system. Chapter 6 treats, in a necessarily tentative way, the problems FRELIMO has confronted in the political arena and the degree to which it has managed to overcome them. The subsequent chapter examines FRELIMO's efforts to set in motion an economic transformation based on broad socialist principles and the serious difficulties that have frustrated many of its programs. The final chapter outlines the new nation's efforts to pursue an independent foreign policy in an increasingly hostile international environment.

Given the book's broad scope, we have tried to organize it to meet the needs of a variety of readers. The discussion, drawn from oral interviews as well as written primary and secondary sources, is pitched at a fairly high level of generalization to make it easily intelligible to readers who have little familiarity with Mozambique. Names and acronyms that recur regularly appear in a glossary and list of abbreviations at the end of the book. The notes contain some long explications and extensive citations for those students and researchers who wish more information on points of particular interest, and we also recommend a small number of books and dissertations in English for those who wish to delve further into various aspects of Mozambican history. Because economic issues are likely to determine the future success or failure of the Mozambican revolution, we have included in an appendix the *Economic and Social Directives* of the Fourth Party Congress of FRELIMO (April 1983), which we obtained just as this book went to press.

2

The Precolonial Period,
1500–1880

Two major revolutions shaped the broad sweep of Mozambican history during this period. Internally, the accelerated process of state formation transformed the political map. Whereas at the beginning of this period most societies were organized into relatively small chieftaincies, by the nineteenth century large states dominated the Mozambican landscape. With these states came increased specialization and social inequality. At the same time, the maritime revolution intensified Mozambique's ties to the wider world. The arrival of successive groups of Swahili, Portuguese, and Indian merchants in search of ivory and slaves marked the beginning of the region's incorporation into the world economy—a process that profoundly distorted the country's economic base and ultimately gave rise to a number of predatory slave-raiding states. Portugal's imperial ambitions, however, extended beyond mere commerce. From the sixteenth century onward, Lisbon periodically attempted to impose its political hegemony. Time and again the indigenous societies blunted Portuguese military advances. Not until the beginning of the twentieth century did Portugal finally prevail, but only after thirty years of overcoming stiff local resistance.

MOZAMBIQUE, 1500–1850

Many centuries before the arrival of the Portuguese in 1498 successive groups of Bantu-speaking people had migrated into Mozambique, either establishing permanent sedentary communities in unoccupied areas or displacing or absorbing nomadic bands of hunting and gathering peoples.[1] These immigrants, in turn, interacted with existing Bantu-speaking groups and subsequent immigrants. These relations, which generally were peaceful, often led to cultural borrowing, intermarriage, and on occasion, the amalgamation of different groups into distinct peoples. Sometimes, however, competition for scarce resources—fertile land, captives, cattle, or minerals—ended in violent confrontation and domination. Although varied in detail and outcome, the processes of population diffusion, economic and social interaction, cultural borrowing, assimilation, and conquest characterized Mozambican history well into the colonial period.

The most striking difference between the early Bantu-speaking immigrants and their hunting and gathering predecessors was the knowledge of iron working and hoe culture that the newcomers brought with them. These innovations, although relatively rudimentary, permitted the organization of self-sustaining agricultural communities that revolutionized their relationship to nature. To meet the labor needs associated with cultivating their land and protecting it from the invasion of weeds and the depredations of animals, permanent kinship groupings replaced roving hunting bands as the principal social and productive unit. The three-generational extended family—with its matrilineal or patrilineal core, concern for reproduction, notions of seniority, sexual division of labor, and veneration of the ancestors—served as the social and ideological foundation of these early Mozambican societies. Agricultural production, in most years, yielded surpluses that, in turn, permitted limited trade and increased contact between peoples. It also facilitated greater specialization than was possible among hunters and gatherers, as the agriculturalists did not have to allocate substantial labor time to transporting their material goods from one location to another and constructing new residences and lightweight, portable commodities. The presence of seasonal or full-time craftsmen, ironworkers, miners, merchants, and fishermen, as well as permanent political and religious leaders, testifies to growing societal complexity.

Before 1500 most Mozambican communities were organized into independent chieftaincies and were governed by land chiefs, who often had religious authority as well. As the direct descendant of the founding or conquering lineage, the chief was the ultimate owner and spiritual guardian of the land, which gave him the exclusive right to alienate parcels to his subordinates and entitled him to an annual tax in either agricultural produce or labor.[2] The chief also received a number of gifts that symbolized his ownership of the land, the most important being the larger tusk of any elephant that died in his territory. The taxes, labor requirements, and symbolic gifts underscored the social differentiation that existed in Mozambican societies well before the arrival of the Portuguese.[3]

Assisting the land chief was a council of elders, composed of village headmen and often cult priests, who, with the royal family, propitiated the ancestor spirits and the gods to bring rain and ensure an orderly universe. Where the chieftaincy encompassed a particularly large region, the land chiefs appointed several territorial chiefs from among either their junior kinsmen or dominant local elders.

At least two large state systems controlled a substantial portion of central Mozambique before the seventeenth century. The kingdom of the Muenemutapa, the older and more important, embraced an area stretching from the southern bank of the Zambesi River to the Save River and into the highlands of contemporary Zimbabwe (see Figure 2.1) and incorporated a number of ethnically disparate peoples. At its high point in the sixteenth century, the Muenemutapa empire was probably the largest and most powerful state in Central and Southern Africa. Elaborate religious institutions and rituals reinforced the position of the king.[4] The aristocracy's control over the gold mines—worked by several thousand subjects[5]—

FIGURE 2.1 States of Central Mozambique, ca. 1650

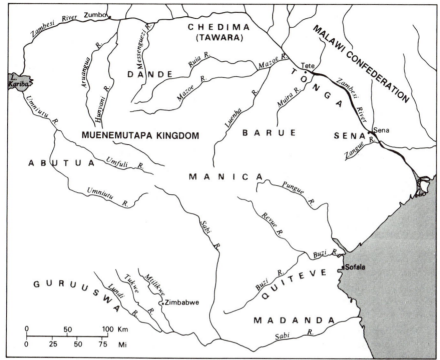

Source: Allen F. Isaacman, *Mozambique: The Africanization of a European Institution, The Zambesi Prazos 1750–1902* (Madison, 1972), p. 6. Reprinted with permission.

access to a portion of the agricultural produce of its subordinates, and virtual monopoly of international trade with Swahili merchants guaranteed its control over the economy and its dominant class position.

The other major power was the Malawi Confederation. Located just northeast of the kingdom of the Muenemutapa, by about 1600 it had begun a century of expansion into and consolidation of control over a vast region bounded by the Zambesi River, Lake Nyasa, the Luangwa Valley, and the Indian Ocean. Here, too, the aristocracy's dominant position rested on its monopoly of foreign trade, primarily in ivory, and its claim to divine power.[6]

The merchants who traded in the Malawian and Muenemutapa kingdoms were part of a Swahili commercial system extending throughout the Indian Ocean between the Middle East and Asia. Attracted by gold and ivory, Swahili traders moving south from the port city of Kilwa had, by the middle of the fifteenth century, established a string of permanent commercial and religious sultanates along the Mozambican coast between the islands of Angoche and Mozambique in the far north and Sofala in the south. Sofala was the principal gateway inland to the gold mines and markets of the kingdom of the Muenemutapa. Swahili traders living in these sultanates often married local women, and over time, their descendants developed a unique ethnic and cultural identity and came to be known, in Mozambique as elsewhere along the East African coast, as Swahili.

The establishment of the Swahili enclaves marked the beginning of the centuries-long process of incorporating Mozambique into a wider world economy. It also permitted the exploitation of Mozambique by foreign merchant capitalists whose profit margin from successful ventures was often several hundred percent. As one historian noted, "What Africans received in exchange for ivory, even though it had little intrinsic value in their own societies, were goods that in no way equalled the value placed on ivory by the merchant capitalists."[7] The same pattern of unequal exchange characterized the trade in gold. The high rate of return helps to explain why the foreign merchants remained content to enter into commercial alliances with the ruling class or dominant local stratum and to remain outside the system of production.

Swahili commercial hegemony was almost immediately challenged by the Portuguese, who moved into the Indian Ocean around 1500. Lisbon was particularly interested in gaining control over Mozambique because of the area's strategic ports and the existence of gold and ivory that Portugal needed to defray the cost of its expansionist policies. In this era of the Crusades dislodging the Muslim infidels also held an obvious attraction.

The Portuguese Crown acted decisively against the Swahili. By 1525 its forces had gained control over Sofala, established a settlement on Mozambique Island, and occupied Angoche. During the following decade Portuguese settlers and merchants founded the inland communities of Sena and Tete and organized a number of interior markets on the frontiers of the Muenemutapa empire, thereby disrupting the Swahili trade network.

Flushed with victory, Portugal attempted to establish its hegemony over the kingdom of the Muenemutapa and gain direct control over the mines. Lisbon initially hoped to achieve this goal by converting the ruling aristocracy to Christianity, but when this tactic failed, it launched a major military expedition in 1567. The European forces, confronting stiff resistance and debilitating diseases, were compelled to retreat, marking the beginning of a long tradition of Mozambican resistance to Portuguese rule.[8] Despite the setback, Lisbon pursued its expansionist policy. After thirty years of court intrigue, efforts at conversion and co-optation, and threats of new invasions Portuguese diplomats in 1607 finally persuaded Muenemutapa Gatsi Rusere to cede all the mines within his territory and, in effect, to acknowledge Lisbon's suzerainty.[9] The following year the Portuguese entered into a formal military alliance with the Malawian king and in 1632 defeated the Malawi ruler Muzura after he had launched a surprise attack on the Portuguese town of Quelimane.[10]

To extend its influence and further consolidate its power, in the seventeenth century the Crown began to distribute to its nationals estates known as *prazos da coroa*. These *prazos*, located in the Zambesi Valley, Sofala, and the Querimba Islands, were expected to become the basis of a permanent white settler community whose members would serve as the Crown's loyal agents. They would be distributed and transmitted only to Europeans who, in return, would pay taxes, provide periodic services, obey all metropolitan laws, and use their slave armies, known as Chikunda, to conquer neighboring peoples.[11]

The first half of the seventeenth century marked the high point of early Portuguese domination. Thereafter, forces opposed to Lisbon's rule seized the initiative. In rapid succession, the sultanate of Angoche regained its independence, the Barue rose up and drove the Portuguese estateholders out of their homeland, and the Malawian empire terminated its alliance with Lisbon. Chope and Tonga chieftaincies in the Sofala hinterland and the Makua polities adjacent to Mozambique Island also refused to acknowledge Portuguese suzerainty. Most devastating was the overwhelming defeat the Muenemutapa and its Rozvi allies inflicted on the Portuguese in 1692, driving them out of the Zimbabwean highlands and the Zambesi interior.[12] Even the *prazo* estateholders, many of whom had become progressively Africanized, refused to acknowledge the Crown's authority. Their independent spirit and antipathy toward Portugal is reflected in the popular expression that among any "group of twenty *prazeiros* each one has nineteen enemies, but all are the enemy of the Governor."[13]

By the middle of the eighteenth century, Mozambique had become to Portugal little more than a backwater malarial zone of minimal value in comparison to Lisbon's holdings in Asia, Brazil, and even Angola. In a half-hearted effort to revive the colony's sagging fortunes, Lisbon gave Mozambique autonomous colonial status in 1752; previously it had been administered as part of Portuguese India (Goa).

Portugal's political setbacks were matched by its failure to consolidate its control over the prosperous Muslim commercial network. The East African trade was very risky and demanded substantial capital. Outfitting the overland caravans with cloth, beads, and other commodities was costly, and considerable capital reserves were needed to absorb the reverses that regularly occurred. Neither the Crown, which maintained a theoretical monopoly on all cloth and ivory imported into the colony, nor the Portuguese settlers, who circumvented the royal monopoly, possessed the capital required to fuel the trade system.

Indian merchants, primarily the Banyans, the Hindu trading caste, quickly filled this vacuum. They gained a foothold by providing manufactured cloth and trading beads on credit to the local settlers, who exchanged them for ivory, gold, and tropical products in the interior. After the middle of the seventeenth century, Asian merchants, based on the northern island of Mozambique, began to organize their own caravans into the Makua homelands. By 1750 they controlled a vast trading network that extended as far south as Quelimane and the Zambesi Valley, earning them the epithet "Jews of the Orient."[14]

Coinciding with the rise of Indian merchant capitalism was a marked shift in the nature of international trade, although agriculture continued as the economic base of all Mozambican societies. Throughout the sixteenth century and much of the seventeenth gold coming from the Muenemutapa was the principal export commodity. During the next century ivory from the northern regions became Mozambique's leading export. This shift was due largely to a decision by Yao elephant hunters and merchants to exchange their ivory for highly prized Indian cloth from Makua middlemen rather than to continue selling the tusks at Kilwa, far to the north. In order to satisfy the increasing Indian demand,[15] Yao hunters and traders extended their activities to much of central Mozambique and as far inland as the Luangwa Valley in present-day Zambia.

If the eighteenth century was the century of ivory, the nineteenth century marked the beginning of Mozambique's transformation into an international labor reserve—a phenomenon that continued throughout the colonial period. As early as the 1760s the growth of sugar plantations on the Indian Ocean islands of Ile de France and Bourbon created a regional demand for slaves that Indian merchants and French traders, as well as the local Portuguese settlers, were eager to satisfy. Drawn by low prices, slavers from Brazil, the United States, and the Caribbean islands were soon trading at Mozambique Island and Quelimane, the colony's two major ports. They also purchased smaller numbers of slaves at the southern towns of Inhambane and Lourenço Marques and on the Querimba Islands to the north. By the early part of the nineteenth century about 10,000 slaves a year were legally exported from Quelimane and Mozambique Island. Contemporary accounts suggest that the number of slaves smuggled out of the colony through illegal markets along the long coastline was even greater. Between 1817 and 1843 more than 100,000 captives were exported to Brazil alone, and during the same period, almost 30 percent of all slaves imported into Cuba identified by national origin came from the Portuguese colony.[16] The illicit commerce continued to flourish even after Lisbon outlawed the slave trade in 1836. The difficulties of curbing this smuggling were described in correspondence between a Portuguese administrator and the captain of an English antislave patrol. "It is not necessary for me to remind you that the number of easily accessible ports both north and south of Quelimane has facilitated the contraband trade. These ports are neither properly guarded by fortifications nor policed by troops, with the result that the slavers have no difficulty making their purchases without the knowledge of the authorities since all the inhabitants have a vested interest in the commerce and do all they can to conceal it."[17]

The skyrocketing demand for captive labor greatly affected commercial activities in the northern half of the country. While continuing their prosperous trade in ivory, the Yao penetrated into the Lake Nyasa region during the first half of the century and, after 1850, entered the Shire Valley in search of new sources of slaves from among the Manganja and Chewa. Indeed, it was common for the slavers to use their captives as porters to carry the tusks to the coastal ports, thereby reducing labor costs. The Chikunda, in the employ of the Afro-Portuguese *prazeiros*, extended their commercial contacts to Zumbo and the Luangwa Valley, while the coastal Makua rulers began to exploit the populous hinterland. Swahili

TABLE 2.1
Legal Slave Exports from Mozambique Island and Quelimane, Selected
Years 1764-1830

Year	Number	
1764	108	(from Quelimane)
1768	158	(from Quelimane)
ca. 1770-79	9,158	(from Mozambique Island to the Mascarene Islands)
1781	9,315	(from Mozambique Island on Portuguese ships)
1784	2,313	(from Mozambique Island on Portuguese ships)
1788	11,016	(from Mozambique Island on Portuguese ships)
1794	3,807	
1803	5,239	(from Mozambique Island)
1818	9,281	
1819	12,953	(from Mozambique Island to Brazil and total Quelimane exports)
1821	15,282	(total exports from Mozambique Island and Quelimane exports to Rio de Janeiro)
1822	9,371	(exports from Mozambique Island and Quelimane to Rio de Janeiro and Maranhao)
1825	7,808	(exports from Mozambique Island and Quelimane to Rio de Janeiro)
1828	11,488	(exports from Mozambique Island and Quelimane to Rio de Janeiro)
1830	10,449	(exports from Mozambique Island and Quelimane to Rio de Janeiro from January through June)

Sources: Edward A. Alpers, Ivory and Slaves in East Central Africa
(Berkeley, 1975), pp. 187, 213; Allen Isaacman, Mozambique: The Africanization of a European Institution, The Zambesi Prazos 1750-1902 (Madison,
1972), pp. 86, 92.

merchants from the sultanates of Angoche, Mossuril, Quissanga, and even
faraway Zanzibar also became prominent slavers. The intensified competition among the slave merchants and their virtual monopoly of modern
weapons, which they obtained from European traders in exchange for
captives, dramatically altered the character of the trade after the 1860s.
Whereas in the preceding period most slaves had probably been obtained
through negotiations between the alien traders and the local aristocracies,
raiding and conquest replaced these transactions as the principal mode of
acquisition.

As late as the last quarter of the nineteenth century slaves continued
to be the dominant export commodity. They were exported to work on
the clove plantations of Zanzibar, the sugar plantations of Madagascar,
and the sugar estates of the Mascarene Islands. After 1890, thousands of
Mozambicans were also sent as corvée labor to the cocoa plantations of
São Thomé. In all, it is very likely that more than 1 million Mozambicans

were forcibly removed from their homelands and sold as cheap bound labor during the nineteenth century.[18]

The slave trade had far-reaching economic and social effects. Fields were ravaged, entire villages destroyed, and survivors often compelled to flee to inaccessible, unproductive locations to avoid slave raiders. The violent disruption of much of the rural economy and the export of many of the most productive members of the indigenous Mozambican societies intensified the process of underdevelopment and impoverishment. The disparity in the value of goods received in exchange for slaves was even greater than it had been for gold and ivory. In return for lost labor power, Mozambican societies received weapons of destruction and a variety of inexpensive perishable commodities such as beads, liquor, and cloth, none of which enhanced production or compensated for the depletion of the work force. The loss of the reproductive capacity of the captives had a profound demographic impact, and in a number of slave-raiding societies slavery increased in scale and intensity during the nineteenth century. Both the Yao and Gaza Nguni, for example, commonly exported male slaves and used female slaves both as agricultural laborers and to augment the reproductive capacity of their master's lineage. The *prazeiro* warlords, on the other hand, filled the ranks of their slave armies with captives, who were closely guarded until they had proved their loyalty.[19]

As the northern half of Mozambique became progressively impoverished, disparities in wealth and social inequality intensified and class distinctions became more pronounced. In stark contrast to the population at large, a relatively small merchant class, often allied with or part of the ruling aristocracy, accumulated substantial profits from the sale of slaves. The wealth and power of the Yao chiefs Makanjila and Mataka, of the sultans of Angoche and Quitanghona, and of the powerful *prazeiros*, such as Bonga, Matakenya, and the Pereiras, were legendary. The slave trade further weakened Portugal's nominal hold on northern and central Mozambique. It precipitated the growth of a number of powerful slave-raiding or conquest states and sparked the resurgence of the Muslim sultanates.

In the south, where the effects of the slave trade were far less pronounced, Portugal faced other problems. There, Gaza Nguni immigrants, who had fled from what is now South Africa during the violent upheavals at the beginning of the nineteenth century, threatened the tenuous Portuguese hold on the Lourenço Marques–Delagoa Bay region. After 1828, the Gaza, under the leadership of Soshangane, migrated north to the Save River, where they forged a powerful state with its capital at Chaimate. Armed with recently developed short stabbing-spears and some European guns, the Gaza extended their hegemony as far east as the Inhambane coast, conquering a number of Tonga and Chopi chieftaincies and virtually eliminating Portuguese influence there. By 1840 Gaza forces had also extended their influence to the southern bank of the Zambesi River. They compelled the *prazeiro* community to recognize the nominal authority of Soshangane and his heirs and to pay them an annual tribute, further eroding Lisbon's claim to this zone.

THE MIRAGE OF PORTUGUESE EMPIRE—MOZAMBIQUE
ON THE EVE OF THE PARTITION OF AFRICA, CA. 1880

After more than three hundred years of nominal rule, Portugal's position in Mozambique was tenuous at best. On the eve of the "scramble," or the partition of Africa by the European powers, Lisbon's influence was essentially limited to a small number of coastal settlements (see Figure 2.2). Some, such as the post at Quissanga or the fort at Sofala, had only a token force to symbolize Portugal's historic claim to the region. In important administrative centers, such as Quelimane, Inhambane, and Lourenço Marques, Portuguese military and civilian personnel, although more numerous, were poorly trained and concerned primarily with self-aggrandizement. Beyond the immediate confines of these towns Lisbon rarely exercised any authority. One colonial official acknowledged that Portuguese influence did not extend more than 2 miles (3.2 kilometers) outside the capital of Lourenço Marques. "No control whatever is exercised over the neighboring chiefs, and the oaths of allegiance sworn by some of them represent . . . a farce."[20]

The Zambesi Valley was the only part of the interior in which there was even a semblance of European rule. Undermanned garrisons at Sena, Tete, and Zumbo, although giving the illusion of a colonial presence, proved no match for the more numerous and well-armed Barue, Muene-mutapa, or Gaza Nguni forces, and as their ranks were further depleted by malaria, they were hard-pressed even to defend their decaying bases. "The state of Tete is horrifying," acknowledged one Portuguese official. "All is reduced to bush and mountains of fire, the inhabitants are all dispersed, the fort has almost completely fallen to the ground."[21] The missionary David Livingstone agreed: "I thought the state of Tete quite lamentable, but that of Sena was ten times worse."[22]

The adamant opposition of African societies to any infringement on their autonomy not only belied Lisbon's claim of empire but prevented the Portuguese from reinforcing their position in the years immediately preceding the scramble. In northern Mozambique, for example, the colonial army was defeated at Tungue Bay in 1853 and a decade later at Angoche. To the south, Portuguese military efforts against the Gaza Nguni proved futile, and local officials were compelled to move the district capital from Sofala to the island of Chiloane, thereby conceding to the Gaza Nguni control over the mainland. Lisbon's most serious setback occurred in the Zambesi Valley. In an effort to dominate this strategic zone between 1867 and 1875 Portugal launched five unsuccessful campaigns against the rebellious *prazeiro* Bonga, ruler of Massangano. In one campaign, only 107 of the 1,000-man force survived.[23]

The growing influence of other foreign powers, especially the British, further eroded Lisbon's tenuous position. By 1853 the sultan of Zanzibar had established direct control over Tungue Bay, which became a center for anti-Portuguese activities extending as far south as Quissanga. Twenty years later he allowed the British to erect a commercial settlement opposite

FIGURE 2.2 The Western Indian Ocean System

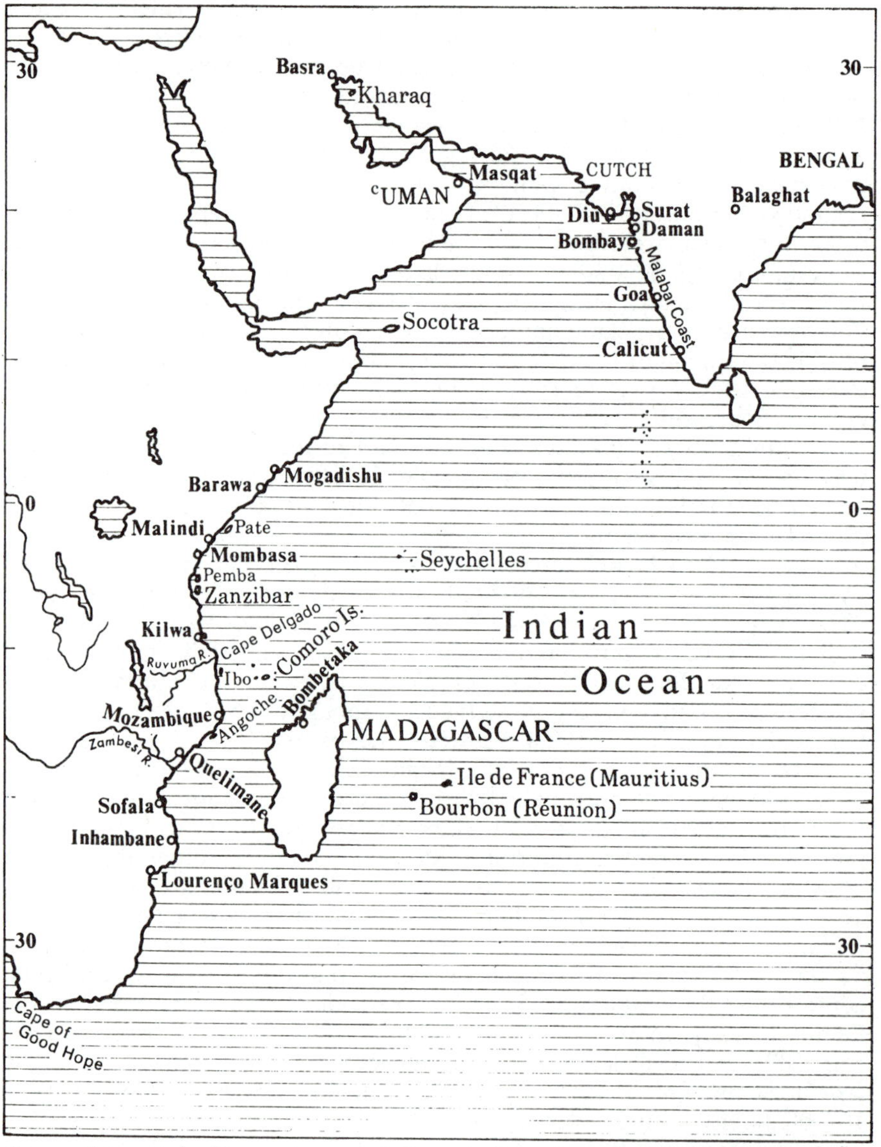

Source: Edward A. Alpers, *Ivory and Slaves in East Central Africa* (Berkeley, 1975). Reprinted with permission.

Tungue Bay, from which they penetrated into the Lake Nyasa region. The British were also becoming increasingly active in the Shire Valley of central Mozambique, while their nationals, Afrikaaners, and Germans sought to settle in the fertile Manica highlands. And in the south British investors consolidated their economic hold over the capital and port city of Lourenço Marques.[24]

THE PARTITION OF AFRICA AND
THE WARS OF RESISTANCE, 1885–1913

If Portugal's position in Mozambique was weak, its international claim to the colony was even weaker. Beset by financial problems, political instability, and a military in disarray, Portugal—the "sick man of Europe"—was no match for the powerful industrial capitalist countries of Western Europe. Jolted by the 1871 depression, they began to compete vigorously for new colonies and new markets. Indeed, at the Congress of Berlin, held in 1884–1885, the Great Powers rejected Lisbon's historic claim to Mozambique and decreed that pacification and effective control were prerequisites for recognition as the colonial power. This decision generated a wave of nationalist sentiment within Portugal, and those factions in the government demanding a more aggressive militaristic policy prevailed. Their symbol became the *mapa cor-da-rosa* ("red map"), a map that envisioned a Portuguese Central African empire linking Angola and Mozambique.

Great Britain posed the most serious threat to Lisbon's territorial dreams. Already controlling key sectors of the Portuguese metropolitan economy, British investors hoped to annex strategic areas of Mozambique itself. They were particularly interested in the fertile Manica highlands adjacent to their holdings in Southern Rhodesia, the Shire Valley gateway to the interior, and the southern port region of Lourenço Marques. Most ambitious was Cecil Rhodes's vision of a Cape to Cairo railroad, which would have established Great Britain's hegemony over much of Southern and Eastern Africa and presupposed control of a substantial portion of Mozambique. After a number of near conflicts, in 1891 London appropriated most of the Manica highlands and the Shire Valley. This humiliating setback brought down the Portuguese government and swept into power a new generation of leaders committed to using the nation's military resources to guarantee Portuguese hegemony.

Portugal's new militancy jeopardized the sovereignty of Mozambican societies. They reacted to this threat in a variety of ways. Some, such as the Gaza Nguni, engaged in diplomatic delaying actions, while others, including a number of Inhambane Tonga chieftaincies, initially collaborated with the Portuguese authorities in an effort to free themselves from the oppressive rule of their Gaza Nguni overlords. Most Mozambican societies, however, took up arms to defend their independence.

The conflict in northern Mozambique centered on the commitment of the ruling class of the coastal Swahili sheikhdoms of Angoche, Quitanghona, Sancul, and Sangage and of adjacent Makua and Yao states to perpetuate the slave trade and retain their independence. Before the scramble Lisbon had fostered a modus vivendi with the coastal aristocracy, who, in return for acknowledging Portugal's nominal rule, were free to engage surreptitiously in slaving. Intensified international pressure, especially from Great Britain, compelled Portugal to give up this arrangement. Pacification and the abolition of the slave trade became minimal preconditions for international recognition. The indigenous aristocracy, who depended on the slave trade for its wealth and arms, could not tolerate such an intrusion. The ruling class was supported by local merchants—Africans, Indians, and Europeans—and it received popular support from much of the Islamized African population by pledging to defend their historic way of life against the alien Christians and to resist all efforts by the Portuguese to impose the dreaded hut tax.

From 1885 to 1896 Lisbon attempted to establish its hegemony by alternating threats and limited military activity with lucrative offers to the ruling aristocracy. This policy proved unsuccessful.[25] Even when Lisbon adopted a more aggressive strategy, the results were the same. In 1896 Portuguese troops launched a major offensive against the Makua, who, reinforced by soldiers from the sultanates of Angoche, Quitanghona, and Marave, defeated the colonial army. During the next decade a number of inconclusive battles were fought in which the colonial army was generally kept on the defensive.

In 1910 a Portuguese force of more than 4,600 men, supported by heavy artillery, simultaneously attacked the positions of Angoche and its Makua allies. The unprecedented commitment of manpower and the deployment of the most sophisticated weapons in the colonial arsenal clearly indicated Lisbon's commitment to impose its rule after nearly thirty years of failure. By the end of the year the Makua had surrendered. Spurred on by this success, Portuguese troops attacked Quitanghona, and within a year they had established their hegemony over this region as well. The defeat of the Makua, Angoche, and Quitanghona ensured Portuguese control over the northern coastal region and left the Yao of Mataka, who had withstood the European advance for more than twenty years, as their only major northern adversary. Determined to finally control the north, in 1912 Lisbon sent an expeditionary force of 3,000 well-armed men, which, after stiff resistance, destroyed Mataka's capital.[26]

Throughout the central part of the country the colonial regime also encountered strong opposition. From the onset of the scramble until the final victory in 1902 there was hardly a year in which Lisbon's troops were not engaged in a military campaign in the Zambesi Valley—scene of numerous confrontations over the past three centuries. Lisbon first attempted to buy the loyalty and assistance of the Afro-Portuguese and Afro-Goan *prazeiro* estateholders by providing them with titles, financial bonuses, sophisticated weapons, and the de facto right to export slaves. The net effect of this policy was to strengthen the military capacity of the *prazeiro* warlords, who controlled virtually the entire Zambesi Valley. Whenever Portuguese officials made a concerted effort to establish their hegemony without the use of large-scale force, however, the *prazeiros* rejected their appeals.

Consider the case of Massangano, the most militant of the conquest states forged out of the *prazo* system. During the decades preceding the scramble, Bonga, the powerful leader of Massangano, had successfully resisted repeated Portuguese assaults on his territory. In 1886, after Bonga's death, Lisbon, believing that Massangano could be pressured into renouncing its independence, sent a delegation to present an ultimatum to Chatara, Bonga's successor. He unequivocally rejected the proposal, declaring Massangano to be an "independent and sovereign state."[27] A year later Portugal attacked with a 7,000-man force, and Chatara and his beleaguered followers fled into the interior. The Massangano royal council and senior religious leaders immediately deposed Chatara for his cowardly action and selected Mtontora to continue the struggle. By June 1888, Mtontora had liberated Massangano and sent an ambassador to the Portuguese to negotiate a treaty of friendship based on mutual sovereignty. In response, Lisbon unleashed a successful offensive with 5,000 men and supporting artillery. Although routed, remnants of the Massangano army joined in 1902 with the neighboring Barue in their unsuccessful struggle for independence.

For thirty years Lisbon had engaged in subversive activities against the Barue nation, located just south of the Zambesi River. In the 1870s it had covertly supported the successful efforts of Gouveia, a Goan *prazeiro* married to a member of the Barue royal family, to usurp the Barue throne. As long as Gouveia remained loyal and was able to maintain his authoritarian rule, Portugal was prepared to allow him to serve as its surrogate. In 1891, however, internal opponents, led by Hanga and other militantly anti-Portuguese members of the royal family, deposed Gouveia. Once in power, Hanga forged a multiethnic coalition of Zambesian peoples living in Mozambique and the adjacent areas of Southern Rhodesia, promising to help the latter drive out the British after he had defeated the Portuguese.

By 1902 Hanga could count on more than 10,000 men, half of whom were armed with guns. Local munitions plants—where rifles, powder, and components for captured artillery were manufactured—a vast network of forts, and a well-developed spy system all enhanced the Barue military capacity. In addition, Barue spirit mediums claimed to have secret medicines that would turn European bullets into water. Although embroiled in military campaigns in the north in 1902, Lisbon diverted some 2,000 troops, supported by artillery, to confront the Barue and its allies. The speed of the Portuguese advance and their superior firepower demoralized the insurgents, who regrouped at the capital, Missongue, for one final confrontation. As the Portuguese commander noted, "The battle of Missongue had a crushing effect on the Barue soldiers who recognized that neither their might nor their magic could counter us."[28]

While Lisbon initially focused attention on the Zambesi region and areas to the north, its position in the southern part of the country, where it faced the formidable Gaza Nguni, grew ever more precarious. Initially, both sides were anxious to avoid a confrontation. Lisbon, immersed in a number of other conflicts, hoped that it could cajole, co-opt, or pressure the Gaza ruler, Gungunyane, to relinquish his sovereignty. Gungunyane, however, had his own imperial ambitions—he initiated a number of campaigns against rebellious Chope subjects; negotiated a treaty with agents of the British entrepreneur, Cecil Rhodes, in which the Gaza received 1,000 rifles and 20,000 cartridges; and entered into secret military negotiations with the neighboring Swazi and Ndebele. At the same time, Gungunyane made a number of symbolic gestures and concessions that he hoped would forestall a Portuguese invasion.

Ultimately, the strategic interests of the two powers collided. An 1894 revolt by several Ronga chieftaincies protesting increased Portuguese taxation and the interference of Portuguese colonial officials in a succession dispute set the stage for the conflict. The leaders of the insurrection—Mahazul and Matibejana—fled to Gungunyane's court after their forces had failed to capture Lourenço Marques. Portuguese officials presented Gungunyane with an ultimatum—turn over the rebels or prepare for war. As the Ronga were his nominal subjects, the Gaza leadership rejected the request as an infringement on its sovereignty.

The first decisive battle took place at Maghul on September 8, 1896. Maguiguane, Gungunyane's war chief, mobilized the bulk of the 20,000-man army for a frontal assault, using the characteristic half-moon battle formation. Although the Nguni forces came within a few yards of penetrating the Portuguese defense, they were ultimately repulsed. They suffered a second major setback at Lake Coolela two months later, which crippled them and convinced Gungunyane that defeat was inevitable. In December 1895 he surrendered and was sent into exile in the Azores, where he ultimately died. The Portuguese victory did not, however, destroy the will of the Gaza people. Two years later they again unsuccessfully took up arms, led by their war chief Maguiguane.[29]

Throughout Mozambique these primary resistance movements had common *raisons d'être*—to drive out the imperialist forces, to protect the indigenous homelands and historic way of life, and to avoid harsh taxes and the expropriation of land and labor. These goals explain the popular support the anticolonial campaigns generally enjoyed. For the ruling classes, especially those engaged in the slave trade, however, economic independence was an equally compelling consideration. The coastal sultanates, the Yao of Mataka, the Namaraal Makua, and the Zambesi conquest states all depended on the export of captives to maintain their privileged political and economic positions. To the extent that a number of wars were fought not only against imperialism but also to perpetuate the slave trade and to preserve the position of a predatory ruling class, these struggles for independence had an ambiguous character.

Whatever their motivation, African leaders recognized the need to neutralize the technological advantage enjoyed by Portuguese forces, and they attempted to do so in several ways. For those states peripherally incorporated into the international trading system, access to arms in exchange for slaves and ivory was relatively easy, and the Zambesi conquest states and the commercial powers of northern Mozambique had no difficulty acquiring large supplies of modern weapons. Other states expanded their arsenals through skillful diplomacy. Gungunyane's efforts to pit the Portuguese against the British were designed, in part, to gain modern weapons. Mozambican societies also relied on internal innovations. The Barue munitions plants, for example, produced an array of weapons, and the people of northern Mozambique developed highly successful guerrilla tactics. Many resisters also sought divine assistance to neutralize the technological superiority of the invading armies—witness the Makua animal tails and Barue medicines, both reputed to turn bullets into water.

Because the resisters did not achieve their ultimate aim, there has been a tendency to minimize or ignore their accomplishments. In fact, however, many Mozambican polities scored impressive, although often short-lived, victories. Others, such as Massangano, successfully held off the Portuguese for more than thirty years, and the northern Mozambican coastal powers withstood repeated attacks from 1888 to 1913.

Despite these victories, African polities were unable to create broad-based anticolonial coalitions that might have countered the technological advantage of the invading colonial forces. Instead of submerging past differences and uniting against a common enemy, neighboring states generally maintained their parochial identities and interests. Competition and conflict generated by the slave trade intensified these divisions.

Internal conflicts resulting from either popular opposition to authoritarian rule or cleavages within the ruling class further compromised the military position of many powerful polities at the forefront of anticolonial activity. The conquest states of the Zambesi Valley, for example, suffered from repeated insurrections by subject populations protesting the harsh rule of the Afro-Portuguese and Afro-Goan leaders and their Chikunda warriors. Armed insurrections by the underclasses weakened the military capacity of the *prazeiro* warlords Kanyemba and Matakenya at the very moment they encountered the invading colonial army.[30] To the south, oppressed Inhambane Tonga and Chope communities rebelled against their Gaza Nguni overlords.[31] Succession crises, court intrigues, and civil wars reduced the defensive capacity of Angoche, Quitanghona, Massangano, Makanga, and the Barue and frustrated efforts to promote a united front.[32]

The existence of these divisions among and within African societies also helps to explain Lisbon's ability to recruit large numbers of collaborators. By playing off historic enemies, appealing to oppressed subject peoples, and offering substantial economic inducements, Portugal filled the ranks of its army with African soldiers, without whom it could not have imposed its rule. More than 90 percent of the "Portuguese" armies that pacified the Zambesi Valley, for example, consisted of African levies and reserves—some of whom were, no doubt, coerced. The force that defeated Gungunyane was also composed primarily of Africans, although the proportion was somewhat lower. The strategic role of collaborators, the technological advantage of the Portuguese military, and the failure of Africans to unite permitted imperialism to triumph and set the stage for formal Portuguese rule.

3

The Colonial Period, 1900–1962

The blacks in Africa must be directed and moulded by Europeans but they are indispensable as assistants to the latter. . . . The Africans by themselves did not account for a single useful invention nor any usable technical discovery, no conquest that counts in the evolution of humanity, nothing that can compare to the accomplishments in the areas of culture and technology by Europeans or even by Asians.

—Portuguese Prime Minister Marcello Caetano,
Os Nativos na Economia Africana (Coimbra, 1954), p. 16

By the beginning of the twentieth century Portuguese rule had been consolidated throughout the strategic southern half of Mozambique, and within a decade Lisbon could claim at least nominal control over the entire colony. Colonial rule transformed the basic fabric of Mozambican society. The imposition of arbitrary and capricious policies informed by the prevailing racial and cultural arrogance of the colonizers and by new labor demands and tax requirements adversely affected all Mozambicans. This is not to say that the impact was uniform. Clearly it was not. Variations, caused by such disparate factors as the local political economy and the personality of particular administrators, profoundly affected the daily lives of the colonized. But these were merely differences in a relative scale of deprivation and exploitation—for even a prosperous African farmer or merchant, of whom there were relatively few, was still a "kaffir."

Despite the broad continuity of colonial policy three discrete periods can be identified. The first, which lasted until 1926, was characterized by a highly decentralized and disorganized colonial government riddled with corruption and mismanagement at all levels. It was a time in which special interest groups within the settler community as well as foreign concessionary companies prevailed. Mozambique's economic dependence on South Africa dates from this period as well. In sharp contrast, the Salazar regime, which came to power in 1928, imposed a highly centralized authoritarian regime. Its objective was to exploit more effectively the colony's resources for the benefit of the metropole, but specifically of the nascent industrial capitalist class that had helped to bring the Salazar government to power. Increasing popular opposition, highlighted by the formation of FRELIMO in 1962,

28

FIGURE 3.1 Major Mozambican States and Portuguese Administrative Centers, ca. 1900

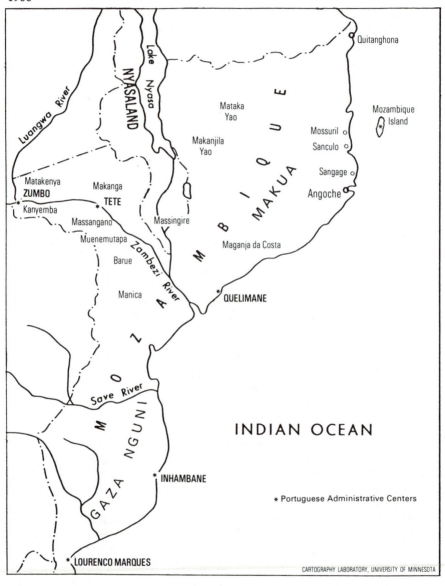

forced Salazar and his handpicked successor, Marcello Caetano, to create the illusion of reforming and rationalizing the colonial system. They ended some of the most exploitative abuses and began to promote the myth of multiracialism. In this chapter we examine the first two of these periods.

PORTUGUESE COLONIAL POLICY
BEFORE THE SALAZAR REGIME, 1900–1926

Four hundred years of ineffectual rule and thirty years of pacification had convinced Lisbon of the need to impose a highly structured, centralized system on the newly conquered colony. Indeed, as early as 1907, well before Portuguese troops had pacified the outlying regions of the colony, the boundaries of the various administrative units had been firmly set in place. In those areas not ceded to European concessionary companies,[1] three levels of Portuguese administration operated subordinate to the governor-general of Mozambique. At the highest level were the district governors, usually military officers appointed by Lisbon. Each district was divided into European and non-European areas. European townships, administered as councils (*concelhos*), enjoyed limited self-government. By the 1920s fewer than 15,000 Europeans resided in Mozambique, primarily in the capital city of Lourenço Marques and the port town of Beira, where they engaged in commerce, crafts, and light industry.[2] Africans lived overwhelmingly in rural subdistricts (*circumscrições*), which for administrative purposes were further subdivided into localities (*postos*). A Portuguese official governed each of these subdistricts and localities.

Poorly educated and poorly trained, these administrators ruled as petty tyrants. They had absolute power to accuse, apprehend, try, and sentence their subjects. The *chefe de posto* could, and often did, commit the most violent acts with impunity. As one European landowner commented in 1907, African "complaints [of mistreatment] never yielded results because most times they are denounced as rebels, and pay for their calls for justice with a march to Tete, Quelimane or Moçambique, where they are imprisoned for an extensive period."[3]

For the administrative system to function, the colonial regime had to depend on African collaborators and mercenaries. Members of the local royal families (*regulos*) became paid functionaries of the state who, exempt from taxation and forced labor, were expected to collect taxes, to settle minor disputes, to recruit labor, and to maintain public order. In addition, many received recruitment bonuses, the right to use forced peasant labor on their own fields, higher prices for their cash crops, and prizes, including bicycles and cloth, for "stimulating" African production. Those *regulos* who were either unwilling or unable to perform their assignments were summarily replaced by more pliant members of the royal family or other collaborators. For those Mozambican peoples, like the Makonde, who had historically lived in localized communities without chiefs, colonial officials created the fiction of chieftaincies and handpicked loyalists to fill the positions.[4]

African police, or *sipais*, initially recruited from among the former

Sipais (African police), Zambézia Province (Credit: P. A. de Sousa e Silva, *Distrito de Tete* [Lisbon, 1927], p. 112; reproduced by permission)

colonial soldiers and sons of loyalist chiefs, constituted the other African component of the state apparatus. To their ranks the colonial government added an assortment of ex-warriors, slavers, and mercenaries, who brought with them predatory skills. Stationed at every post in the colonial administration, their principal function was to intimidate the local population. *Sipais* were used to collect taxes, recruit labor, transmit the administrators' orders, and arrest dissidents. As long as they satisfied the *chefes de posto*, they were given license to prey upon the rural population. Accounts of their pillaging are legendary. One elder, who had fled to Southern Rhodesia in 1917, recalled with disgust how the *sipais* "have been ravishing children who are too young for a man to sleep with. Many of the girls were very ill and had to be sent back. One *sipai*, Nyakatoto, actually cut the girl's private parts so that he could penetrate her."[5]

The colonial regime also maintained separate legal systems for the "civilized" Europeans and the "uncivilized" *indigenas*. The former lived under a version of the metropolitan legal code, designed to maintain harmonious relations within the settler community, guarantee its privileged racial and class position, and protect the interests of both Portuguese and foreign capital. The indigenous population, with the exception of a small number of *assimilados* (see next section), were expected to continue to live according to the rules of their "traditional" legal systems, which the colonial administrators, aided by local chiefs, interpreted and applied. These customary regulations were necessarily subordinate to and modified by specific state legislation to meet the needs of the colonial-capitalist system.

The formal legal system in the colony derived from metropolitan law. In most cases the Mozambican Provincial Assembly ratified, with only minor modifications, legislation passed in Lisbon. Even before the 1926 coup in Portugal, which ultimately brought Salazar to power and ushered in a half century of fascism, legislation had been enacted to enshrine conservative social values and, above all else, to defend the interests of the colonial bourgeoisie and the various fractions of capital. An elaborate family code that guaranteed the primacy of patriarchal values, a criminal code that placed priority on protecting property, and labor regulations that limited the efforts of white workers to strike all reflected these concerns. The legal system, firmly in the hands of the colonial bourgeoisie, was highly formalized, with an emphasis on procedures, rules, paperwork, litigation, and professional adjudication.[6]

If 99 percent of the African population remained outside the formal Portuguese legal system, they were nevertheless subject to some of its most pernicious features. Their lives, and in many cases their very survival, were profoundly shaped by the regime's tax laws and labor codes. This legislation was designed primarily to create an abundant supply of cheap labor.

From the outset of the modern colonial period, Portugal could extract Mozambique's resources only by mobilizing and controlling bound labor, because its own economy, which was both archaic and on the verge of bankruptcy, lacked the capacity to export the fixed capital necessary for development. Even in the colony's major city, Lourenço Marques, only

European being carried by African porters on a *machila* (Credit: Alexandre Lobato, *Lourenço Marques, Xilunguine* [Lisbon, 1970], plate 222)

27 percent of the investments in 1900 consisted of Portuguese capital. The city's electrical system, trolley system, and first modern wharf complex were all financed by foreign, primarily British, capital—a situation not unlike that in Lisbon itself.[7] An 1899 government commission, whose task it was to analyze the prospects for development in Mozambique, concluded: "We need native labor, we need it in order to better the conditions of these laborers, we need it for the economy of Europe and for the progress of Africa. Our tropical Africa will not grow without the Africans. The capital needed to exploit it, and it so needs to be exploited, lies in the procurement of labor for exploitation. Abundant, cheap, solid labor . . . and this labor, given the circumstances, will never be supplied by European immigrants."[8]

Even before this commission was established, the state had introduced a number of tax laws[9] designed to force many African agriculturalists off their land and to create a pool of cheap labor. Colonial officials anticipated that, by forcing male members of the rural population to pay a tax in European currency or through service, they would be compelled to seek employment, at least on a temporary basis, on European plantations, in the embryonic light industrial sector, or in the port towns of Lourenço Marques and Beira. To ensure sufficient labor, the colonial state also attempted to strangle peasant agricultural initiatives by imposing artificially low prices for their commodities and by restricting the activities of the Asian merchants to whom the peasants had historically sold their cash crops. In some regions, such as the lower Zambesi, colonial officials also required rural cultivators to work on European company plantations in lieu of taxes.[10]

Although the tax laws did provide the state with a new source of revenue, they initially failed to generate a cheap labor force on a sufficient scale. Many peasants were able to circumvent the labor requirement by cultivating new or additional cash crops to pay their taxes. Others opted to work in the mines and plantations of neighboring South Africa and Southern Rhodesia at wages that were 200–300 percent higher than those offered by the undercapitalized Portuguese firms and planters. In 1912, for example, more than 91,000 Mozambicans legally worked in the South African gold mines, whereas only 5,300 Africans chose employment in Lourenço Marques[11] (see Table 3.1).

Because the nascent capitalist sector in Mozambique was unable to

TABLE 3.1
Mozambican Mineworkers in South African Gold Mines, Selected Years
1902-1961 (legal exports)

Year	Mozambican Mineworkers	Total number of Mineworkers
1902	38,635[a]	
1903	43,595	
1904	50,997	77,000
1905	59,284	81,000
1908	81,920	149,000
1909	85,282	157,000
1912	91,546	191,000
1913	80,832	155,000
1915	83,338	198,000
1918	81,306	158,000
1920	96,188	173,000
1922	80,959	183,000
1927	107,672	215,000
1929	96,667	205,000
1931	73,924	226,000
1932	58,483	233,000
1933	88,499	318,000
1939	84,335	323,000
1942	74,507	310,406
1945	78,806	320,147
1946	96,300	305,400
1951	106,500	306,100
1956	102,900	334,500
1960	95,500	396,700
1961	100,200	413,900

[a]From February to December

Sources: Centro de Estudos Africanos, The Mozambican Miner (Maputo, 1977), p. 24; A. Rita Ferreira, O Movimento Migratorio de Trabalhadores Entre Moçambique e a Africa do Sul (Lisbon, 1963), p. 68.

attract workers, the colonial state had to resort to undisguised coercion. As early as 1899 the first native labor code was introduced. Article One documented the legal rationale for forced labor, known as *chibalo*, which continued under varying guises until 1961: "All native inhabitants of the Portuguese overseas are subject to the moral and legal obligations to seek to acquire through work those things which they lack to subsist and to improve their own social conditions. They have full liberty to choose the means through which to comply with this obligation, but if they do not comply in some way, the public authorities may force them to comply."[12]

And force them they did. Local administrators had complete discretion to determine who was "idle," and virtually all *chefes de posto* supplemented their modest salaries with gifts and favors from European planters, merchants, factory owners, and farmers in return for African labor. As a result, the rural areas were transformed into large labor reserves. When workers were needed to plant sisal, sugar, tea, or cotton; to build roads; to expand the ports of Lourenço Marques and Beira; to lay railroad lines; to serve as domestics; or for any other private or public tasks, local administrators readily provided them. It was not uncommon for men, captured and bound by African police, to be sent to distant areas to work on state or private projects for a year or two, even though the theoretical limit for *chibalo* labor was six months. Moreover, Africans could expect to be conscripted many times in the course of their lives.[13] Women, although legally exempt from *chibalo*, often suffered a similar fate. An American sociologist visiting Mozambique in 1924 observed that

> women, even pregnant or with a nursling, are taken for road work by cipaes. In out-of-the-way places the Government builds little barracks to house them. No pay nor food. According to the circumscription the term is from one week to five but a woman may be called out again in the same year. Others in the village bring food to them, in some cases a day's journey away. Girls as young as fifteen are taken and some are made to submit sexually to those in charge. They work under a black foreman who uses a stick. They begin work at six, stop an hour at noon and work til sunset. There are some miscarriages from heavy work.[14]

Chibalo laborers worked under grueling conditions. They were entitled to neither food nor lodging, were subjected to repeated physical abuses, and received little or no remuneration. Skilled *chibalo* workers, such as carpenters, earned barely 10 percent of the salaries of their free counterparts. In rural areas planters and merchants regularly withheld remittances from their workers' wages and often bound them through a system of debt peonage.[15]

Besides providing a regular source of cheap labor, *chibalo* offered several benefits to private employers and the state. It "encouraged" Africans to enter the labor market, it helped keep wages down, and it reduced the bargaining position of free African labor. On a number of occasions, most notably during the Lourenço Marques port strikes of 1918 and 1921, state officials used *chibalo* laborers to undercut the effectiveness of defiant

Magaiças, or Mozambican mineworkers, stripped for inspection before going off to South Africa (Credit: Santos Rufino, *Albuns fotográficas*, 4 [Munich, 1929], p. 110)

strikers. Colonial officials also regularly intimidated "troublemakers" and "malingerers" by threatening to send them off to *chibalo*.[16]

Despite the obvious appeal forced labor held for undercapitalized Portuguese employers and European firms, it exacerbated the existing shortage of labor by driving thousands of additional Mozambicans clandestinely to the plantations and mines of South Africa and Southern Rhodesia. Indeed, farmers in southern Mozambique and planters along the coast bemoaned this loss of labor and regularly mounted campaigns to restrict such movement.

The settler community became particularly incensed when the colonial government, anxious to secure "rent" for the loss of its nationals, signed a formal agreement in 1901 with the Witwatersrand Native Labour Association (WNLA), official representative of the South African mining industry. Under this accord, the colonial government received 13 shillings per worker plus 6 pence more for each month's service beyond the initial one-year contract period. In addition, half of each worker's salary was paid directly to the colonial government in gold at a fixed rate of exchange that was appreciably below the market price of gold. This permitted the Portuguese government to resell it on the world market at a substantial profit. Throughout the colonial period, the recruitment tax, together with the sale of gold, was a major source of income and ensured Mozambique's continued economic dependence on South Africa.

The 1901 treaty also laid the foundation for another form of dependence on South Africa. In return for cheap labor, the South African state agreed to divert to the port of Lourenço Marques a specified percentage of imports to and exports from the Transvaal. By 1917 the customs duties and related transshipping charges, about $700,000 per year, constituted almost one-third of the state's revenue and was the single largest source of colonial income. Eleven years later an amendment to the original agreement set the Transvaal export-import figure at 47.5 percent. If for some reason this figure was not reached, South Africa agreed to pay the difference to the Mozambican Port and Railway Authority.[17]

While southern Mozambique became an economic satellite of South Africa, the central part of the country grew increasingly dependent on Southern Rhodesia. The 1914 Tete Agreement permitted that country to recruit 25,000 Mozambican laborers annually. In addition, the port of Beira, Mozambique's second largest port, became the principal link between landlocked Southern Rhodesia and the world. Although small by comparison to the volume of trade with South Africa, by 1913 rail and port revenues had reached almost a quarter of a million dollars.[18]

Just as the shortage of capital necessitated the export of labor to South Africa and Southern Rhodesia, it compelled Lisbon to turn over to foreign concessionary companies the direct administration and exploitation of much of central and all of northern Mozambique. The most important of these firms were the Zambesi, Mozambique, and Nyasa companies. The companies were expected to administer their areas under the theoretical supervision of the governor-general[19] and to develop large-scale agricultural and mining operations. Because they themselves were underfinanced, however, they made little effort to do either. Instead, they were content to use their monopoly of police power to extract taxes from the Africans living on their land, to purchase agricultural products at depressed prices, and to export African labor to neighboring colonies.

Consider the case of the Mozambique Company, founded in 1888 and the oldest of the concessionary firms. Capitalized at only £40,000, its stated objective was to exploit the rich mineral deposits in the central regions of Manica and Sofala. Although Lisbon tried to stimulate the interest of Portuguese investors, British and French concerns quickly dominated the firm. Rather than develop the region, the company derived handsome profits from speculating in stocks, collecting taxes, compelling men to work on wild rubber and coconut plantations, forcing women to grow cotton that company agents purchased at depressed prices, and selling conscripted labor to adjacent settler estates. By 1928 company officials estimated that 95 percent of the able-bodied men in its territory were "gainfully employed." To minimize expenses the directorship kept salaries of local European employees low, expecting them to supplement their wages by pillaging the local population. Forced labor and related abuses precipitated two major uprisings in 1902 and 1917. In both cases the company refused to assume the cost of containing the rebellions, despite its legal mandate, and Lisbon had to intervene at substantial expense. In short, the Mozambique Company in no way achieved its objectives. This sorry state of affairs was acknowledged by the governor of Manica and Sofala after the state refused to renew the concession in 1942. "They did nothing," he observed, "to develop the potential wealth of this entire region, preferring to plunder it and alienate the natives."[20]

If the Mozambique Company failed to live up to Lisbon's expectations, the experience of the Nyasa Company in the northern third of the country was even more disastrous. Granted 73,000 square miles (190,000 square kilometers) of remote territory in 1891 without infrastructure or port access, the company failed to attract any investment capital. The directorate therefore discarded any pretense of development and transformed its holdings into a massive labor reserve and tax farm from which the company's European and African employees violently extracted peasant surplus. One horrified observer writing in 1914 commented, "So far as the native is concerned, this is a land of blood and tears, where the most brutal ill treatment is no crime and murder merely a slight indiscretion."[21]

Thousands of young men living within the company's territory were bound and exported to such diverse locations as the gold mines of South Africa, the copper mines of Katanga, the port of Mombasa, the sugar estates of the lower Zambesi, and the cocoa plantations of São Thomé. Company officials obtained additional profits by progressively increasing the hut tax that every adult male was forced to pay. Those who failed to meet this obligation were beaten by the company *sipais* and their families brutalized and held hostage. "The tax," reported one British official in 1912, "is collected by the simple expedient of sending out the native soldiers from the post at collection time to round up all the women on whom they can lay their hands. The women are brought to the posts and kept there until the husbands and fathers rescue them by paying taxes."[22] Nyasa Company officials also permitted Arab and Swahili slavers to operate freely within their territory, profiting from the sale of guns, powder, and chains. It is little wonder that during World War I, when German forces from Tanganyika conquered portions of northern Mozambique, they were often hailed as "liberators."

The Zambesi Company, which in 1892 had received as a concession the decaying *prazo* system in Zambezia district and part of Tete district, served primarily as a regional landlord. It subleased most of its holdings to European estate owners and agricultural companies controlled by British, French, and German investors, who continued their profitable operations after the Zambesi Company's concession had expired. The most significant of these agricultural firms were the Madal Society and the Boror Company, which planted large copra plantations on the Quelimane coast, and the Luabo Company and Sena Sugar Estates, Mozambique's largest sugar producers. The individual estate owners and larger companies both received a de facto monopoly of political power, which they used to extract labor and produce at artificially depressed prices. The Zambesi Company, like the Nyasa Company, also exported conscripted labor to São Thomé, the South African gold mines, and adjacent settler estates.[23]

The fact that the colonial state failed to revoke the concession of any of the companies, even though all failed to meet their contractual obligations, is just one indication of its fragile position and many problems. Indeed, by the early 1920s, a serious economic and political crisis had gripped Mozambique. Runaway inflation, devaluation of the Mozambican currency, and a dramatic decline in the price of agricultural commodities together exacerbated the colony's tenuous economic position.[24] The prevailing sense of pessimism is reflected in the assessment of a Portuguese settler that "only fools or careless people who have a passionate love for the colony, those who were called good colonists, because they bury there everything they make, frequently losing it, dare to use their wealth here in new undertakings." Everyone else, he noted, "takes from the province all that he makes and invests it where he may have the certainty of greater and surer gain without work or worry."[25] To make matters worse, South African investors and officials, anxious to maintain and expand the republic's economic hegemony over Mozambique, blocked British loans that might have permitted some economic growth.

Mozambique's political crisis stemmed from more than twenty years of mismanagement, corruption at all levels of the colonial bureaucracy, and financial manipulation by special interest groups. In an effort to turn this situation around, in 1920 the republican government in Lisbon reorganized and centralized the administrative structure by appointing a high commissioner to replace the governor-general. In theory, the high commissioner had much greater authority than his predecessor, including the power to make critical economic and political decisions, thereby avoiding the long delays involved in communicating with Lisbon. It also created local legislative councils to give a greater voice to the settler community. The appointment of Manuel Brito Camacho, a highly regarded "reformer," as the first high commissioner held out the hope that corruption would disappear and development begin.

The high commissioner had a clear vision of how Mozambique should progress. He favored an emphasis on agriculture and industry in the south, sharp curtailment of the "ruinous labor exports" to South Africa, improved working conditions for Africans, and reduced influence of special interest groups. By the time of his death in 1924, he had achieved none of these objectives—South Africa vigorously campaigned against reducing labor exports and even threatened direct annexation of southern Mozambique; settlers in the south and planters in the north opposed any reform in labor laws; and the powerful Overseas National Bank was still able to engage in currency manipulation.[26]

Moreover, the high commissioner received little assistance from the republican government in Lisbon, which, facing increasing political instability itself and on the verge of bankruptcy, was forced to channel all its energies into thwarting a right-wing coup. On May 28, 1926, a conservative alliance of the Catholic Church, large landowners, bankers, industrialists, and important segments of the military brought down the metropolitan government. In 1928 an obscure professor of economics, António Salazar, became minister of finance. Over the next four years he consolidated his dictatorial power, thereby ushering in forty years of fascism.[27]

MOZAMBIQUE UNDER THE SALAZAR REGIME, 1928–1962

"The distinguishing feature of Portuguese Africa . . . is the primacy which we have always attached to the enhancement of the value and dignity of man without distinction of color or creed."[28] So proclaimed Salazar in 1962. But colonialism, like slavery, is scarcely understood by reference to official ideology. Stripped of its rhetoric, Salazar's colonial policy rested on three interdependent propositions. First, the colonies had to remain under the firm grip of Lisbon. Salazar rejected decentralization, local autonomy, and democracy in favor of highly centralized, authoritarian rule. For Salazar the colonies were merely an extension of Portugal, "like the Minho or Beira," he asserted. "Angola, or Mozambique or India is under the single authority of the state."[29] Second, the human and natural resources of Mozambique had to be more effectively and directly exploited, for the benefit of the metropole and the nascent Portuguese capitalist class rather than for the benefit of foreign investors. To achieve this goal he promoted a neomercantilist policy in which state intervention figured prominently at all levels of the economy and that included the introduction of a new labor code to rationalize the *chibalo* system. Finally, Salazar reaffirmed that the colonial state in alliance with the Catholic Church had a civilizing mission—to bring Christianity and Portuguese culture to the "primitive" Africans—that would also bind Africa to the Portuguese empire. This interplay of factors is represented in the commonly repeated slogan, "One state, one race, one faith, and one civilization." These guiding principles were enshrined in the Colonial Act of 1930, which Salazar himself wrote, and the slogan was incorporated verbatim into the 1933 Portuguese Constitution.

The Salazar regime acted almost immediately to increase state power in Mozambique. In 1928 it refused to renew the contract of the Nyasa Company, and two years later it abolished the *prazo* system, thereby regaining direct administrative control over more than 100,000 square miles (260,000 square kilometers)—more than one-third of the entire country. At the same time Lisbon imposed a highly centralized, uniform administrative code that, among other things, reaffirmed its hegemony over subject populations and formalized the *Regime do Indigenato*, which ensured that the overwhelming majority of Africans would be legally frozen into a subordinate race, class, and cultural position.[30]

Under the *Regime do Indigenato*, Africans and mulattoes were divided into two groups. The tiny minority who could read and write Portuguese, had rejected "tribal" customs, and were gainfully employed in the capitalist economy were classified as *assimilados*. In principle, they enjoyed all the rights and responsibilities of Portuguese citizens. Africans and mulattoes who could not satisfy these requirements had to carry identity cards, fulfill stringent labor requirements, and live outside European areas. These persons, known as *indigenas*, were not considered citizens, and they remained subject to customary law.

Although it was theoretically possible for any African or mulatto to change his or her legal status, the constraints imposed by the colonial-capitalist system—including the lack of schools, the limited opportunities for paid employment, and the culturally arrogant and racist assumptions of the authorities—effectively precluded this. Colonial Minister Armindo Monteiro, speaking to a conference of administrators in 1935, revealed the state's hypocrisy: "We do not believe that a rapid passage from their African superstitions to our civilization is possible. For us to have arrived where we are presently, hundreds of generations before us fought, suffered and learned, minute by minute, the intimate secrets in the fountain of life. It is impossible for them to traverse this distance of centuries in a single jump."[31] As late as 1961 less than 1 percent of the African population had been legally assimilated.

Under Salazar the settler community lost the relative autonomy it had enjoyed during the republican era. The high commissioner's office, which had been responsive to their interests, was replaced by a governor-general who merely administered policies formulated by the Overseas Ministry, while the local municipal governments and the Mozambican Provincial Assembly became rubber stamps for the Portuguese dictatorship. As one prominent white jurist recalled, "All the major decisions (and the tiny ones) which guided the life of the courts were taken in Lisbon. It was there that the main laws were worked out and it was in terms of those laws that the courts had to define their activities and to which they had to confine themselves. That is to say, the laws forged in the colonizing metropole were exported just like wine or cloth to the colonies and constituted a body of foreign norms."[32]

The Salazar regime also added a veneer of corporatism and a new level of political repression. Although the corporatist ideology was never as firmly entrenched in Mozambique as it was in the metropole, the fascist regime dismantled the independent white trade unions and replaced them in 1937 with state-controlled corporate syndicates, which became the sole legal representatives of the white workers. "The labor organizations, sindicatos," observed the U.S. vice-consul in Lourenço Marques in 1955, "are kept under very close government control, in accordance with the Portuguese Corporate State concept of the position of labor in the economy, and in society. . . . Strikes are prohibited, and key sindicato officials are appointed, and may be removed, by the government."[33]

To ensure the social harmony envisioned by corporatist ideology, the state in Mozambique, as in Portugal, employed numerous instruments of oppression. Censorship, informers, secret agents, police, the military, and the court system were used to repress any opposition—black or white—that surfaced. The secret police's reign of terror remains legendary to this day.

Colonial economic policy hinged on Salazar's conviction that the territories should produce raw materials and send them to the mother country in exchange for manufactured goods. State officials considered Mozambique, with its fertile lands, good rainfall, accessible ports, and largely "unproductive" population, ideally suited to producing agricultural commodities that, in turn, would be either consumed in Portugal or transformed there into finished goods, some of which would be reexported to the colonies. Rather than selecting one system of production, colonial officials sought to maximize output by stimulating the existing plantation system in the central part of the country, encouraging Portuguese peasants to migrate to and settle in southern Mozambique, and compelling African peasants, primarily in the north, to produce cotton and rice.

In all parts of the colony, however, the state's economic policy depended upon the continued exploitation of cheap African labor. Greater administrative centralization facilitated more effective social control and labor recruitment—through census taking, tax collection, and vigorous enforcement of labor laws. At the same time increasing international pressure convinced Lisbon to issue a new labor code in 1928, which ostensibly put an end to forced *chibalo* labor except for purposes of penal correction and necessary public works. This code echoed earlier theoretical guarantees that Africans had "full liberty of choosing the work which best suits them" in order to "fulfill their moral duty . . . of working to secure their livelihood and of thereby contributing to the welfare of humanity."[34]

Yet behind this moral rhetoric, legislation passed in 1930 had the effect of obligating the overwhelming majority of African men to work as contract laborers at least six months a year, either for private employers or the state, in order to pay their taxes. To facilitate enforcement, each adult male had to carry a passbook that recorded his last date of employment and when he had paid taxes. To close existing loopholes and provide greater clarity, in 1942 the governor-general issued a decree that expanded the definition of who was "idle," and therefore eligible for contract labor, to include all men between 18 and 55 who had not worked in South Africa or Southern Rhodesia under a legal contract for the past six months, who were not currently employed by European firms or the state, and who were not cultivating cotton or rice. Africans self-employed in a profession or commerce or who owned a minimum of fifty head of cattle were also exempt. As there were only 600,000 African-owned head of cattle in the entire country, only 12,000 farmers could have possibly been protected under this clause. The governor-general offered the following rationale for this legislation: "The rendering of work in Africa cannot continue to depend upon the whim of the Negro, who is, by temperament and natural circumstances, inclined to spend only the minimum effort necessary to meet his basic needs."[35]

The effect of this legislation was to formalize the collaboration between local administrators and agricultural company recruiters, planters, and farmers, all of whom depended on African labor despite the official prohibition on *chibalo*.[36] When private employers needed workers, they merely contacted the local administrators, who were eager to meet their requests in return for a substantial bonus. In 1950, the well-known American traveler, John Gunther, described the system as follows:

> An up-country planter informs the government that he will be needing so many men, these are provided for him by the local *chefes de posto*, or District Officers. Native recruiters go out into the villages, and collect the necessary

number of men, who are then turned over to the planter. But the planter, to be sure of getting all the recruits he needs, usually has to pay off ten times the contract laborers' wages for six months. Nothing more vicious can be imagined.[37]

Those members of the rural population who refused to work or tried to flee were whipped or beaten. Those who managed to escape generally returned when they heard that their families were held hostage or their wives and daughters sexually abused.

If the number of contract laborers recruited in this manner proved inadequate, the *chefes de posto* merely sent *sipais* to neighboring villages to detain "troublemakers," "tax evaders," "malcontents," and other undesirables. The detainees were then reclasssified as *chibalo* workers. Pruan Hassan, a peasant from Cabo Delgado, was recruited in the 1950s in this fashion. He recounted his experiences as follows:

> I was in my village at Nawana quite ill. The *sipais* entered my hut and beat me because I had not completed planting my cotton field. One raped my wife. Then I was bound and taken with other villagers to Nangoro [sisal plantation] where I was given a strip of land to work each day. Because I was still ill, I could not finish, so the overseers beat me. At Nangoro we only received food once a day and only if we completed our task. The porridge often had sand and pulp in it. On occasion they gave us corn with a bit of dried fish but it was never enough to go around. Many workers died.[38]

The account of a peasant conscripted to work on a tea plantation at Gurue in central Mozambique is strikingly similar.

> I was arrested by *sipais* at my house and taken to the administration. There were many others there. We were marched to Gurue 3 days away. . . . The overseers supervised our labor and if we did not finish our assigned daily tasks, we were considered lazy and punished. For six months we picked tea, filling large bins which we had to lug on our backs. There in the tea fields many people became ill. Few were treated in the hospital. Many died. On most days we were given porridge full of red ants and nothing else. At the end of six months we received 150 *escudos* [US $6.00].[39]

As in the earlier period, contract laborers not only worked under grueling conditions and were often subjected to physical abuse by African *sipais* and European planters, but they received almost no remuneration for their labor. As late as the 1950s the fixed salary for six months of labor was often as little as $3 per month, and the workers were responsible for arranging their own food, clothing, and lodging, as well as taxes and "gifts" for the chief when they returned home. Numerous accounts exist of sexual abuse by European and African overseers against the workers' wives and daughters, who came to give them their daily rations.

To meet the needs of the settler community, local administrators regularly provided penal labor to supplement the work force. Peasants incarcerated for violating the Criminal Code were shipped under guard to European estates. Unlike the contract and *chibalo* laborers, they received no remuneration, and their services often extended beyond the six-month period.

State intervention and organization of the labor supply provided substantial benefits both to Lisbon and to private local capital. The state gained additional revenue by issuing recruiting licenses and attaching salaries of contract workers to guarantee that current as well as past taxes were paid. In addition, the bonuses to local administrators served as wage supplements that permitted the Salazar regime to retain its low salary structure. For private capital, access to a supply of cheap and constant bound labor held an obvious attraction. Moreover, by relying on short-term migrant workers, management was able to adjust its labor requirements during the slack period and to avoid allocations of food and clothing to maintain the workers. While large agricultural firms, like Sena Sugar, provided minimal food and housing, many plantations and farmers offered neither. Thus, by purchasing the labor power of their employees at depressed rates and minimizing expenses, the various fractions of the capitalist agricultural sector were able to extract extremely large profits. By the 1950s government estimates, as well as those of contemporary observers, placed the number of contract and *chibalo* workers at well over 100,000.[40]

The Salazar regime's labor policies, coupled with the sharp expansion of the post-Depression international agricultural commodity market, contributed to a resurgence and expansion of the plantation sector. Sugar, sisal, and copra estates located in central and northern Mozambique substantially increased their output. Between 1939 and 1958, for example, sugar exports increased from 79,000 to 165,000 tons, sisal from 10,000 to 32,000 tons, and copra from 14,500 to 25,000 tons. In addition, settlers and foreign investors resuscitated the tea industry centered at Gurue in Zambézia district. Production jumped from 117 tons in 1934 to 40,000 tons in 1958.[41] By 1960 these commodities constituted 60 percent of the total value of all Mozambique's exports (see Table 3.2).

Lisbon also used the availability of bound African labor as an incentive to attract Portuguese peasants to Mozambique. In addition, the immigrants received choice tracts of land, cash bonuses, livestock, low-interest credit, and substantial technical assistance. Between 1937 and 1959 the number of new arrivals rose from 1,900 to 10,000 a year. Most settled in Lourenço Marques and Beira; the remainder established farms in the interior—primarily on expropriated African lands in the fertile southern Limpopo Valley and in the Manica highlands, where they cultivated citrus fruits, bananas, and vegetables. By the 1960s the 3,000 European planters and farmers controlled more land than 1.5 million African peasants. The average European holding was 1,405 acres (562 hectares) as compared to 3.5 acres (1.4 hectares) for an African family (see Table 3.3). Portuguese peasants had no difficulty adjusting to their relatively privileged class position. "Availability of native labor," a U.S. consular official disdainfully noted, "does not make farm labor appealing to the average European farmer who would rather supervise and direct the black man than engage himself in physical work."[42]

TABLE 3.2
Agricultural Exports as a Percentage of Total Exports, Selected Years
1955-1964

	1955	1960	1962	1964
Cotton	25.41	32.47	23.43	18.65
Cashew	8.46	11.12	10.49	19.99
Sugar	12.60	13.25	13.19	8.07
Copra	8.26	9.26	7.82	6.84
Sisal	7.16	8.47	6.37	9.03
Tea	9.15	8.40	6.87	5.39
Vegetable oils	5.27	2.43	2.24	4.92
Fruits	0.34	0.52	1.27	1.15
Tobacco	0.37	0.65	1.24	0.95
Remaining exports	22.98	13.43	27.08	25.11
Total exports (thousand escudos)	1,695,766	2,099,250	2,615,832	3,042,973

Sources: United Nations, General Assembly, Summary of the work of the
Special Committee of Twenty-Four, United Nations and Decolonization:
Report of the Special Committee on the Situation with Regard to the
Implementation of the Declaration on the Granting of Independence to
Colonial Countries and Peoples (New York, 1965), Annexes, p. 435 (de-
rived from Moçambique, Comércio Externo (1955-1962); Moçambique, Anuário
Estatístico (1964); and Moçambique, Boletim Mensal (December 1964).

TABLE 3.3
Farming Units by District, 1967

	Number of Units		Area Occupied (1,000 hectares)		Average Size of Unit (in hectares)	
	tradit.	devel.	tradit.	devel.	tradit.	devel.
Lourenço Marques	53,628	567	77.4	329.5	1.4	581
Gaza	156,432	1,779	248.0	348.7	1.6	296
Inhambane	159,019	185	279.1	121.5	1.8	657
Manica and Sofala	135,446	451	224.3	676.8	1.7	1,501
Tete	99,865	61	152.3	46.2	1.5	757
Zambezia	277,961	308	219.0	376.5	0.8	1,222
Moçambique	419,745	553	688.9	302.9	1.6	548
Cabo Delgado	149,946	106	173.1	49.3	1.2	465
Niassa	62,975	33	107.8	20.7	1.7	628

Source: Standard Bank Group, Annual Economic Review, Mozambique 1968
(London, 1968), p. 3.

TABLE 3.4
Cotton Exported to Portugal, 1926-1946 (in kilograms)[a]

1926	337,967
1927	291,654
1928	165,873
1929	249,558
1930	189,994
1931	159,251
1932	1,083,805
1933	1,057,214
1934	1,919,420
1935	1,829,277
1936	3,247,105
1937	8,226,107
1938	7,492,406
1939	6,576,288
1940	4,473,328
1941	5,012,612
1942	14,146,295
1943	13,245,704
1944	22,659,989
1945	17,256,570
1946	29,003,688

[a]These figures represent cotton after it had been pressed and cleaned. In general, there was a two-and-one-half ratio between raw cotton and ginned cotton.

Source: Arquivo do Instituto de Algodão, Junta de Exportação de Algodão Colonial, "Elementos para o seculo," Gaspar de Mello Furtado, Chefe da Delegação, June 15, 1954.

The most far-reaching economic change introduced by the Salazar regime was the imposition of forced cotton production in 1938 and of compulsory rice cultivation four years later.[43] The purpose of introducing cotton was to benefit Portugal's fledgling textile industry and to ease Portugal's acute balance-of-payments problem. In 1926 Portugal's factories had used 17,000 tons of cotton, 95 percent of which had to be imported from foreign countries. By 1945 more than 1 million Mozambican peasants,[44] primarily in the north, were producing enough cotton to meet the demands of the metropole, and cotton had become the colony's principal export (see Table 3.4).

Unlike most other agricultural activities, all aspects of cotton production and marketing were organized and controlled by the colonial state. It issued concessions to twelve Portuguese companies, each of which had both a buying monopoly within a specified part of the country and the responsibility to gin the cotton. In each region state officials established the minimum area a family had to cultivate as well as a timetable for planting, imposed a daily work schedule, mandated how often the cotton had to be weeded, instituted production quotas, and supervised the inland markets. The state-controlled Cotton Marketing Board also fixed prices paid by the concessionary companies to the peasants for raw cotton at artificially depressed levels in order to maximize the profits of the concessionary companies. This policy permitted the Portuguese textile industry to obtain Mozambican cotton at about half the world price. In 1939 the average price paid to African cultivators for first-class raw cotton was two cents per kilogram (just under one cent per pound), which rarely provided sufficient remuneration for peasants to pay their taxes. By 1957, after a number of highly publicized reforms and price increases, the average yearly income derived by a family from cotton production in northern Mozambique was $11, barely covering its tax obligation to the state; and family income in the least prosperous regions was often less than $4.[45]

Because of the onerous nature of the system and the minuscule financial return, the state had to use highly coercive tactics to ensure even partial peasant compliance. "If we refused to grow cotton they arrested us," recalled one elder; "they put us in chains, beat us and then sent us to a place from where we did not come back."[46] Peasants who rejected the seeds the state-appointed chiefs distributed or who failed to produce the established minimum quantity were compelled to work on sisal, tea, or sugar plantations for little or no remuneration or were deported to the cocoa estates on São Thomé. When sipais, who regularly patrolled the fields, noted that a particular cotton plot was not properly cared for, they beat the guilty party and, if it was a woman, often sexually abused her. Repeat offenders went to jail for sixty days or more, depending on the whim of the company overseers and local administrators. Samora Machel, who was to become Mozambique's first president, recalled that his own political education began "not from writing in a book. Nor from reading Marx and Engels. But from seeing my father forced to grow cotton and going with him to the market where he was to sell it at a low price— much lower than the white Portuguese grower."[47]

That the cotton could not be legally manufactured into textiles in Mozambique but had to be sent to Portugal was part of a broader state strategy to block the development of any transforming industries in the colony. This policy, together with a high protective tariff, ensured that Mozambique would remain a major market for the relatively backward and inefficient Portuguese industrial sector. In the period from 1928 to 1962, for example, industrial output was limited essentially to consumer commodities used by the growing Portuguese settler community—cigarettes, beer, cement, ceramics, and flour (see Table 3.5). By 1961 there were only eighty-one enterprises in the entire country capitalized at more than $150,000, and the total value of all manufactured goods was a meager $14 million.[48]

Salazar's policies, although they distorted the Mozambican economy, were extremely profitable for Portuguese capital. Throughout the 1940s and 1950s products from Portugal accounted for more than 30 percent of the total value of imports, almost double those from Great Britain, its nearest competitor (see Table 3.6). In the early 1960s this figure jumped

TABLE 3.5
Industrial Production, 1928-1946

Commodity	1928	1938	1946
Cement (tons)	14,049	24,297	26,275
Mineral water (liters)	129,280	1,200,000	1,511,443
Beer (liters)	22,780	609,115	2,254,186
Maize flour (tons)	2,718	11,668	32,944
Ice (tons)	2,960	4,609	6,612
Pasta (tons)	87	180	422
Cigarettes	263,708,860	256,120,000	--[b]
Soap (tons)	388	2,309	4,296
Butter (tons)	--	27	12
Cordials (liters)	--	4,178	28,496
Bricks (1,000)	--	6,559	13,538
Rice (tons)	--	100[a]	7,338
Dry fish (tons)	--	--	714
Ceramics (pieces)	--	71,680[a]	212,653
Leather art (tons)	--	--	201

[a]Figures for 1939

[b]Figure unknown

Source: David Wield, "Some Characteristics of the Mozambican Economy Particularly Relating to Industrialization" (University Eduardo Mondlane, Center for African Studies, Working Paper, 1976), pp. 4-5.

TABLE 3.6
Origin of Imports, Selected Years 1949-1961 (percentage of total value)

Year	Portugal	Britain	South Africa	United States	West Germany
1949	28.9	26.5	6.0	14.5	1.0
1950	29.2	19.3	7.9	11.4	2.6
1952	25.0	16.6	7.6	11.8	3.0
1954	26.5	15.8	7.5	18.0	7.3
1955	28.3	15.6	8.1	8.5	14.0
1956[a]	30.1	17.5	9.00	8.3	10.3
1957[b]	31.5	16.2	8.6	6.7	9.3
1961	29.7	12.3	10.7	7.1	9.3

[a]through October 1956

[b]through September 1957

Source: Compiled from Moçambique, Comércio Externo (Lourenço Marques, 1950-1962).

TABLE 3.7
Destination of Exports, Selected Years 1949-1960 (percentage of total value)

Year	Portugal	South Africa	Britain	U.S.	West Germany	India	Southern Rhodesia
1949	30.0	6.0	2.7	2.7	3.0	--	2.1
1951	34.8	5.3	2.0	6.1	4.9	--	1.6
1953	41.6	13.8	3.4	4.8	--	--	--
1954	41.5	5.9	3.4	6.0	3.5	--	3.7
1955	43.8	6.4	8.2	6.1	3.6	8.3	3.8
1956	40.2	5.5	8.1	5.5	3.3	9.0	3.4
1957	42.3	5.3	7.2	4.0	3.4	13.5	5.2
1958	45.0	3.4	7.7	4.2	--	12.5	--
1960	48.0	2.9	7.7	5.8	2.4	9.2	3.8

Source: Compiled from Moçambique, Comércio Externo (Lourenço Marques, 1950-1961).

to more than 40 percent. Throughout this period the colony imported from Portugal appreciably more than it exported, thereby serving as a net contributor of foreign currency to the embattled Portuguese economy while suffering itself from a progressively worsening balance-of-payments problem. In 1950 Mozambique's balance-of-payments deficit was $17.45 million, and a decade later this figure had more than tripled (see Table 3.8).

As this balance-of-payments deficit expanded, Mozambique's dependency on "invisible" income from South Africa and Southern Rhodesia grew proportionately. This income came primarily from wage remittances for Mozambicans who worked in the gold mines of South Africa and on the farms and mines of Southern Rhodesia and from the port and transit fees these two countries paid for the use of Lourenço Marques and Beira,

TABLE 3.8
Balance of Payments, Selected Years, 1950-1960
(in $ million)

1950	-$17.45
1955	-$35
1956	-$38
1957	-$37.5
1958	$42.6
1959	$45.8
1960	$53.6

Conversions from escudos are based on rate published in World Currency Charts (San Francisco, 1969), p. 57.

Source: Instituto Nacional de Estatística, Anuário Estatístico do Ultramar (Lisbon, 1951-1960).

Railroad maintenance crew (Credit: Mozambique, *Documentário Trimestral*, 2 [1935], p. 9)

respectively. Indeed, until 1957 invisible earnings offset the colony's negative balance of trade and thereafter reduced it to only a few million dollars.[49]

Thus, for all the rhetoric of economic nationalism, the Salazar regime failed to eliminate Mozambique's dependency on its English-speaking neighbors. Despite complaints from farmers, planters, and colonial officials about the shortage of African labor, the Portuguese government renegotiated new labor contracts with the South African mineowners and permitted substantial numbers of workers to go to Southern Rhodesia. Thus, throughout the period the number of Mozambicans legally employed in the South African mines hovered around 100,000, and an additional 100,000 Mozambicans worked legally in Southern Rhodesia. Colonial officials also estimated that 190,000 workers annually crossed clandestinely into Southern Rhodesia and South Africa during the late 1950s to seek employment.[50] Although the state derived no immediate benefit, a portion of the income the migrants brought home ultimately ended up in the colonial coffers.

As Africans represented solely a source of cheap labor, there was no need for the Salazar regime to do more than pay lip-service to its claim of a "great civilizing mission," and it made little sense to waste government resources on developing an educational infrastructure. Only a handful of *assimilados* and loyalists merited more than the most rudimentary education. The objective was to provide some members of the indigenous population with a veneer of Portuguese culture and minimal reading and writing skills, which would make them more effective clerks, low-level bureaucrats, industrial workers, and craftsmen. The first major piece of educational legislation promulgated in Mozambique in 1930 anticipated that "indigenous instruction would gradually lead the African from a savage to a civilized life, making him more valuable to society and to himself."[51]

In adopting this strategy the Salazar regime was simply reaffirming the policies and practices dating back to Mouzinho de Albuquerque—one of the leading late-nineteenth-century architects of Portuguese colonial policy. "As far as I am concerned, what we have to do in order to educate and civilize the 'indigena,' " he proclaimed, "is to develop in a practical way his aptitude for manual labor and take advantage of him for the exploitation of the province."[52] Thus, even before Salazar came to power, African educational opportunities were limited to a few rural missionary schools. In 1924 a delegation from the Phelps Foundation observed that "the failure to formulate and execute sound policies for the development of the native people is evidenced by the almost negligible provision for native education."[53] An enlightened official of the Mozambique Company echoed this assessment: "In our territory, as throughout the province, native education has been badly neglected. This neglect of one of the most important duties of colonialism by the state was never as glaring as it is now."[54]

From the outset of the Salazar period state officials, anxious to limit social expenditures on Africans, entrusted the training of virtually all *indigenas* to the Catholic Church. A central feature of this alliance between church and state, formalized in the Missionary Act of 1941, was the policy of severely limiting Protestant schools. By 1955, 2,000 of the 2,040 "rudimentary" schools were operated under the direct auspices of Catholic missionaries. Besides a spiritual monopoly, the church received substantial material benefits, including tax exemption on all its property and pensions for senior officials.[55]

In practice, African education was organized in three stages, each of which was designed to eliminate most students and to serve as a barrier to higher education. The *ensino de adaptação*, or rudimentary schools, theoretically introduced African children to Portuguese language and culture in order to bring them to the level of Portuguese children entering primary school. Teaching was exclusively in Portuguese. As a result, many children failed the examination normally given after three years and had to repeat the course one or more times. Even for the small percentage who ultimately passed, there was no certainty of advancing, as the law barred Africans over thirteen from entering primary school. Those who completed their primary program were theoretically entitled to go on to a fifth-year program that prepared them for either high school or technical training. That few mission schools offered the fifth-year courses effectively blocked all Africans from attending secondary school. Moreover, the maximum age for entrance into secondary school was fourteen, and it was rare indeed for any but

TABLE 3.9
State of Education, 1960

Type of School	Number of Students
Rudimentary (for Africans only)	361,966[a]
Primary	25,472[a]
Vocational	11,324[a]
Teacher training	574
Secondary	3,129[a]
Nongovernment and not subsidized by the state	9,075
Total	411,540

[a]Primarily students of European descent

Source: Eduardo de Sousa Ferreira, Portuguese Colonialism in Africa: The End of an Era (Paris, 1974), p. 77.

the most privileged Africans to have completed the three-year rudimentary program and five years of primary schools by that age.[56]

Thus, for the overwhelming majority of Mozambicans the deterrents to education were powerful—a limited number of rural schools, excessive entrance fees (equivalent to several weeks' salary per child), instruction in an alien language, age restrictions, and an alarmingly high failure rate— almost 70 percent. In addition, many peasant families, short of labor to grow cash and food crops due to the colonial labor policy, preferred to keep their children at home, where they provided an important source of domestic labor. By 1960, only about 400,000 children out of a total school-age population of approximately 3 million attended classes; more than 90 percent of these were enrolled in the first three grades and only 1 percent in high school (see Table 3.9).

Predictably, the quality of education was appreciably inferior to that offered in the state and private schools attended by the children of settlers and assimilados. Under the direction of stern missionaries, much of the school day was devoted to religious education, with only a smattering of Portuguese-language training, reading, writing, and elementary mathematics. The schools suffered from a lack of qualified teachers, most of whom were themselves graduates of a three-year missionary program, and from an acute shortage of books and other educational materials, which further increased the possibility that few children would advance beyond the preprimary "adaptation classes." The state acknowledged by 1958 that almost 98 percent of the population was still illiterate (see Table 3.10).

Although the schools failed to educate the overwhelming majority of Mozambicans, they did serve as disseminators of colonial ideology.

TABLE 3.10
Estimated Illiteracy Rates in the Portuguese Colonies, 1950

Colony	Total Population	Illiterate Population	Percentage of Illiteracy
Angola	4,145,266	4,019,834	96.97
Cape Verde	148,331	116,844	78.77
Guinea	510,777	504,928	98.85
Mozambique	5,738,911	5,615,053	97.84

Sources: Instituto Nacional de Estatística, Anuário Estatístico do Ultramar (Lisbon, 1958); Eduardo de Sousa Ferreira, Portuguese Colonialism in Africa: The End of an Era (Paris, 1974), p. 71.

Because the educational curriculum was controlled by the state, children learned about the heroic efforts of Portuguese adventurers and the richness of Portuguese culture while their own traditions and history were debased or ignored. Through experience, they also learned about the virtues of hard work, as they spent a good portion of their day in the fields where, like their parents, they were often compelled to cultivate cotton and rice for the benefit of the church.

Gabriel Maurício Nantimbo, who attended a mission school in Cabo Delgado, recalled his frustrating experiences: "I studied at the mission, but we weren't taught well. In the first place, they taught us only what they wanted us to learn—the catechism; they didn't want us to learn other things. Then every morning we had to work on the mission land. After 1958 our parents even had to buy the hoes with which we cultivated the mission land."[57]

Medicine, like education, was organized to serve the privileged white settler community. As one doctor recalled, health care "was characterized by the total absence of medical facilities in the rural areas. But in the three main towns—Lourenço Marques, Beira and Nampula—you can see sophisticated hospitals with sophisticated equipment. The inequality between town and country is a consequence of the political situation in the colonial days. Medical care was intended only to be given to a privileged group."[58] The fact that more than 90 percent of the doctors practiced in urban centers supports this contention. Even within the cities, very few blacks and mulattoes could afford to consult doctors, all of whom were European. A survey completed in 1957 indicated that the overwhelming majority of the Africans residing in Lourenço Marques had never been to a hospital and those who had were placed in overcrowded, segregated wards and "were treated like animals without any respect."[59]

Health conditions in the rural areas were even worse. The handful of doctors could not possibly serve the 80 percent of the population that lived outside the major cities. The minuscule allocation of state funds for rural health services further handicapped their efforts. Without proper medical facilities, decent housing, and sanitary facilities, Africans suffered acutely from a number of infectious and parasitic diseases. Many of these illnesses, such as tuberculosis, malaria, and smallpox, could have been treated at a relatively low cost by distributing prophylactics and by organizing rudimentary programs of health education. Although precise statistics are unavailable, one doctor who worked in Nampula Province estimated that the infant mortality rate in outlying regions often approached 700 per 1,000.[60]

THE SOCIAL COSTS OF COLONIAL-CAPITALISM

The central feature of Mozambique's colonial experience was the extraction of cheap African labor through state intervention. As a result of the imposition of contract labor, the system of *chibalo*, the use of penal labor, and the treaties with South Africa and Southern Rhodesia, Mozambique lost hundreds of thousands of the most productive members of rural society. Their departure, in turn, created serious demographic imbalances, profoundly altered the structure of rural society, and resulted in a sharp decline in agricultural productivity. Forced cotton and rice production further compounded the daily problems faced by most Mozambican peasants. Disruptions in the cycle of household production with an attendant decline in food production, increased debt, famines, disease, and soil erosion were all directly related to the state's imposition of forced cotton and rice cultivation. In short, the extraction of African labor on such an unprecedented scale profoundly changed the human and natural environment of Mozambique in ways that will take generations to overcome.

Although it is impossible to determine how many people actually left Mozambique, both legally and clandestinely, scattered references suggest the enormous scale. Emigration was, after all, the most common response to economic exploitation and political oppression during the colonial period. About 200,000 peasants, for example, resettled in southern Nyasaland between 1920 and 1945 to avoid contract labor requirements and the accompanying threat of *chibalo*. It is estimated that by 1950 there were more than 100,000 Mozambicans living in permanent exile in Southern Rhodesia, and a smaller but significant number had fled to Nyasaland, Tanganyika, and even Kenya. To the south, migration was almost entirely to South Africa. The average legal migration from 1920 onward hovered around 100,000 annually, and official government sources estimated that a somewhat larger number fled clandestinely each year. Generally, this flight was to avoid forced labor, which was particularly oppressive in southern Mozambique, the location of most of the European farms and therefore of the greatest need for conscripted workers. Migration from the south consisted almost entirely of adult males between the ages of twenty and forty, most of whom renewed their contracts several times. Many spent large portions of their most productive years outside the country or settled permanently in South Africa. The introduction of forced rice and cotton production precipitated a new wave of clandestine migrations (see Chapter 4).

The immediate effect of this large-scale and continued migration was the loss of Mozambique's most productive human resources. In the southern districts of Gaza, Inhambane, and Maputo, between 40 and 50 percent of the male population was absent at any one time, and in some subdistricts, such as Jangamo, the figure approached 65 percent.[61] Although the situation was not as extreme in the parts of Tete district near the Southern Rhodesian border, it was not uncommon for colonial administrators to report census figures reflecting appreciably more women than men. Whether the migration was individual or by family, the migrants tended to be the younger and stronger, precisely those members of rural society who were responsible for much of agricultural production. Left behind were the children, the crippled, the elderly, and most women.

Although the consequences have never been studied in depth, it is not unreasonable to assume that this large demographic imbalance reinforced tendencies toward polygamy and probably substantially depressed the birth rate. Moreover, in southern Mozambique, access to mine income and "target items" strengthened the exploitative *lobolo* (bride-price) system, and fathers greatly inflated the amount that had to be paid for their daughters. This, in turn, meant that more and longer periods of migration were necessary before young men could amass sufficient wealth to purchase their wives, to satisfy their debts, and to meet ritual and ceremonial obligations, obligations that became increasingly monetarized as the twentieth century progressed.

The sustained absence of men also altered the nature and structure of the family all over Mozambique. Women had to assume most of the socializing functions and supply almost all of the productive labor. A 1941 survey in Gaza revealed that women, many of whom were elderly, represented 80 percent of the agricultural labor force.[62] The long-term absence of men left them, in addition to performing their historic roles of producing and preparing the family's food and fetching firewood and water, with the responsibility of burning and clearing the fields, guarding the cattle, and thatching the huts. The colonial regime added additional duties—namely, forced labor and forced cultivation of cotton or rice. When women were rounded up to perform *chibalo*, there was no one to work on the family plot, prepare the food, and care for the children.[63]

The absence of men, who historically had played a critical role in clearing the fields and harvesting the crops, led to a decline in agricultural production in many rural areas—a development exacerbated by forced cotton or rice production. Because cotton and rice demanded great attention, it was impossible for the women to grow sufficient food for their families. A 1941 survey in Gaza Province concluded "that 50% of the women could not produce the forced cultures without seriously reducing food production."[64] Faced with this subsistence crisis in most parts of the country, women were compelled to reduce grain cultivation in favor of collecting manioc, which, although drought resistant and requiring little

Women carrying 50-kilogram bales of cotton to market (Credit: Portugal, *A Companhia de Moçambique; Monografia* [Lisbon, 1929])

attention, was much less nutritious. Studies analyzing the diets and nutritional status of the Mozambican population in 1955 concluded that the diets were neither adequate nor well balanced. "They lack energy foods, proteins, and fats and the animal/vegetable protein ratio is unsatisfactory." Furthermore, "during many months of the year, the amount of fresh vegetables and fruit consumed failed to provide satisfactory doses of minerals and vitamins."[65] Throughout the 1940s and 1950s famines were extremely common. As late as 1959 a confidential government report acknowledged that "the majority of the population is underfed" and warned that "it is absolutely necessary that cotton producers have sufficient food to enable them to work."[66] Moreover, the extremely low price the state established for rice and cotton made it impossible for families to purchase sufficient food supplies to supplement their meager harvests.

State health authorities failed to give serious consideration to the consequences of inadequate diets even though they undoubtedly affected productivity. Fragmentary data, based on limited reports from hospitals and rural clinics, suggest that nutritional diseases recurred with regularity. Kwashiorkor, rickets, scurvy, beriberi, and pellagra, in that order, were the most common, although there were some variations from one region to another. Rickets, caused by a deficiency of vitamin D, appears to have been most prevalent in the cotton-producing regions of northern Mozambique. Pellagra, commonly found among migrant laborers who were unable to maintain gardens and had little access to fresh vegetables, posed a serious problem in Zambézia, home of the large sugar, tea, and copra plantations.[67]

TABLE 3.11
Agricultural Wages, 1962-1963

Race	Number Employed	Average Wage (escudos)
White	803	49,644
Chinese	40	32,640
Mixed	82	27,102
Africans		
(over 18 years)	82,878	5,156
(under 18 years)	10,631	1,595

Source: Moçambique, Anuário Estatístico, 1966 (Lourenço
Marques, 1967), pp. 284-285.

Moreover, the income the men earned as contract laborers, when
they brought any home, was hardly enough to pay their taxes, much less
to purchase food or other basic commodities. In 1951 the average salary
for a contract agricultural laborer in the northern half of the colony ranged
from $1.73 to $3.46 per month.[68] Eleven years later, after several highly
publicized reforms, the monthly salary had increased to about $15 per
month—barely 10 percent of the salary paid to Europeans doing the same
work.[69] That Asians and racially mixed employees fared appreciably better
than their African counterparts demonstrates a convergence of race and
class (see Table 3.11).

Although most Mozambicans lived in a state of poverty, commodity
production and employment on the South African Rand provided the
preconditions for the formation of a small, nascent class of capitalist
farmers. From the moment the state sought to promote cotton and rice
production the indigenous authorities, like their European planter counterparts, were allowed—indeed encouraged—to recruit corvée labor to
work their fields. Their victims—the most destitute members of the local
communities accused of vagrancy, tax fraud, or some other petty offense—
lacked any legal recourse. With land and labor readily available it was
not uncommon for the chiefs qua capitalist farmers to plant 25 to 75 acres
(10 to 30 hectares) of cotton or rice for which they received substantially
higher payments than did peasants. There are also indications that in
southern Mozambique some members of the rural population who worked
on the South African mines accumulated sufficient capital to purchase
oxen and ploughs and to employ local labor on a seasonal basis.[70]

Although the vast majority of Mozambique's population remained
rural throughout the colonial period, major urban zones developed in
Lourenço Marques and Beira. They served primarily as service centers for
South Africa and Southern Rhodesia respectively, and their pattern of
development was conditioned by this role. From the outset of the colonial

period each was a foreign enclave in which British capital played the dominant role. Foreign capital requirements also determined the types of employment opportunities for African workers. Most males who migrated to these urban areas were employed in the ports, in related service areas, on the railroads, in light industry, or as domestics (see Table 3.12). A smaller number, often recruited as *chibalo* labor, worked for the municipalities themselves. Women seeking to support their rural households or to escape bad marriages worked in low-wage industries or more often as nannies or prostitutes.[71]

Even though both cities grew substantially during the twentieth century, the major foci of migration continued to be South Africa and Southern Rhodesia. In 1912, for example, only 5,000 Africans worked in Lourenço Marques while more than 91,000 were on WNLA contracts in South Africa. Thirty years later, only 47,000 Africans lived in Lourenço Marques, and not until 1957 did its African population equal the number of Mozambicans working in South Africa on WNLA contracts. As of 1962, Mozambique was still overwhelmingly rural; only 2.5 percent of the total population, consisting of most Europeans, Asians, mulattoes, and some Africans, resided in these cities and the other seven provincial capitals; 3.5 percent, almost entirely Africans, lived on the outskirts of towns; and 94 percent lived in the rural areas.

Within the cities the colonial regime vigorously enforced segregation by race and class. Europeans lived in modern apartment buildings or spacious private homes in the "city of cement." In Lourenço Marques, the small number of *assimilados*, who enjoyed protection under civil law and could therefore register their property, were grouped into two communities: Xipaminine, built in 1921, and Munhuanna, completed two decades later. In Xipaminine, the more fashionable of the two, rents were higher than the monthly salary of middle-range civil servants, which meant that only the most affluent *assimilados* could afford to live there. Although the residents had been promised free water, a garden, a market, and regular bus service, they had to pay for water, the garden never materialized, and the bus rates were so exorbitant that most had to walk to work.

TABLE 3.12
African Urban Employment, 1950

	Domestics	Fishing	Business	Industry	General Service	Construction and Public Works	Transportation and Communications
Lourenço Marques[a]	13,610	1,246	1,929	9,024	4,780	2,175	2,825
Beira[a]	14,924	1,038	3,935	14,924	6,196	3,350	3,935

[a]Includes the hinterland regions adjacent to the city

Source: United States, Department of State, NEA 4, "The Labor Movement in Mozambique-- Basic Report," Ralph W. Richardson, U.S. vice-consul, March 29, 1955.

Conditions in Munhuanna, located in a swampy region, were even worse, and high rents made the area almost as inaccessible as Xipaminine.[72]

Whatever the shortcomings of Xipaminine and Munhuanna, these communities must have seemed idyllic to the vast majority of Africans, who lived in makeshift shantytowns ringing Lourenço Marques and Beira. Because the colonial government defined cities as enclaves for the civilized and designated *indigenas* as temporary residents, no efforts were made to provide social services for the "migrant" communities, which as late as the 1950s "lacked the usual urban facilities such as made-up roads, street lighting, drainage and water-borne sanitation."[73] A smaller number of workers rented shacks or rooms from their Portuguese employers or from *cantineiros* (shopkeepers), and *chibalo* laborers lived in compounds run by the state and private firms, which health officials and contemporary observers agreed were unfit for human habitation.[74]

Until the 1960s a combination of rigorously enforced laws and social conventions prohibited Africans from entering "white" restaurants, theaters, and bathrooms, or for that matter from being in the city after dark without explicit permission. *Assimilados* stopped by police in the evening were also detained and abused if they were not carrying the identity cards that indicated their "privileged" status.

Laws that prohibited urban African workers from organizing unions together with de facto job reservation trapped them in the most menial jobs, if they were fortunate enough to find employment at all. The arrival of thousands of illiterate Portuguese, who received preferential hiring treatment, made their position even more precarious. "Each boat-load of metropole peasants," commented one foreign diplomat in 1960, "aggravates the unemployment problem and increases the African–unskilled white competition."[75] By the early 1960s it was estimated that white workers, regardless of their qualifications, earned twenty times as much as African workers, and mulattoes earned fourteen times as much.[76]

Unsatisfactory housing, the high level of unemployment, and the low wage scale created social problems characteristic of most colonial urban slums. Alcoholism, prostitution, and a wide range of poverty-related diseases were all products of colonial-capitalist oppression. In the evenings and especially on the weekends residents of the urban shantytowns plied themselves with liquor in order to escape the harsh realities of their daily lives. "Throughout the entire region from Matola [a suburb of Lourenço Marques] to Marracuene," reported a disgruntled colonial administrator, "it is common to encounter men, women, and even children in a drunken stupor weaving through the streets, paths, and even to the doors of the secretariat."[77] Portuguese *cantineiros*, anxious to attract African wages, stocked their shops, located on the fringes of the shantytowns, with cheap wine, beer, and brandy. By the late 1950s Mozambique was importing 8 million gallons (30 million liters) of Portuguese wine per year—a major source of income for metropolitan capital as well as a powerful mechanism of social control in the colony.[78]

Prostitution flourished in the urban centers and was probably the major source of income for most women, who found few other possibilities for employment. Indeed, for many widows and women whose husbands had abandoned them, prostitution offered almost the only opportunity for employment. Their clients included colonists, migrant laborers, and white tourists from South Africa and Southern Rhodesia, who flocked to Mozambique to sleep with black women. With the arrival of large numbers of Portuguese colonial troops after 1960 and their deployment throughout Mozambique, the evils of prostitution spread as well. Prostitution also prospered in way-stations for the miners returning from South Africa, such as Ressano Garcia, where miners were besieged by women eager to relieve them of their money.[79]

Yet despite the severity of the impact of colonial-capitalism, the people of Mozambique—peasants and workers, old and young—were more than merely victims of oppression and objects of ridicule. In a variety of different ways they asserted their dignity and struggled to limit colonial exploitation. This overlooked, but highly significant, chapter of Mozambican history merits far more attention than it has received to date.

4

Popular Opposition to Colonial Rule, 1900–1962

The native is by nature indolent. After four centuries of contact with the Portuguese he is still not even capable of copying him.

—Albano Augusto de Portugal Durão,
"Considerações sobre a Zambésia,"
Congresso Colonial (Lisbon, 1903), p. 9

I am coal
and you wrench me brutally from the ground,
and make me your mine, boss;
I am coal
and you light me, boss
to serve you eternally as a moving force
BUT NOT ETERNALLY, boss.
I am coal
and I have to turn, yes,
and burn everything with the force of my combustion.
I am coal
the exploitation burns me,
burns me alive like tar, by brother,
until I am no longer your mine, boss.
I am coal
I have to burn,
burn everything with the fire of my combustion.
Yes!
I will be your coal, boss!

—José Cravereinha, "Grito Negro."
Translated in Luís Bernardo Honwana,
"The Role of Poetry in the Mozambican Revolution,"
Lotus: Afro-Asian Writings, 8 (1971):151

"Indolent," "incapable," and "incompetent" are typical of the adjectives both colonial planners and local officials used to characterize Mozambique's African population. But as "Grito Negro" [The shouts of blacks] powerfully testifies, a simmering spirit of insurgency had long existed. Often submerged, rage periodically surfaced in acts of defiance even in the face of oppression. They took the form of tax evasion, work

61

slowdowns, desertions, and sabotage, which the authorities perceived as merely prima facie evidence of the docility and ignorance of the subject population. These perceptions notwithstanding, protests by peasants and rural laborers, strikes and work stoppages in urban centers, the apocalyptic anticolonial vision of independent African churches, and the protest writings of Mozambican intellectuals demonstrate that the subordinate classes were not just passive victims of oppression. In small but often significant ways they could, and did, alter both their working conditions and the quality of their lives.

RURAL PROTEST

Peasant opposition posed a recurring challenge to the colonial-capitalist system. To be sure, not all, or perhaps even most, peasants resisted. Resistance was not a knee-jerk reaction. It was a decision, carefully considered, with very serious consequences. In such a repressive environment it is hardly surprising that many people were intimidated. "How could we resist?" asked one former worker on a sisal plantation incredulously. "The *sipais* and overseers were always on our backs."[1] Many other peasants and urban and rural workers could think only of the immediate survival of their families and channeled all their time and energy into trying to eke out a living.

Moreover, divided from each other by space, ethnicity, religion, primordial kinship affiliations, the tyranny of their work schedule, and a host of other factors, individual peasants were relatively powerless to mount the sort of large-scale opposition that lends itself to detailed historical analysis. Their actions tended to be isolated, diffused, and sporadic; their limited aims and systemic importance hard to measure and easy to ignore. Yet, acting within the serious constraints imposed by the colonial-capitalist system, Mozambican peasants and conscripted rural workers did, to varying degrees, minimize the disruptive effects of Portuguese domination by struggling against the appropriation of their labor as well as the ravaging of both their culture and the basic social fabric of their communities. In so doing, they were also helping to build a powerful cultural legacy of resistance that would inspire later generations.

Throughout the colonial period, but especially before the Salazar regime, tax evasion recurred with great regularity. The rural population developed a variety of strategies to reduce or avoid the annual payments and thereby diminish both the likelihood of being conscripted and the amount of time they had to devote to commodity production instead of food crops. Peasants commonly falsified their age or marital status to reduce their financial burdens. Many young adults claimed to be minors, sometimes temporarily residing in prepuberty huts when the revenue officials arrived. Others sought exemption because of advanced age or serious affliction. Husbands often hid their junior wives or claimed that they were either sisters-in-law or wives of friends who had gone away to work. In Inhambane, where hut taxes were the norm, extended families gathered together in one hut, which they claimed to be their exclusive domicile. As neither the large concessionary companies nor the local administrators possessed precise census data, these efforts often proved successful.[2] Even after they were assessed, the peasants used duplicity to postpone, or even avoid, paying the taxes. As one frustrated Portuguese official in Marávia noted in 1928:

> The headmen and peasants belonging to the populations of Chiefs Cussarara, Chuau, and Capanga are engaged in an incredible campaign of passive resistance. When they are called to bring their taxes they come without any money and negotiate long postponements which they invariably exceed, necessitating the use of *sipais* to bring in the *fumos*, each of whom only brings in a small percentage of the taxes from their respective villages, and thus it takes many months, often an infinite period, before the obligations are liquidated.[3]

Other members of the rural population, warned by their neighbors, fled into the interior just before the arrival of the collector. Official reports indicate that women often claimed that their husbands were dead when, in fact, "they [had] temporarily fled, returning to the village shortly after the tax collectors or census officials had left."[4] In other cases, virtually the entire village would leave. "It remains unknown," a Quelimane official acknowledged, "how many times six or more adults will flee from their kraals, leaving only a blind, ill or elderly individual who is exempt from taxes."[5] These examples suggest the operation of a subterranean communications network extending between, and perhaps beyond, adjacent villages.

Africans living close to an international frontier moved back and forth, avoiding tax obligations on both sides. Peasants residing near the Tanganyikan border pursued this strategy with great skill, as did those located in the Malange region along the Nyasaland border.[6] The expansive, unmanned Southern Rhodesian frontier proved an equally inviting refuge. As early as 1904 one border official complained that the Africans "never paid taxes and are reported to be in a very wild state," concluding that "the natives invariably run away on the approach of the police or messengers and would appear to be ill disposed toward both the Portuguese and British administrators."[7]

The colonial regime used a variety of coercive techniques to try to curtail such activity. Some *sipais* were sent to villages to intimidate the local peasantry while other platoons were placed at strategic locations to block any mass exodus. Peasants who were caught or failed to pay their taxes on time were beaten in public and carted off to jail for periods ranging from six months to a year. In the territory of the Nyasa Company soldiers preemptively arrested large numbers of women, who were kept in jail until their husbands or fathers paid the appropriate taxes.[8] Despite these repressive tactics, the governor of Inhambane acknowledged in his 1909 annual report that tax resistance "cost a great deal of time and precious money."[9]

Thousands of rural Mozambicans compelled to work on settler farms, plantations, and state public works projects or to grow cotton and rice attempted to limit the amount of labor they provided to the colonial-capitalist system. The most extreme action was withholding their labor entirely by fleeing to neighboring colonies. Flight represented the harshest blow an individual peasant or rural laborer could strike against the productive demands of the colonial state. Despite the arduous and dangerous nature of clandestine emigration, by 1919 it was estimated that more than 100,000 Mozambicans had resettled in Nyasaland alone.[10] Twenty-five years later an official Nyasaland census placed the number of Mozambican immigrants at more than 380,000.[11] Even in the south, where the state exercised the greatest control, Portuguese authorities expressed concern that large numbers of Africans were fleeing the province of Sul de Save "because of cotton. . . . It was reported that many natives abandoned their lands after setting fire to their huts."[12] By 1960 probably more than one-half million Mozambicans had escaped Portuguese colonial rule.[13]

Other deserters, reluctant to break all links with their families and historic homelands but anxious to regain their autonomy and reconstruct the social fabric of their society, fled to sparsely populated backwater areas. There they created communities that bear a striking resemblance to the maroon societies organized by runaway slaves in the Americas and the Caribbean. In general, the refugees regrouped in rugged mountainous zones or in coastal swamps, where the difficult topography served as a natural barrier to Portuguese penetration. Several of these communities were able to remain free throughout the entire colonial period, surviving both the harsh environment and armed assaults by the colonial state. Pruan Hassan recounted a confrontation with the colonial authorities in the mountains near Meloco in northern Mozambique in the 1950s:

> As we were on the top of the mountain when the Portuguese came we allowed them to climb half-way before we rolled boulders down on them, killing some. Some of our people hid themselves in caves. When the Portuguese arrived they placed scrub and wood in the front and set it alight, thinking that all those inside would suffocate to death with the smoke—then they left. But as our people were deep inside the cave the smoke didn't reach them; no one died. So we continued to live there.[14]

Not content to remain outside the sphere of the colonial system, some of these bands of fugitives periodically returned to their homelands to attack the specific symbols of rural oppression—the plantation overseers, labor recruiters, tax collectors, collaborating chiefs, and African police—in an effort to protect their kinsmen and reestablish the preexisting order. Like the social bandits of Sicily and northeastern Brazil, these bands were led by individuals who, although branded as criminals by the state, were regarded as heroes by their own societies. Such confrontations continued sporadically until the 1950s, but they were most common in the early part of the century when Lisbon's position was tenuous.

Consider the career of Mapondera, the best-known social bandit of South-Central Africa. For more than a decade, at the turn of the century, his "outlaw" band of more than 100 men and a handful of women operated along the rugged Southern Rhodesian–Mozambican frontier in the Fungwe-Chioco region. It protected the local peasantry from abusive Portuguese and Southern Rhodesian tax collectors and labor recruiters and robbed the warehouses, stores, and fields of the concessionary companies. Indeed, Mapondera's own career as a social bandit had begun when he urged his followers not to pay taxes, which he considered to be the unjust demands of alien interlopers. According to the reminiscences of a British official: "About the year 1894 when the collection of the hut tax commenced and the general administration of the native was definitely assumed the Chief Mapondera gave a great deal of trouble by openly resisting the authorities and committing various crimes. The then Native Commissioner of the District, the late Mr. Pollard, attempted to arrest him but Chibaura [a praise name of Mapondera] and a small band of followers fled northward."[15]

Although British and Portuguese propaganda portrayed the rebels as outlaws alienated from the rural population, Mapondera and his followers benefited from material assistance by the peasantry. As their mobile existence made it impossible for them to always grow their own food and government attacks periodically destroyed the fields they did manage to cultivate, the grains and other foodstuffs that the peasants provided were critical. The rebels also received strategic assistance, ranging from surveillance of British and Portuguese patrols to warning of enemy attacks.

In 1901 Mapondera, convinced that oppression would end only with the defeat of the colonialists, entered into a broad anticolonial alliance with the neighboring Barue and the Muenemutapa. His goal, to "regain our homelands and our women and kill all the white men," struck a popular chord among peasants who longed for a return to the old order free from colonial exploitation. As a British commander admitted in 1901:

> At the time I wrote it [my earlier assessment] there existed a doubt as to whether the natives in the majority of the cases who had joined Mapondera had done so from force or not. I am in a position to positively state now that the majority did not do so by force but willingly so. In fact, all information I have received since my early reports goes forcibly to show that these natives only waited for the first opportunity [to rebel], and in getting such a leader as Mapondera a better opportunity . . . could not have arisen.[16]

By the time of his capture and execution in 1904, stories of Mapondera's heroic deeds had spread throughout a vast region of Mozambique and Southern Rhodesia. Like the famed tales of Robin Hood, oral traditions to this day recount his exploits, not only against the privileged and powerful Europeans, but also against authoritarian chiefs and African collaborators.[17] Embedded in the pages of Mozambican history are other examples of men and women like Mapondera, whom the colonial state contemptuously dismissed as "vagrants" or "outlaws."

Covertly withholding a portion of their labor was the most widespread expression of defiance by peasants and rural workers during the colonial period. This strategy was less risky than desertion or banditry and provided peasants with additional opportunity to cultivate badly needed foodstuffs.

In the 1920s European planters in the south bitterly complained about the "unreliability" and "ignorance" of their grossly underpaid laborers, who broke equipment, pilfered, and dragged their feet.[18] The governor of Inhambane also deplored the reluctance of the Nguni men to engage in agricultural labor, which they claimed to be "women's work."[19] Thirty years later a colonial official in northern Mozambique noted with disdain, "The Africans in this part continually fabricated excuses why they have not seeded any cotton. This year it is the lack of rain."[20] Workers on the Sena Sugar Estates acknowledged that at great personal risk some of their coworkers feigned illness, others illegally marked their tools with an "X" in stolen chalk indicating that they had finished a day's labor, while still others managed to convince the overseers that they had completed a line of sugar cane actually cut by someone else. A number of cunning laborers were also able to avoid their daily assignment by buying off the African overseers with a variety of favors.[21]

Occasionally this covert labor resistance flared into the open. Perhaps the most spectacular of the documented examples occurred at Buzi in 1947, when 7,000 women organized a strike and refused to accept the cotton seeds that the administrator ordered to be distributed. They maintained that with their men absent working on nearby sugar plantations, they had neither sufficient time nor labor to produce both cotton and food. As a token compromise, the administrator offered to exempt pregnant women and mothers of more than four children from forced cultivation.[22]

In addition to limiting the amount of time they allocated to cash crops, many peasants withheld the products of their labor. In the systems of forced rice and cotton cultivation, in which the state fixed the price at artificially depressed levels, many made the minimum contribution to the market, and some succeeded in covertly boycotting the system entirely. Rice growers consumed a large portion of their output. Cotton cultivators often roasted a portion of their seeds before planting them, let the crop rot in the ground, or scattered it in the bush. In Gaza Province cotton producers organized large-scale boycotts in 1955 and 1958 until local officials agreed to raise the prices paid for rice and cotton. Peasants who grew cash crops not under state control often sought to maximize their profits by selling their products at illegal markets or across international borders where prices were higher. Officials in Tete repeatedly complained that grain grown in the region ended up in Southern Rhodesia and Nyasaland, and a substantial clandestine commerce in cashew nuts existed between Mozambique and Tanganyika. Doctoring the weight of the commodities by hiding foreign objects in the sacks brought to market and pilfering from one warehouse and reselling to another also occurred with some frequency.[23]

Given the factors that tended to individuate the peasantry—the dissolution of collective work groups, the decline of supra-household kinship affiliations, heightened economic and social differentiation, and increasing numbers drawn into migratory labor—and frustrate any sense of class solidarity, it is hardly surprising that rural resistance rarely took a collective form. Nevertheless, several armed uprisings occurred even after pacification.

Of these, the Pan-Zambesian insurrection was most significant in terms of both its scale and its degree of success. From 1917 to 1921 peasants from seven different ethnic groups, angered by forced labor, increased taxation, mandatory cotton production, sexual abuses, and military conscription, united in an effort to dismantle the colonial system. In the words of one of the insurgents, "The Portuguese take our children away every day by force. I pay taxes, my people go to work, yet they send policemen to ravish our women. This is the reason we are fighting the Portuguese."[24] The rebels numbered more than 15,000 armed men. They were led by descendants of the Barue royal family and the transethnic network of spirit mediums, who appealed to the rich traditions of the past and to a common cultural heritage and who claimed that they had sacred medicines to turn European bullets into water. By June 1917, two months after the insurrection had begun, the rebels had destroyed the colonial administrative network throughout the southern zone of the Zambesi Valley and were confidently proclaiming that they would soon help liberate Southern Rhodesia.[25] Despite such heroic efforts, peasant-based movements were ultimately defeated, not only in the Zambesi Valley but throughout the colony, for the same reasons that the earlier ones had been—the extremely unfavorable balance of power. Even so, two decades later, smaller peasant uprisings were reported in Erati, Moquincal, and Angoche in northern Mozambique and in 1953 in Mambone just south of Beira.[26]

Throughout this section we have briefly examined the various forms of rural defiance without specific reference to the ways in which the protests varied either over time or space or among various segments of the population. With regard to changes in the forms of rural defiance over time, two contradictory tendencies seem to have been operating. On the one hand, virtually all types of resistance—permanently withholding all labor, regularly withholding a portion of one's labor, and short-term boycotts and insurrections—were reported throughout the entire period, and it is impossible to determine quantitative changes from one decade to another. On the other hand, collective violence, such as social banditry and rebellions, occurred most frequently before the 1920s. Taken together, these facts suggest that as the state began to consolidate its power through more careful surveillance and intensified intimidation, it was able to contain or eliminate insurgent activities that explicitly challenged the system. Similarly, increased surveillance and border patrols in the 1950s may have reduced peasant flight and surely made it a more difficult type of protest. The data suggest that there were somewhat greater opportunities to resist in the northern districts of Cabo Delgado and Niassa than anywhere else, although in no part of the country did the state or the concessionary companies have sufficient staff to mount a campaign of constant surveillance. "Free social space,"[27] within which peasants and rural workers could plan collective action undetected, existed or could be created more easily in both districts. Because they were considered marginal backwater areas, the state apparatus was appreciably weaker than in the more effectively policed southern districts, such as Gaza, or in the adjacent district of Moçambique. Moreover, the transportation and communications systems in Niassa and Cabo Delgado were largely undeveloped, and both had vast unpopulated areas—further reducing the potential for state or company surveillance and facilitating the establishment of maroonlike communities.

Although rural opposition tended to be generalized, there are indications that age and sex criteria were important in determining participation in one specific form of resistance—flight. Although there are numerous oral accounts and colonial reports of entire families fleeing, most commonly men deserted alone, and there are only a few indications of women opting for a similar strategy. In part, this reflects the fact that once free and across international borders, men had greater employment possibilities. Moreover, they probably had, or thought they had, a better chance to survive the rigors and dangers of clandestine flight. On the other hand, women, with stronger ties to their children and greater responsibility for feeding their families, were undoubtedly more reluctant to abandon their homelands except as part of a larger group. Elderly people also had stronger ties to the land, were less likely to survive the flight, and had fewer job possibilities abroad. Thus, the rate of defection was probably highest among young men. Apart from flight, however, there is no evidence that age, sex, or ethnicity per se were important factors in determining who resisted.

Should the fact that most of these acts of rural defiance were limited in scale and short in duration consign them to oblivion as futile and transitory gestures with no systemic importance? Clearly they failed to undercut or paralyze cash-crop production and plantation output. Nevertheless, flight, work slowdowns, and sabotage did pose serious problems for the plantations and European farmers as well as for the cotton and rice concessionary companies. And boycotts and circumvention of designated markets reduced the profit margins of investors and the state. In short, the evidence suggests that these protests not only narrowed the freedom of action of the state-capitalist alliance but also, when successful, blunted some of the most pernicious aspects of colonialism.

Where fear or coercion prevented opposition at the level of production, peasants and rural workers often manifested their hostility through cultural symbols unintelligible to the authorities. For example, the Chope, living in southern Mozambique, developed an entire repertoire of songs denouncing the colonial regime in general and the hated tax official in particular:

> We are still angry; it's always the same story
> The oldest daughter must pay the tax
> Natanele tells the white man to leave him alone
> Natanele tells the white man to leave me be
> You, the elders must discuss our affairs
> For the man the whites appointed is the son of a nobody
> The Chope have lost the right to their own land
> Let me tell you about it.[28]

The work songs of laborers employed by Sena Sugar Estates were even more explicitly hostile, often depicting the European overseers in the most unflattering, sexual terms. Themes of suffering and humiliation ran through a whole body of songs about Paiva, a hated European overseer, replete with obscene references to his genitals.

You are making us suffer
Beating me up
You, beating me up
You, Mr. balls owner
Your penis
You are making us suffer for nothing
Me, working for nothing
We've seen hardship with the sugar
Look we're getting just two hundred only
Getting three small cruzados only, your penis.[29]

To the north the Makua and Makonde artists ridiculed state officials, both African and European, in highly stylized carvings that distorted their features and eliminated their humanity.[30]

THE STRUGGLE OF URBAN WORKERS

Urban workers, like their rural counterparts, initially engaged in individual and sporadic actions to escape from or minimize the effects of the new capitalist economic order. They fled before the labor recruiters arrived at their villages, deserted in large numbers, "loafed," and on occasion, sabotaged machinery or raw materials. Although such actions continued to be the dominant mode of protest for *chibalo* laborers, by the second decade of the twentieth century urban wage earners had begun to shift their tactics and to organize within the new system in order to improve their conditions of employment.

Several factors militated against the organizing efforts of African workers during this period. First, their numbers were extremely small. Mozambique's retarded capitalist sectors employed relatively few full-time laborers. Moreover, the state explicitly prohibited Africans from forming unions, and government informers infiltrated the ranks of workers, who were in any case closely supervised by European overseers. The white labor movement, although struggling for better conditions of employment for its members, remained indifferent and often hostile to the needs of African workers, reflecting the racial and cultural prejudices that were part of official state ideology.[31]

Nevertheless, as early as 1911, a small group headed by Francisco Domingos Campos, Alfredo de Oliveira Guimares, and Agostinho José Mathias attempted to organize the African Union (União Africano) for all African workers in Lourenço Marques. They maintained that black workers had to organize if they were to survive, and they specifically warned against the divisive tendencies of tribalism and the danger posed by the refusal of workers in better-paying jobs to unite with common day laborers: "In order to avoid capitalist exploitation it is necessary that we all unite and organize the African Union, which will be composed of all classes from the humblest porter to the ordinary worker to the civil servant. In our association there will be no distinctions. . . . Let us unite and struggle forward side by side."[32] On the point of working-class struggle and solidarity they were equally unequivocal. Despite their eloquence and the power of their critique, strong opposition from the colonial-capitalist state and the white trade union movement, plus the lack of organizing skills and the high rate of labor migration to South Africa, undercut the African Union even before it got started.

There were a number of other sporadic attempts to organize African workers in Lourenço Marques. Strikes and work stoppages occurred among employees of the Merchants Association in 1913, tram workers in 1917, railroad technicians in 1918, and employees at an engineering firm in 1919.[33] In 1916, several thousand domestic laborers in Lourenço Marques refused to comply with registration laws. For almost two years, working through an informal underground network, they continued their boycotting even though more than 2,000 domestics were arrested.[34]

As in other parts of Africa, port workers were the most militant and best-organized sector of the labor force. During the first two decades of the twentieth century the port of Lourenço Marques had grown into a regional entrepôt for international commerce, linking the Transvaal and

Lourenço Marques dockworkers unloading rails, 1910 (Credit: *Relatórios sobre Moçambique,* 5 [Lourenço Marques, 1948], p. 48)

Swaziland as well as southern Mozambique to the larger world economy. Despite the strategic economic importance of the port and the state's efforts to prevent any dislocation of traffic, there were seven major strikes between 1918 and 1921, precipitated by the refusal of the shipping and forwarding companies to increase African wages to keep up with the spiraling postwar inflation. All strikes at the port followed the same broad pattern. Disgruntled workers, organized through informal grassroots networks, refused to work unless their wages were adjusted. As soon as they gathered in front of the main entrance to the port demanding better salaries and working conditions, the colonial governor sent in troops to smash the demonstration and arrest the leaders and used *chibalo* workers as strikebreakers to keep the port going. The strikes were always quickly broken, and even when the employers agreed to pay increases, they often reneged, as they did in the 1919 strike. Nevertheless, there were several port strikes in the 1920s and a number of less publicized work stoppages.[35]

Perhaps the bitterest port confrontation was the Quinhenta strike in 1933. Port officials and handling companies, suffering the effects of the world depression, decided to reduce the already inadequate wages of wharf workers by 10 to 30 percent. This was five times the amount they had gained from the 1921 strike. When the announcement was made, workers walked off the job and refused to return after lunch, leaving the port paralyzed. Leaders of the strike vowed that they would not go back to work until the cuts were rescinded. Faced with a paralyzed port, employers agreed to the demands, and port workers returned, only to find themselves locked in the port and surrounded by police, who forced them to unload all the ships. Thereafter, it was announced that the cuts would not be restored. One Lourenço Marques newspaper captured the anger and frustration on the wharf: "Workers with empty bellies faced their boss, who, with his full belly, answered them with empty promises."[36]

After the Quinhenta strike the Salazar regime intensified its repression. Even so, there were periodic reports of port disturbances in the late 1940s and 1950s. Stevedore strikes at the port of Lourenço Marques in 1947, which spread to neighboring plantations, culminated in an abortive uprising in the capital a year later and resulted in more than 200 arrests. In 1950 police had to be called in to break another strike at the port, and in 1957 dock workers again walked off the job, paralyzing the port and forcing colonial officials to use *chibalo* laborers as strikebreakers and to bring in troops to reestablish a semblance of order. As in the earlier labor protests, the police clubbed to death a number of workers, and insurgent leaders who survived were deported to São Thomé.[37] In 1963 strikes broke out not only at the port of Lourenço Marques but also on the docks of Beira and at the northern port of Nacala. Despite the growing scale of these strikes and the increased militancy of the port workers, one observer close to the scene noted that "the strike action itself was very largely spontaneous and for the most part localized . . . and ended in the death and arrest of many participants." He candidly acknowledged that the "failure and brutal repression which followed in every instance must have temporarily discouraged both the masses and the leadership from considering strike action as a possible effective political weapon in the context of Mozambique."[38]

Mozambicans employed beyond the borders of the colony sometimes joined in labor struggles with their fellow workers. They participated in a number of work stoppages at Southern Rhodesian mines in the first decade of the century, in major strikes on the Rand in 1913, and in strikes at the ports of Tanganyika and Kenya.[39] There are also indications that they organized covert acts of sabotage on the cocoa plantations of São Thomé, to which thousands had been sent as conscripted labor.

Returning workers brought with them a new militancy and a heightened sense of racial and cultural oppression. A number of miners carried home the message of Marcus Garvey, who was very popular in South Africa, and even tried to organize branches of Garvey's United Negro Improvement Association in Beira and Tete.[40] Others, in still greater numbers, channeled their rage into separatist churches.

INDEPENDENT CHURCHES

As in other parts of Southern and Central Africa, independent churches offered another opportunity for workers and peasants to vent their hostility against the new social order and the hypocrisy of the established Christian churches. A 1957 report prepared by the Portuguese secret police noted that the popularity of the separatist churches was due "both to the racial discrimination within the larger society and the insensitivity of the European missionaries with regard to the natives."[41] As early as 1918 seventy-six separatist churches were known to exist in Mozambique. Twenty years later the number had jumped to more than 380.[42] Membership ranged from a mere handful of adherents to more than 10,000 in the case of the Christian Ethiopian Mission, whose network extended throughout four provinces.

Virtually all independent churches traced their origin to the separatist church movements (Zionist and Ethiopian) in neighboring South Africa and Southern Rhodesia. Mozambican migrant laborers there found refuge in these churches, and when they returned home, they either organized branches or formed autonomous sects modeled after their South African and Southern Rhodesian counterparts. Samuel Belize, the moving force behind the powerful African Methodist Episcopal Church, for example, had long been associated with a black offshoot of the Wesleyan Mission in South Africa, and Sebastião Piedade de Sousa modeled the Christian Ethiopian Mission after the Ethiopian church to which he belonged in Durban.[43] In other cases, the reputation of a particular apostolic leader provided sufficient incentive for Mozambicans to join his flock. Because most of the migrant laborers came from the southern half of the colony, the independent churches enjoyed their greatest support in the districts of Lourenço Marques, Gaza, Inhambane, and Sofala.

The Ethiopian churches were relatively autonomous institutions in which Mozambicans could elect their own officials and have their own budgets, constitution, flag, and even paramilitary forces. They represented another arena of "free space" within an enclosed authoritarian system, in which oppressed workers and peasants could enjoy a modicum of self-rule and racial and cultural dignity. The Zionist churches, on the other hand, derived much of their appeal from their apocalyptic vision of divine intervention and the destruction of the oppressive colonial order.

In terms of explicit anticolonial activity, Mozambican independent churches ran the gamut from radicalism to quietism. According to secret government reports, the Methodist Episcopalian Church, based primarily in Gaza and Manica districts, was a center of subversive activities. Government infiltrators reported that the church fostered antiwhite sentiments and explicitly attacked the opppressive colonial regime in its services and at clandestine meetings. Church officials also reputedly maintained links with South African nationalist movements, including the African National Congress.[44] Its members attacked colonial authorities and loyalist chiefs on several occasions, and the sect was subsequently accused of helping to organize a major peasant uprising in Mambone in 1952. Such insurgent activities, however, seem to have been the exception. Most independent churches chose instead to limit their opposition to verbal criticism and, in some cases, an apocalyptic vision.[45]

There are also tantalizing suggestions of Islamic revivalist movements in northern Mozambique, where the Muslim population had historically opposed colonial rule. In the 1920s Islamic holy men protested against the abuses of forced labor, low wages, and land expropriation in the area of Quelimane. A number of Muslim chiefs and their followers were also involved in uprisings in the early 1930s, although their exact causes remain unknown.[46]

THE VOICE OF PROTEST

Urban intellectual protest, although not as deeply rooted in Mozambique as in Angola, nevertheless was an important forum for reformist discourse. The first, somewhat tentative, call for change came in 1908 with the publication of the Lourenço Marques newspaper, *The African (O Africano)*, the official organ of the African Union—a social and civic group founded by the leading mulatto and African families (*grande famílias*) two years earlier. Despite their relatively privileged position and their self-conscious sense of importance, these families took as their mandate the responsibility to speak for oppressed Africans. Indeed, the masthead of *The African* boldly proclaimed that it was "devoted to the defense of the native population of Mozambique." Its successor, the *African Voice (O Brado Africano)* was a similarly self-defined guardian of African peasants and workers. On the occasion of its seventh anniversary, it affirmed that "Africans have in *Brado Africano* their best defense, indeed, their only weapon against the injustices which fall upon them."[47]

In their news stories and commentaries both papers highlighted four recurring abuses—*chibalo*, the poor working conditions of free African labor, the preferential treatment given white immigrants, and the lack of educational opportunities for Africans—that, to the editors, symbolized colonial oppression. Throughout this period editorials vigorously denounced and carefully documented the abuses inherent in the *chibalo* system, protesting against the brutal methods used by African *sipais* to recruit forced labor, the low wages and poor working conditions of the *chibalo* laborers, and the arbitrary and capricious actions of European overseers. The editors were particularly incensed by the common practice of seizing "African women to repair and construct roads, not even supplying them with food nor paying them a salary," while "forcing them during the rainy season to sleep in mud-huts, beside the road, like slaves."[48]

The newspapers also unleashed broadside attacks against the conditions of employment of free African workers. They deplored the fact that peasants and nominally free agricultural workers were compelled to work on European estates "from sunrise until sunset earning hardly a shilling a month," that Mozambicans working in the South African mines were "denied the right to select their own employers . . . and die like flies in the mines," that African workers were arrested and beaten if they lacked proper identification, and that the state used *chibalo* laborers to break strikes and drive down the wages of free workers.[49] The informal color bar, which froze Africans in the lowest paying jobs while reserving the most desirable employment for white immigrants, was a target of several editorials. In one scathing commentary, the *African Voice* questioned the colonial regime's logic in underwriting the expensive white "riff-raff," who contributed nothing to the colony.

> The common Portuguese, who is known as *mumadji* [common Portuguese immigrant] among the African population, always leaves Portugal with the fixed intention of a short stay in the land of the blacks to gather enough savings; and then to escape it all to return to Portugal, settle in and enjoy the wealth which he managed to accumulate, with God knows what sacrifices over 2, 3 or 4 years.
>
> Are they aware there [in Portugal] of the deprivations that these men suffer in order to save that 300 or 400$000 reis? It is a poem of pain and misery. A veritable madness that some of them live through in an effort to fill their suitcases—with those paltry pieces of metal. Gold Fever!
>
> They live in pigsties, without light, without air, some 4 or 5 together in order to cut costs. They customarily eat three persons from the same meal, because it costs less. In a squalid dinner, soups or stews . . . are more accurately puddles of warm water in which some five beans swim hopelessly in search of company.[50]

Although the tone of the editorials in both newspapers was cautious and reformist, appealing to the goodwill and sense of justice of the colonial government, mounting frustrations sometimes produced outbursts of anger. This occurred with greater regularity in the period immediately after Salazar's rise to power, which generated a sense of despair even among the most privileged members of the African and mulatto community in Mozambique. An editorial in the *African Voice*, entitled "Enough," represents the clearest expression of their rage:

We are fed to the teeth.
Fed up with supporting you, with suffering the terrible
consequences of your follies, your demands, with the
squandering misuse of your authority.
We can no longer stand the pernicious effects of your
political and administrative decisions.
We are no longer willing to make greater and greater
useless sacrifices. . . .
Enough.[51]

Yet for all their criticisms of colonial abuses and their self-image as
guardians of oppressed Africans, the *grande famílias* lived in a social and
cultural milieu totally separate from that of the workers and peasants who
returned after a hard day's labor to their shantytowns, barracks, and
villages. Moreover, as members of a nascent colonial bourgeoisie, they
had very different class interests that often placed them at odds with their
less privileged compatriots and precluded a more radical critique of colonial-
capitalism. Intense rivalries between mulatto and African segments of the
colonial elite further reduced the influence of the *African Voice* and
precipitated its demise.[52] In 1936 the Salazar regime imposed extremely
stringent censorship laws that effectively silenced it.[53]

The decline of the *African Voice* marked the end of three decades
of organized literary protest. After a hiatus of about ten years, a new
generation of young poets and writers emerged. Influenced by anti-Nazism,
antiracism, Negritude, Pan-Africanism, Marxism, and nationalism, activist
writers such as José Craveirinha, Noemia de Sousa, Marcelino dos Santos,
Gwante Valente, and Rui Nogar began to express the hopes and frustrations
of the Mozambican people through their writings. Their poetry, denouncing
the capricious abuses of colonialism, was angry and aggressive, a substantial
departure from the more restrained tone of earlier protest writers. Craveirinha's poem, "Grito Negro," cited at the beginning of this chapter,
reflects their collective sense of hostility and rage. Unlike the patronizing
African Voice, these poets of the post–World War II era reasserted the
cultural dignity of their past and the common suffering that bound all
the people of Mozambique. As with Craveirinha's anthropomorphic coal,
however, this suffering was not eternal, but ready to burn everything
repressive with the fire of its combustion.

Noemia de Sousa, like Craveirinha, created strong images from the
natural environment and a common African heritage. In her poem, "If
You Want to Know Me," her metaphor for exploitation and suffering was
the grotesque figure carved in black wood by the inspired hands of a
"Makonde brother" from the north:

. . . Ah, she is who I am:
empty eye sockets despairing of possessing life,
a mouth slashed with wounds of anguish,
enormous, flattened hands,
raised as though to implore and threaten,

body tattooed with visible and invisible scars
by the hard whips of slavery . . .
tortured and magnificent,
proud and mystical,
African from head to toe,
—ah, she is who I am![54]

This empty-eyed and despairing figure, fashioned largely by the
cruelty of colonialism, is nevertheless rebellious and strong. In de Sousa's
final images are heard the groans of dock workers, the melancholia of an
African song, and the sounds of frenzied dancing.

for I am no more than a shell of flesh
in which the revolt of Africa congealed
its cry swollen with hope.

As with West African and Caribbean Negritude poets of an earlier
generation, metaphors of land, fertility, and ancient Africa informed this
new poetry. Consider the images of Marcelino dos Santos in his poem
"Here We Were Born."

[Our forefathers] like the coarse wild grass
were the meagre body's veins
running red, earth's fragrance.
Trees and granite pinnacles
their arms
embraced the earth
in daily work
and sculpting the new world's fertile rocks
began, in colour,
the great design of life.[55]

Dos Santos fused past and present, the land of the forefathers to the land
in which the present generation was born. It was a hot land, a "green
land of fertile fields," a soft land that surrendered itself to the Africans
who loved it. Even the ravages of colonialism could not destroy the love
for this land:

We grew up lulled
by the Chirico's song
and as we reached in this way the level of Man
the impetus was such it generated
waves pregnant with crystal.
And when the wind
whips the sky
and the sword falls
tearing the flesh
and horror touches

the naked face
Our love is not shaken
This is the land
where we were born.[56]

At the same time that these writers reasserted their cultural identity, they never shied from attacks on the contradictions of colonial "civilization." The Mozambican people, in whose shell of flesh "the revolt of Africa congealed," whose bodies bore the "visible and invisible scars [made] by the hard whips of slavery," were the same people who, like Craveirinha's coal, would "burn everything with the fire of my combustion" and become the boss of coal.

The deeply felt, and at times overly romantic, racial and cultural pride extended beyond the borders of Mozambique to oppressed peoples of color throughout the world. Noemia de Sousa's poem "Let My People Go," inspired by the Harlem renaissance and the growing civil rights movement in the United States, was typical:

. . . I turn on the radio and let myself drift, lulled . . .
But voices from America stir my soul and nerves
And Robeson and Marion sing for me
Negro spirituals from Harlem
"Let my people go
—oh, let my people go
let my people go—"
they say.
I open my eyes and can no longer sleep,
Anderson and Paul sound within me
and they are not the soft voices of a lullaby
Let my people go.[57]

The heightened political and cultural consciousness of these writers compelled them to shift the arena of debate from condemnation of particular forms of oppression to an attack on the creator of oppression—the system of colonialism itself. This recognition permeated a poem written by Noemia de Sousa after a strike by dockworkers at the port of Lourenço Marques in 1947 had been brutally repressed. João was the collective memorialization of the arrested dockworkers.

João was young like us . . .
João was the father, the mother, the brother of multitudes,
João was the blood and the seat of multitudes
and suffered and was happy like the multitudes
. . . .
João and Mozambique were intermingled
João would not have been João without Mozambique
João was like a palm tree, a coconut palm
a piece of rock, a Lake Niassa, a mountain

an Incomati, a forest, a macala tree . . .
a beach, a Maputo, an Indian Ocean
. . . .
Ah, they have stolen João from us
But João is us all
Because of this João hasn't left us
And João "was" not, he "is" and "will be"
For João is us all, we are a multitude and the multitude
Who can take the multitude and lock it in a cage?[58]

If these poets became progressively more militant, why did the colonial regime permit them to publish? For a relatively short period following World War II, according to the Mozambican writer Luís Bernardo Honwana, the Salazar regime was a victim of its own antifascist rhetoric. Although privately sympathetic to the Nazis, its formal ties to the Allies did not permit it to censor or prohibit antifascist and antiracist literary works. This ambiguity created a small opening for Mozambican intellectuals to have their poetry published in both the metropole and the colony. Moreover, as very few workers and peasants could read Portuguese and fewer still could comprehend much of the poetry, the impact of the intellectuals was necessarily minimal. Cut off from and probably distrusted by most of their compatriots, they did not pose an immediate threat to the state.[59]

By the mid-1950s, however, the situation had changed. Colonial officials began to comprehend the long-term political ramifications of this literary movement and were concerned by the writers' impact on and influence over a new generation of secondary-school pupils fluent in Portuguese, who had formed a national organization known as NESAM (Nucleus of African Secondary Students of Mozambique). Under the guise of promoting social and cultural activities, NESAM members—including Eduardo Mondlane, Joaquim Chissano, and Mariano Matsinhe, all future leaders of the liberation struggle—clandestinely began to organize politically "to spread the idea of national independence and encouraged resistance to the cultural subjection which the Portuguese imposed."[60] At meetings held in African suburbs of Lourenço Marques, they debated a wide range of social and political issues, studied Mozambican history, performed African dances, and reaffirmed their Mozambican identity.[61] They even managed to launch a magazine, *Alvor*, which, though severely censored, subtly addressed these social and political concerns.[62] The colonial regime responded by apprehending several of the leading literary figures. Noemia de Sousa, among those detained, ultimately fled to Europe, where she was joined by Marcelino dos Santos and other dissidents. Many leaders of NESAM were also arrested in the early 1960s. Some managed to escape to Tanganyika, where they joined Eduardo Mondlane, Marcelino dos Santos, and groups of younger insurgents and helped to organize the Front for the Liberation of Mozambique, more commonly known as FRELIMO. It is the story of FRELIMO's birth and the subsequent armed struggle for independence to which we now turn our attention.

5

The Struggle for Independence, 1962-1975

I was interested in the nationalist struggle against the Portuguese for many, many years back. I could trace it to my own childhood, when my mother, who was a traditional woman insisted that I go to school in order to equip myself to be able to face the Portuguese because my father had died trying to recover the power of the traditional people in Mozambique. My uncle, a paramount chief in the South, died after serving 25 years in a Portuguese prison because he opposed the Portuguese system.

—Eduardo Mondlane,
quoted in Ronald Chilcote,
"Eduardo Mondlane and the Mozambique Struggle,"
Africa Today 12 (1965):4

I did not know either of my grandparents, maternal or paternal. But I was lucky enough to know those who saw my grandfather, who by 1920 was more than 100 years old. He was a soldier in the wars of resistance against the Portuguese invasion, including even the last war of occupation. My parents told me he had many bullet wounds. This is how my father knew his father and he used to tell us about him. He used to tell us stories about the brutality of the invasion, the inhumanity of the invasion, the way they treated people who were taken prisoner.

—Samora Machel, in a 1975 interview
with Iain Christie

The establishment of FRELIMO on June 25, 1962, marked the beginning of a new phase in the struggle against Portuguese colonial rule—a phase characterized both by creative experimentation and demoralizing setbacks. During the struggle FRELIMO's leaders had to grapple with complex political, economic, and social issues whose resolution radicalized the movement. This process shaped the socialist path of development the country has pursued since it became independent on June 25, 1975.

THE ORIGINS OF FRELIMO

As early as 1960 the nationalist fervor sweeping through Africa had captured the imagination of a small but growing number of Mozambicans, who organized UDENAMO (National Democratic Union of Mozambique),

MANU (the Mozambican-Makonde Union), and UNAMI (National African Union of Independent Mozambique). From the outset, however, each organization had a relatively narrow regional and ethnic character. In a country with a multitude of ethnic and language groups, parochialism posed obvious organizing problems. As its name suggests, MANU emerged from a cluster of Makonde self-help and cultural associations. UDENAMO attracted its supporters exclusively from the southern half of the country. UNAMI was composed of militants almost entirely from Tete province.[1] All three parties, founded by Mozambicans who had been in exile for several years and headquartered far from the colony, were disconnected from those they purported to represent. UDENAMO was based in Bulawayo, Southern Rhodesia, far from the Mozambican border; MANU's initial support came from Makonde dock and plantation workers in Kenya and Tanzania, many of whom had lived abroad for more than a decade; and UNAMI, the least significant of the movements, had its office in Blantyre, the capital of Malawi, and directed its appeal to other exiles residing in that country.

The one effort at political mobilization by these organizations proved disastrous. In 1959 activists in the process of organizing MANU sent Zacarias Vanomba into the Makonde highland "to mobilize peasant support and raise their political consciousness."[2] Working clandestinely through the network of agricultural cooperatives, he was able to build a substantial base of popular support and sympathy for MANU. In June 1961, five months after its birth, MANU supporters, who had held late-evening meetings deep in the bush, helped to stage a large peaceful demonstration in front of the Portuguese administrative center at Mueda. A bloodbath ensued.

> The governor invited our leaders into the administrator's office. I was waiting outside. They were in there for four hours. When they came out on the verandah, the governor asked the crowd who wanted to speak. Many wanted to speak, and the governor told them all to stand on one side.
> Then without another word he ordered the police to bind the hands of those who had stood on one side, and the police began beating them. I was close by. I saw it all. When the people saw what was happening, they began to demonstrate against the Portuguese, and the Portuguese simply ordered the police trucks to come and collect these arrested persons. So there were more demonstrations against this. At that moment the troops were still hidden, and the people went up close to the police to stop the arrested persons from being taken away. So the governor called the troops, and when they appeared he told them to open fire. They killed about 600 people. Now the Portuguese say they have punished that governor, but of course they have only sent him somewhere else. I myself escaped because I was close to a graveyard where I could take cover, and then I ran away.[3]

Immediately thereafter the colonial state formally prohibited all African organizations with more than thirty members.

The Mueda massacre revealed MANU's lack of a coherent strategy for gaining independence, a problem shared by all the exile organizations.

Influenced by nationalist gains in the neighboring British colonies, all believed in the efficacy of petitions, protest letters, and nonviolent demonstrations. They failed to anticipate the inflexibility of the regime they confronted. Even after the massacre at Mueda none of the organizations even seriously considered the possibility of armed struggle, and MANU leaders Matthew Michinis and Mamole Lawrence Malinga confidently testified before a United Nations Special Commission that "complete independence and the elimination of Portuguese colonial and imperial rule" would be achieved "before the end of the year 1963."[4]

Small in numbers, detached from internal bases of support, lacking a coherent strategy, and periodically engaging in divisive exile politics, the three organizations hardly posed a credible threat to the Portuguese colonial regime. In an effort to overcome the mutual suspicion that divided them, President Nyerere of Tanzania invited the three in 1962 to establish their headquarters in Dar es Salaam and work toward the creation of a unified movement. Prodded by Nyerere, Kwame Nkrumah (the president of Ghana), and the Conference of Nationalist Organizations of the Portuguese Colonies (CONCP), the three movements—UNAMI rather reluctantly—agreed to merge into FRELIMO under the leadership of Dr. Eduardo Mondlane.

Insurgency ran deep in Mondlane's family. The examples of his father and his uncle, who had both fought in anticolonial struggles at the end of the nineteenth century, as well as his mother's quiet militancy, had obviously inspired Mondlane. After attending missionary schools in southern Mozambique and South Africa, Mondlane received a scholarship in 1947 to Witwatersrand University, where he came into contact and collaborated with students opposed to racial segregation, causing his deportation two years later. Back in Mozambique, he helped to organize and was a leading force in NESAM, the Mozambican student movement. His powerful critique of Portuguese colonialism and the value he attached to Mozambican culture and history inspired a whole generation of younger high school students, a number of whom subsequently became prominent members of FRELIMO. His activities brought police surveillance, interrogations, and harassment. Anxious to reduce his influence and simultaneously to co-opt him, the colonial regime in 1950 sent Mondlane to Portugal to continue his education. There he encountered other militant African students trying to forge a coherent anticolonial ideology out of Pan-African, Pan-Negro, Marxist, and antifascist philosophies. Among his cohorts were Amilcar Cabral and Agostinho Neto, who subsequently led the liberation struggles in Guinea-Bissau and Angola respectively, and Marcelino dos Santos, who was to become secretary general of CONCP and a founding member of and leading figure in FRELIMO. In the face of intensified police surveillance, Mondlane fled Portugal and continued his education in the United States. The doctoral degree he received in 1960 made him Mozambique's first Ph.D.[5]

In 1961, protected by diplomatic immunity as a United Nations employee, Mondlane returned home a hero. In shantytowns on the outskirts of Lourenço Marques and in his rural Gaza homeland he met secretly

First FRELIMO president, Eduardo Mondlane (*right*), with Samora Machel, who succeeded Mondlane after he was assassinated (Credit: American Committee on Africa, reproduced by permission)

with dissidents, who detailed the increased oppression and urged him to organize a nationalist movement.[6] He was also courted by Portuguese officials. Mondlane rejected their advances and left Mozambique inexorably committed to the struggle for independence. A little more than a year later he arrived in Dar es Salaam and was elected president of FRELIMO.

Mondlane's immediate objective was to forge a broad-based insurgent coalition that could effectively challenge the colonial regime. This meant not only unifying the three opposition groups but drawing into FRELIMO militants who had recently fled Mozambique and either were unattached to any of the older exile groups or opposed them because of their narrow regional and ethnic character. A younger generation of Portuguese-trained, Marxist-oriented intellectuals also demanded that their voice be heard. At FRELIMO's First Congress in September 1962, a platform designed to be acceptable to all the diverse interests was adopted. The overarching concern—independence—dictated unity. According to FRELIMO documents, unity in 1962 was extremely fragile.

The existing, externally-based organizations which joined hands to form FRELIMO at that time did so reluctantly, and largely at the urging of younger, unattached militants with more direct and recent experience of the harsh realities which existed inside Mozambique itself. The causes which kept these organizations separate in the past—namely, tribalism, regionalism, lack of a clear and detailed set of goals and of agreed and relevant strategies—continued to exist. The only thing which was common to them was their opposition to Portuguese colonialism. On all other particulars, including the actual aims of the struggle, the mode of military activity to be undertaken or the very definition of the enemy, there was no consensus.[7]

Unity also meant incorporating into the movement all Mozambicans of whatever social class or stratum—peasants, workers, merchants, artisans, and chiefs—who supported the common struggle. Thus, its objectives and composition made FRELIMO a fairly typical Third World nationalist front uniting ideologically divergent groups on the basis of patriotism and opposition to foreign domination.

Strains within the Front quickly surfaced. As official FRELIMO documents acknowledged, "The early days of FRELIMO were marred by mutual recriminations, expulsion, withdrawal, . . . [and] futile in-fighting of an irrelevant brand of nationalist politics."[8] Although personal ambitions and ethnic rivalries certainly contributed to this divisiveness, deep-seated strategic and ideological differences concerning the propriety of protracted armed struggle seem to have been the underlying cause. One group, which included some of the leaders of the three former groups, favored dialogue with the Portuguese and appeals to the United Nations. Opposed to them were younger militants newly arrived from Mozambique and radicalized exiles who, aligned with Mondlane and dos Santos, rejected a reformist strategy as illusory and self-destructive and emphasized the need to restructure social and economic relations.[9] This faction dominated the Executive Committee of FRELIMO; when the minority realized it could not prevail, it defected and organized an array of splinter groups.[10]

Infiltrations by the Portuguese secret police, shortages of war material, and the overt hostility of the Western countries that were Portugal's NATO allies compounded FRELIMO's initial difficulties. Despite increased Portuguese surveillance and repression within Mozambique, however, FRELIMO organizers, appealing to smoldering anticolonial sentiment and the region's long tradition of defiance, was able to create a nascent rural network in the northern provinces of Cabo Delgado and Niassa. Ali Thomas Chibudu recounted the difficulties he and other cadres had had to overcome.

> When I first began to organize, the people did not know about politics. They only knew that they had been miserable all of their lives. I had many troubles in those days and I walked only during the night because the Portuguese knew my name and sometimes came looking for me. They called me a bandit.
>
> By day I remained hidden in the bush and my contact man in the village sometimes gave me food. Usually I lived on mealie and cassava and bush rats. I held meetings at night and the ones who joined us went to their villages to organize. I worked a year and a half like this before the war finally started in 1964, and always lived in the bush.[11]

The "contact men" to whom Chibudu referred were generally respected elders or chiefs not compromised by the colonial regime. They served as an important link between the first FRELIMO cadres and the villages.

> The old man Banganamana, who became a FRELIMO chairman, had met secretly in the night with the militants. Over the next few weeks he spoke with several people in our village and explained to them that only by joining and aiding the fighters could we hope to end the suffering brought about by Portuguese rule. We purchased [FRELIMO] cards for 5 escudos which he warned us to hide carefully. On a designated night he organized a *reunião* where we met FRELIMO for the first time.[12]

Even at this early stage rural supporters provided the cadres with food, strategic information, and recruits, confirming the potential anticolonial energy of the peasants.

THE ARMED STRUGGLE, FORMATION OF LIBERATED ZONES, AND RADICALIZATION OF FRELIMO, 1964–1972

In the dead of night on September 25, 1964, FRELIMO soldiers, with logistical assistance from the surrounding population, attacked the Portuguese administrative post at Chai in Cabo Delgado Province. Despite reports by a collaborationist chief of guerrilla movement in the area, the colonial authorities were taken by surprise, and the guerrillas were able to damage the post and kill one policeman and wound several others before they melted back into the forest. The colonial regime responded quickly. It dispatched heavily armed troops and secret police (PIDE) agents to Chai and arrested and beat a number of suspected FRELIMO sympathizers, but it was unable to track down the guerrilla band or crack the FRELIMO network. In retaliation, colonial troops committed a number of atrocities. According to Amade Sique Ibraimo, an African policeman, "The Portuguese went to Micalo where they murdered many people. Villagers were herded into huts which were set afire. As they tried to escape, they were shot down by Portuguese soldiers positioned nearby."[13]

The raid at Chai marked the beginning of the armed struggle against the colonial regime. Employing classic guerrilla tactics—ambushing patrols, sabotaging communication and railroad lines, and making hit-and-run attacks against colonial outposts—and then rapidly fading into inaccessible backwater areas, FRELIMO militants were able to evade pursuit and surveillance. In the two northern provinces of Niassa and Cabo Delgado, FRELIMO's peasant network provided critical supplies and ammunition. Rural supporters, both men and women, also carried war material great distances from bases in Tanzania. This was not only a long but also an arduous task. "Everything must be brought in from outside, on our heads, and we must plan these routes according to our geographical position. Most nearby countries are unfriendly to us, it takes a month to carry a box of ammunition into Niassa province from the frontier, for example, because the distances are enormous. Since we cannot ride, we must walk. And on the way, the guerrillas and carriers are contending with hunger,

FRELIMO soldiers (Credit: FRELIMO)

thirst and sickness."[14] The peasants also provided strategic information and food in what, one guerrilla explained, became a mutually supportive relationship.

> The people are united and help us. Otherwise, for instance, we couldn't go into enemy areas; it is the people who give us all our information about the movements of the enemy, their strength and their position. Also, when we start working in an area where we have no food, because we have not yet had the opportunity to grow any, the people supply us and feed us. We also help the people. Until militias have been formed in a region, we protect the people in their fields against the action and reprisals of the colonialists; we organize new villages when we have to evacuate the people from a zone because of the war; we protect them against the enemy.[15]

Gradually, although not without setbacks, FRELIMO consolidated its power and drove the colonial forces out of the surrounding regions, progressively expanding the liberated zones (see Figure 5.1). By 1968 the insurgents claimed to control approximately 20 to 25 percent of Mozambique and had opened a third front in the strategically important central province of Tete.[16]

The expansion of the liberated areas, however, created new problems for FRELIMO, problems that required creative solutions. Having dismantled the colonial state apparatus and exploitative colonial institutions, the liberation movement faced the more difficult task of introducing new economic, social, and political structures. For these there were no precedents. Moreover, to guarantee the active involvement of the peasants in both the liberated zone and the areas of conflict, FRELIMO had to offer them more than just the end of the colonial order. What was demanded was a vision of hope for a new and just society.

Despite the united front FRELIMO presented to the world, it was really two entities throughout much of this early phase—"a conventional nationalist movement unable to secure an easy transition to power and a revolutionary movement struggling to be born."[17] The demands placed on FRELIMO by its successes intensified the ideological conflict that had been submerged since its inception. The first, rooted in a narrow nationalist tradition, sought merely to capture the colonial state. The second increasingly saw the struggle as an opportunity to transform basic social and economic as well as political relations. The conflict surfaced in debates over the resolution of the three basic questions facing FRELIMO: (1) Who was the enemy? (2) What were the best tactics for waging an armed struggle? (3) What type of alternative society should be constructed in the liberated zones?

The definition of the enemy was extremely important as it required FRELIMO to grapple with the issues of racial and class antagonisms and permitted the war to be seen in broader anti-imperialist terms. Some FRELIMO leaders perceived the struggle exclusively in racial terms, arguing "that only the white was an exploiter." They therefore opposed participation of whites and even racially mixed Mozambicans in FRELIMO and favored the harsh treatment of captured Portuguese soldiers. Leo Milas, FRELIMO's

FIGURE 5.1 The Progress of the War, 1967

Source: *Africa Report*, November 1967 (adapted from *Standard Bank Review* [London]).
Reprinted with permission.

first secretary of information and an outspoken proponent of this view, complained publically that "Jorge Rebelo, a leading member of the Central Committee is an Indian from Goa" and "much of the direction of FRELIMO is carried by Helder Martins, a Portuguese, and Janet Mondlane," Eduardo's white, American-born wife.[18]

In sharp contrast, Mondlane and a majority of the Executive Committee defined the enemy as Portuguese colonialism. Indeed, FRELIMO's initial declaration of principles stated unequivocally that its struggle was against the "fascist colonial administration" and invoked "the noble democratic tradition of the Portuguese people,"[19] whose support it sought. This group welcomed sympathetic whites and mulattoes into the movement and believed that captured Portuguese soldiers should be humanely treated because they often came from humble peasant backgrounds and they, too, suffered from the Salazar dictatorship. To expose the limits of the racial analysis, they pointed to the sharp increase in the number of Africans from Portuguese colonies fighting in the colonial army, especially in elite volunteer units. This latter definition of the enemy emphasized economic and social relations rather than pigmentation.

Moreover, in the face of vigorous Western support of Portuguese colonialism, FRELIMO adopted a more explicitly anti-imperialist posture. As early as 1964, at a conference held in Italy, Mondlane expressed profound disillusionment with the West for aiding the Salazar regime. He warned his audience: "It does not matter how many soldiers the Western NATO powers pour into our country; it does not matter how many tons of weapons they supply to Portugal; it does not matter how many millions of dollars the United States gives to the Portuguese military and commercial interests, the Mozambican people are determined to rid themselves of colonialism and economic imperialism once and for all and they will win."[20]

The rejection by the majority of the FRELIMO leadership of a racial analysis had a direct impact on what tactics should be used. In the first instance, it undercut the position of those who advocated urban guerrilla warfare and random attacks on the European community. According to Mondlane, such a strategy was ultimately rejected because "the Portuguese secret police . . . had always been exceptionally alert in the cities and often paid blacks to infiltrate the underground organizations."[21]

A second strategy envisioned a general and largely spontaneous insurrection in the countryside. Several FRELIMO leaders, influenced by the writings of Che Guevara and proponents of the "focal theory," believed that once guerrillas entered a region the peasants would spontaneously follow them, even if they were not politicized and did not understand the goals of the revolution. The uprisings, they argued, would crystallize world opinion against Portugal. FRELIMO employed this strategy in the 1964 military campaigns in Tete province, but the results were disastrous. The peasants failed to rally behind the liberation forces, Portugal proved to be less impotent than some had thought, and international public opinion was not a particularly powerful force. After a reassessment of tactics and goals, the Executive Committee concluded that, without mass mobilization and popular support, the guerrillas could not hope to overcome the superior firepower of the colonial forces. In a frank statement of self-criticism, FRELIMO acknowledged that the setbacks "revealed an even more negative aspect: that there were among the leadership people who accepted the principle of armed struggle but considered it merely a technical and mechanical experience. Such leaders, in effect, refuse to consider armed struggle as a process of people's participation and as the fundamentally political undertaking which it is."[22]

By 1966 those leaders intimately engaged in the fighting had called for a new strategy predicated on popular mobilization and faith in the rural masses. It involved forging permanent bonds between the guerrillas and the peasants based on mutual respect, shared political goals, and popular involvement in all aspects of the struggle. FRELIMO first addressed this question publicly in an editorial in *Voz da Revolução* (Voice of the Revolution), the internal organ of the Front, in April 1966: "Political mobilization consists of explaining to the people WHY IT IS that we are fighting and FOR WHAT IT IS that we are fighting. The people must know that we are fighting for the expulsion of the Portuguese colonialists and for the liberation of Mozambique, so that Progress, Liberty and Equality should return to our country. An end to misery, slavery and discrimination."[23]

Integrating peasants into the struggle became a central feature of FRELIMO's strategy. "The people are to the guerrillas as water is to fish," emphasized a military command bulletin. "Out of the water a fish cannot live. Without the people, that is to say, without the support of the people, the guerrillas cannot survive."[24] President Mondlane articulated a similar sentiment: "The army leads the people, but more importantly yet is the fact that the army is the people, and it is the people who form the army."[25] To make this union work, FRELIMO had to protect the peasants, involve them in the political and military struggle, and improve the quality of their lives. Such objectives could be achieved only by creating liberated zones, a free terrain in which FRELIMO and the peasants could together develop an embryonic form of the new society for which all were fighting. FRELIMO militants established liberated zones in inaccessible areas, generally deep in the bush or in mountainous regions, that would be relatively free from Portuguese land and air attack. FRELIMO guerrillas exploited their knowledge of this rugged terrain and by 1966 had demonstrated that they could not only protect the peasants against Portuguese reprisals but also inflict heavy losses on the colonial troops. This show of force instilled a new sense of confidence and strengthened the commitment of the peasants. Many agreed to move to more secure areas; others took up arms.[26]

Integrating the peasants into the political process and institutionalizing the principles of mass participation and popular democracy proved to be more difficult than gaining new recruits. Most peasants, intimidated by the colonial regime, were initially reluctant to participate in the weekly public meetings that became the hallmark of FRELIMO efforts to stimulate direct popular decision making. As Marcelino dos Santos noted, "Even

Peasants aiding FRELIMO fighters in the liberated zones (Credit: Robert Van Lierop)

now for us the basic problem is not guns; the Portuguese have guns, too, but that does not make a revolution. The problem is man. It is not because you give a Mozambican a rifle that he becomes a revolutionary, the problem is a political one. Political consciousness is the base."[27]

The refusal of most "traditional authorities," supported by a faction within the Executive Committee, to give up their privileged positions complicated the democratization process. Even after villagers had moved to the liberated zones, chiefs often continued to rule—now as FRELIMO chairmen—sometimes exacting tribute and labor from their subordinates while espousing nationalist rhetoric. The prominence of these chiefs posed a serious dilemma for FRELIMO. Although many indigenous authorities in the north rallied popular support behind the struggle for independence, an end to exploitative relations—be they "colonial" or "traditional"—was becoming progressively more central to the movement's ideology. The behavior of the chiefs reinforced the belief among the radical wing of the leadership that they had to be removed from positions of authority within the movement.[28]

Equally contentious was the debate over the role to be played by women in the liberation struggle. During the colonial period Mozambican women endured double exploitation. Under customary law, they were not persons in a legal sense. They could not, for example, appear before the courts on their own behalf but were always represented by a male protector, and women spent their whole lives under the tutelage of a senior male member of the lineage to which they belonged. They were reduced to units of production and reproduction and subjected to a number of exploitative practices, ranging from bride price to polygamy. Women also suffered, like men, from the oppressive nature of the colonial regime; they too had to be integrated into the liberation struggle.[29] From the beginning teenaged girls had been moved by the words of FRELIMO recruiters, and many had fled to join the struggle for independence. Initially, their role was limited to transporting material, producing food for the FRELIMO forces, working in health and education facilities established by FRELIMO, and spying on Portuguese troops. Female militants also were important in mobilizing support for the insurgents in areas still under Portuguese domination and in convincing young people to join the liberation movement.

Nevertheless, within FRELIMO women remained in subordinate positions. After a particularly acrimonious debate in 1966 on this issue, the Central Committee issued a communiqué in which it "condemned the tendency which exists among many male members of FRELIMO to systematically exclude women from the discussion of problems related to the Revolution, and of limiting them to executing tasks."[30] The document emphasized that appropriate measures would be taken "to assure the participation of women in the direction of work" at all levels, including the Central Committee. The following year, in response to continued pressure from female militants and from members of the Central Committee, FRELIMO organized a women's detachment.[31] In villages, both inside and outside the liberated zones, women cadres encountered strong opposition and skepticism from rural men. Even within the army, their position

Members of the Women's Detachment (Credit: FRELIMO)

remained ambiguous at best. Recalled one militant who had joined the women's detachment in 1967:

> Our relationships with men were always difficult to figure out because many of them would promise marriage, but it rarely happened. Even when it happened it did not mean the end of problems. For example, I finally stayed with one man from whom I became pregnant, but then he refused to accept the child, saying that the child was not his. He even suggested that I take medication to induce abortion. I refused and I had the child. I realized then how difficult it was going to be with 2 children. How to work and take care of 2 children at the same time.[32]

Over time, a sense of camaraderie born of common struggle and political discussion began to develop among militants, and gender distinctions became less significant. Said Rita Mulumba, "The revolution is transforming our life. Before I was ignorant, while now I speak in front of everyone at meetings. We are united. We discuss our problems among ourselves and that reinforces our unity."[33]

Just as the army became a school in which problems of sexism, racism, and tribalism were addressed, if not completely overcome, so

FRELIMO used the weekly meetings (*reuniões*) held at villages in the liberated zones as a forum for political education and a context for collective decision making. Western observers stressed the number of hours spent discussing problems and the fact that everybody had to speak on a subject before any action could be taken.[34] The militants chairing these meetings elicited accounts of the ways in which particular chiefs had collaborated with the colonial regime and had abused their traditional position. They also tried to convey the ways in which both men and women were exploited and the fact that in the liberated zones all Mozambicans were equal.

At varying speeds peasants in the liberated zones gained self-confidence in their decision-making abilities. For the peasants, who had lived under the tyranny of the local administration, this represented an important advance. "African villagers will sit for hours, days, if necessary, until a solution can be agreed upon," noted a Western journalist visiting Cabo Delgado. She continued, "There is no time limit for speakers, which leaves everyone with the impression that he has gotten his point across, and all aspects of an argument are examined. Anyone may express his ideas, however irrelevant or nonconstructive they may be."[35] Ultimately the villagers elected a committee to replace the chiefs as chairmen. These leaders, both men and women, organized collective production, presided over public meetings, sat as local courts that helped to establish new guidelines of sanctioned behavior, participated in district and provincial assemblies, and helped to organize people's militias.[36] In short, popular participation became a central feature of FRELIMO's state-in-the-making.

Popular democracy required also that the tyranny of illiteracy and superstition be destroyed. "We have always attached such great importance to education," noted President Mondlane, "because in the first place, it is essential for the development of our struggle, since the involvement and support of the population increases as their understanding of the situation grows; and in the second place, a future independent Mozambique will be in very great need of educated citizens to lead the way in development."[37] Yet mass education posed a number of serious problems— not the least of which were the lack of qualified teachers and the absence of books and other educational materials.[38]

Through experimentation, FRELIMO militants, in conjunction with the local population, created at least an embryonic educational infrastructure in rural areas where few schools had previously existed. Within the liberated zones those who could read and write, however minimally, taught those who could not. It was not uncommon, for example, for children who had the equivalent of a third- or fourth-grade education to lead kindergarten and first-grade classes in the day, as well as adult education classes in the evening. As a result, large numbers of children as well as adults previously denied access to learning because of their race and class received some formal education. By 1966 more than 10,000 students were attending FRELIMO primary schools in the liberated zones, and by 1970 the number had tripled. A larger number of adults participated in the literacy program.

FRELIMO soldiers in the liberated zones giving inoculations (Credit: United Nations/ Robert Van Lierop)

To be sure, many classes were overcrowded, and there were never enough books or teachers, but this was a small price to pay for the democratization of education.[39]

At all levels, the schools, along with teaching basic skills, helped to instill a new set of values. They attacked the colonial myths that negated Mozambican culture and divorced Mozambicans from their own history. Students learned about Mozambique's heritage and were also taught to appreciate the unique traditions of different ethnic groups. In this way schools became an important instrument for liberating Mozambicans from the colonial myths of their past and setting in motion the creation of a new cultural identity.

FRELIMO's ability to organize a minimal health care delivery system in the liberated zones helped to improve the quality of life of peasants and thereby increased popular support. As with education, attempting to confront the serious health problems endemic among the rural population required FRELIMO to improvise. Recalled one doctor, "At that time we didn't have personnel, we didn't have materials. We were obliged to discover new solutions to our problems."[40]

The democratization of medicine was also at the core of FRELIMO's policy. Throughout the liberated zones the colonial emphasis on curative medicine, both expensive and impractical, was abandoned in favor of preventive medicine for all peasants. In 1966 more than 100,000 peasants in Cabo Delgado were inoculated against smallpox. FRELIMO also opened first-aid stations and district medical centers in Cabo Delgado and Niassa[41] at which peasants were treated for illnesses and war wounds, inoculated against infectious diseases, instructed in personal hygiene, and taught to build latrines to prevent water pollution. In addition, FRELIMO nurses periodically visited villages to discuss nutrition, proper breast-feeding techniques, and other matters that affected the rural population.

For the liberated zones to be viable FRELIMO had to revitalize and restructure agricultural production. The flight of colonial administrators, European planters, and cotton concessionary company officials facilitated the shift from a forced-labor, cash-crop economy to one based primarily on the production of staples needed to feed both the peasants and the militants. The departure of the Europeans did not, however, resolve questions concerning the organization of labor or the ownership of property. These arose almost immediately as members of FRELIMO who had accumulated modest amounts of capital during the colonial period—chiefs, farmers, and petty traders—began to organize their own plantations and marketing schemes to replace those of the departed European landlords and merchants.[42]

> The landowners in the province of Cape Delgado started in 1966 to put the people to work on their lands. They began to put people to work in the cashew plantations. And after working on the cashew harvest for a month, a person would receive only a shirt. Then, after having marched for eight days up to the Rovuma River with a sack of cashew, he would receive one capulana [a cloth]. Thus began the contradictions. And after he reached the Rovuma and took the piece of clothing which the landlord was going to use for sale, he received salt, he worked for a week on the landlord's fields and received in payment salt and a tin of condensed milk.[43]

Such actions generated peasant opposition and reinforced the position taken by most members of the FRELIMO Central Committee that the collectivization of labor was a precondition to improving the material conditions of everyone in the liberated zones. The FRELIMO response was for cadres to hold long meetings with the peasants in which they discussed and debated the advantages of collective labor and an equitable distribution of production and the threat posed by the nascent "black elite."

By the end of 1966 FRELIMO had begun to experiment with a variety of agricultural cooperative systems. In some regions peasants worked the land jointly and shared the produce and profits equally. Even after they allocated a portion for the guerrillas, their profits were appreciably more than what they had previously received from the European concessionary companies or planters. In other areas peasants retained control over their own plots but worked collectively a designated number of days each month on a communal field growing food for the army, whose members worked side by side with the civilian population.[44] The collectivization of labor, however limited, reinforced the sense of common purpose, of identity, and of class solidarity among the peasants and between the peasants and the army. In this sense, the work experience became an important source of new values, which helped to shape FRELIMO's emerging ideology. As Samora Machel observed, "Through work we are becoming more united, cemented in our unity. If I am a Nyanja and cultivate the land alongside an Ngoni, I sweat with him, wrest life from the soil with him, learn with him, appreciate his effort and I feel united with him . . . tangibly living the unity of our country, the unity of our working class."[45]

When peasants complained in 1966 that the flight of most Portuguese and Asian merchants had precipitated shortages of basic commodities, FRELIMO organized People's Shops. By 1966 stores were operating in the liberated areas of Cabo Delgado, Niassa, and Tete. In addition, mobile shops visited particularly remote areas. To stimulate agricultural production, the People's Shops offered short-term credit and barter arrangements, served as collection centers for commodities to be exported to Tanzania, and facilitated interregional trade between one liberated zone and another. In a 1968 interview, Calisto Mijigo, military commander in Cabo Delgado, noted the benefits of this new commercial system:

> Before FRELIMO began the war, the people always got the short end of the bargain in any barter with the Portuguese. All shops belonged to the colonials and when the revolution started they stationed troops inside the posts where the shops were. After the Europeans fled, they began to exchange their crops across the Ruvuma River at barter points operated by the movement. They are better off now and can produce more for trade unless their crops have been bombed in the meantime. But their food supplies to us throw an additional burden on them which we want to alleviate.[46]

Disquieting reports soon began to circulate that senior officials were siphoning off profits and speculating in products in short supply. Increasingly, peasants living in Cabo Delgado identified Lazaro Nkavandame, FRELIMO's party secretary in Cabo Delgado Province and director of the Department of Commerce, as the principal culprit. Others complained that Nkavandame was also exploiting laborers in his private fields. These recurring charges against him and his lieutenants raised the specter of an embryonic black capitalist class within FRELIMO's ranks that would stifle basic social and economic changes. As Nkavandame came under increasing attack, he sought to manipulate tribal loyalties by appealing to "Makonde consciousness," and he began to plan a separatist Makonde movement to gain independence for Cabo Delgado Province.[47]

At about the time that popular protest against Nkavandame was surfacing, FRELIMO became embroiled in a conflict over student elitism. A key cause of this crisis was the Mozambican Roman Catholic priest, Father Mateus Gwenjere, who had joined FRELIMO at the end of 1967, bringing with him a number of seminary students from Beira. At the FRELIMO-run Mozambican Institute in Dar es Salaam, where he taught, Gwenjere encouraged students to expect scholarships for university study abroad and to defy the 1966 decision of FRELIMO's Central Committee that, upon completion of high school, all students spend at least a year inside Mozambique actively participating in the struggle. He also rekindled the issue of race, demanding the removal of four of the institute's teachers as well as the director, Janet Mondlane, because they were white and therefore not Mozambicans. The Central Committee, after an acrimonious debate, censored Gwenjere in March 1968. His supporters, who had temporarily forced the closing of the Mozambican Institute and were probably involved in the sacking of FRELIMO headquarters two months later, fled to Kenya. A number of Mozambicans studying in the United States also defied the 1966 decision and refused to return home and join the ranks of the militants. Instead, they organized a vitriolic public campaign against Mondlane, charging, in effect, that FRELIMO's education policy reflected Mondlane's desire to safeguard his own intellectual position as the country's only Ph.D.[48]

By mid-1968 popular criticism of Nkavandame, the attack by Gwenjere, and fundamental disagreements over the issues of race, tribalism, and nationality brought to a head the deep-seated ideological divisions within the Central Committee. Two different "lines"—as FRELIMO periodicals came increasingly to refer to them—each with a different vision and class orientation, openly contested for power. One group, including Nkavandame, Gwenjere, and Uria Simango, the FRELIMO vice-president, maintained a narrow nationalist posture with racialist and tribalist overtones. Its members argued that southerners dominated the leadership of FRELIMO, "while the Portuguese were determined through cunning ways to infiltrate the Central Committee as members. Marcelino dos Santos played a very important role to achieve this, on the basis that they were also Mozambicans as the black masses—a definition which was not established by any organ of FRELIMO."[49] For this group the ultimate objective was to create an independent black nation run by an educated black elite that would replace the white colonialist regime.

In opposition stood the majority of the Central Committee, led by Marcelino dos Santos, secretary for foreign affairs; Samora Machel, head of the army; Joaquim Chissano, a senior member of the Executive Committee; and President Mondlane, who himself had been radicalized by the struggle. According to a long-time associate, Mondlane, "initially obsessed with the desire to maintain the unity of the movement,"[50] by 1968 had come to recognize the futility of that desire. The Mondlane–dos Santos–Machel group argued that Lisbon's defeat would mark only the first step in transforming Mozambican society, and it saw the experiences of the liberated zones as establishing a model, however embryonic, for the way in which collective action and collective ownership could lead to a more equitable distribution of Mozambique's resources. Rejecting the notion that an educated elite should guide the country and appropriate its wealth, and bitterly attacking the racialist posture of the other line, it asserted instead the primacy of peasants and workers and an analysis based on class.

At the Second Party Congress, held in July 1968, the latter group, committed to what is termed a "revolutionary line," prevailed. Despite the staunch opposition of Nkavandame, the congress was held in liberated Niassa Province, Mondlane was reelected president, and the Central

Committee's size was doubled, from twenty to forty. New members came almost exclusively from popularly elected constituencies inside Mozambique and from the military—both of which supported the revolutionary position. The enlarged Central Committee adopted a new program emphasizing the eradication of all forms of social and economic inequality and committing FRELIMO to forge ahead with the process of national reconstruction begun in the liberated zones. In an explicit statement of the ideological path along which FRELIMO was moving, the Congress affirmed that "the struggle is part of the world's movement for the emancipation of the oppressed peoples, which aims at the total liquidation of colonialism and imperialism, and at the construction of a new society free from exploitation of man by man."[51]

Although defeated, the minority faction led by Nkavandame was not prepared to yield power without a struggle. A few weeks later Nkavandame organized a meeting of FRELIMO dissidents in southern Tanzania at which he elaborated his plan to establish an independent Makonde nationalist movement. Makonde guerrillas rejected his appeal. As one scholar noted, "Nkavandame had little support among the ethnic group he claimed to represent. But like Gwenjere, he tried to use appeals to ethnic solidarity and discrimination to advance his own position."[52] Undeterred, Nkavandame conspired in the assassination of the deputy chief of the Defense Department, Paulo Samuel Kankhomba. On January 3, 1969, the Central Committee stripped him of all his official responsibilities. A month later a letter bomb killed President Mondlane at his office in Dar es Salaam. Evidence implicated Nkavandame, along with Silvério Nungu, a senior FRELIMO member, in the assassination, which had been orchestrated by the Portuguese secret police. Nkavandame fled across the border with the help of PIDE agents and defected to the colonial regime. Throughout the rest of the war, Nkavandame served as one of Lisbon's leading propagandists.

Widespread doubts about Vice-President Simango's loyalty enabled the revolutionary faction to block his immediate assumption of the presidency until the Central Committee could convene in April 1969. After severely criticizing him for not explicitly attacking the Gwenjere-Nkavandame line, the Central Committee created the Council of the Presidency, to be composed of Simango, Marcelino dos Santos, and Samora Machel. These latter two were committed to pursuing a radical path.

Increasingly isolated, Simango made a desperate bid for power. In a polemic entitled "Gloomy Situation in FRELIMO," he publicly attacked the Central Committee, flattered the Mozambican students studying abroad, subtly attacked whites and mulattoes in the movement, and claimed that the Machel–dos Santos group was dividing FRELIMO by demanding ideological clarity instead of merely adhering to the fundamental principle of independence through armed struggle. Simango also rejected as irrelevant any analysis of the struggle in class, rather than racial terms, asserting that "if there is an indigenous bourgeois class at the moment and if it is willing to contribute for the liberation of our struggle we must accept its cooperation."[53] In November 1969 the Executive Committee of FRELIMO suspended him from the Council of the Presidency, and in May 1970 the Central Committee elected Samora Machel as president of FRELIMO and Marcelino dos Santos as vice-president.

Like his assassinated predecessor, Samora Machel came from a family steeped in a long tradition of anticolonial struggle. His grandparents and great-grandparents had fought in the wars of resistance at the end of the nineteenth century in southern Mozambique, and his paternal grandfather was one of the leading figures in the Maguiguane rebellion in 1896. His family had also suffered for its outspoken opposition. Both maternal grandparents had been deported to São Thomé, where they had died in exile.

From his earliest youth Machel had experienced exploitation. At missionary school he was forced to spend most of his day cultivating cash crops for the benefit of the church. When he completed his primary education, his teachers decided to send him to seminary, rather than to high school, where they hoped his rebellious nature would be tamed. Machel refused to go. Instead, he took a nursing course and then completed secondary studies at night, paying the cost from his meager wages. His father not only suffered all the indignities of forced cotton production but in the early 1950s had his land confiscated and given to a Portuguese immigrant. Machel's eldest brother and many other close relatives died in the South African gold mines.

When FRELIMO was formed, Machel fled Mozambique and joined the movement, rising quickly within its ranks. In 1963 he went with a small group of militants to Algeria for military training, and after his return to Tanzania, he was placed in charge of FRELIMO's first military training camp. In this capacity he played a central role in planning and organizing the initial phase of the armed struggle. A year later he directed the military campaign in the eastern sector of Niassa, and in 1966, after the death of FRELIMO's first defense secretary, Filipe Magaia, he took over this post. In the hotly contested ideological debates within the Central Committee, to which he was soon after elected, Machel aligned himself with President Mondlane and Marcelino dos Santos, emerging as one of the principal protagonists of the revolutionary nationalist position.[54] The selection of Machel as president and dos Santos as vice-president marked the final victory for the forces of revolutionary nationalism within FRELIMO and set the stage for a more explicit adoption of a socialist agenda.

Between the end of 1969 and 1972 FRELIMO formalized the principles and practices developed in the liberated zones and extended the war zone. FRELIMO's clearer ideological stance facilitated the destruction of the last vestiges of traditional authority. It also highlighted the fact that a black bourgeoisie, if left unchecked, could co-opt and ultimately destroy the revolution. The need to emancipate women received greater emphasis, and advances were made in the fields of health and education. On the military front, guerrilla forces expanded their operations in Tete Province and, for the first time, began making significant inroads in the southern half of the country.

Reflecting on this period, Samora Machel recently noted, "We evolved a theory out of our practice and then we found that this theory of ours evolving out of our practice had already acquired theorization under different circumstances. This theory and this theorization is Marxism-Leninism."[55] In a conversation with us, he was particularly emphatic about the importance of FRELIMO's experiences in the liberated zone during the armed struggle. "Marxism-Leninism did not appear in our country as an imported product."[56]

THE REACTION OF THE COLONIAL STATE

Intransigent in its opposition to Mozambican independence, the Salazar regime acted swiftly to blunt FRELIMO's advances and to isolate the liberation movement. Lisbon initiated a far-reaching counterinsurgency campaign within Mozambique and an external diplomatic offensive designed to attain increased support from its NATO allies by redefining the independence struggle within a Cold War framework.

Portugal's military strategy hinged on its ability to isolate the guerrillas from the larger African population by confining the fighting to the frontier regions in the far north of the colony. These remote areas in Cabo Delgado and Niassa were the least profitable and most sparsely populated and had only a handful of European settlers. In 1960, for example, only 2,400 Europeans lived in the two provinces, and most of these resided in the adminstrative centers of Porto Amélia and Vila Cabral. Above all else, military planners agreed that FRELIMO's advances had to be checked north of the Zambesi River so as not to jeopardize the large community and major investments to the south.

Forced relocation of peasants into strategic hamlets (*aldeamentos*) and the creation of a *cordon sanitaire* along the Tanzanian and Malawian borders were key elements of Lisbon's counterinsurgency program. Although the colonial government and the state-controlled press claimed that the establishment of strategic hamlets was part of a broader policy to improve the social and economic conditions in rural areas, the elimination of the peasant's covert assistance to FRELIMO was the overriding consideration. Portuguese officials also hoped that the militias being organized in each hamlet would serve as a first line of defense and would also help to "win over" the inhabitants.

In 1965 Portugal began a "scorched-earth" policy along the Tanzanian border in Cabo Delgado and simultaneously herded thousands of peasants into villages encircled by barbed wire. According to one colonial official, "The people were ordered to enter aldeamentos. They were given short notice, which varied from three to fifteen days, to abandon everything and to resettle. If they failed to heed the warning they were automatically considered terrorists and the troops had been instructed to kill all of them."[57] Despite the promise that these villages would be located in fertile areas with abundant supplies of water and other social amenities, this was rarely, if ever, the case. As one Roman Catholic priest observed, "The places are badly chosen; the huts are too close to one another; the compulsory transfer is made too quickly, and, in fact, is made before the huts are ready. Then there are all the other moral, social and hygienic problems."[58] Not the least of these, according to a United Nations Commission of Inquiry, was starvation, "because of the lack of sufficient land for farming . . . and the propagation of contagious diseases owing to the absence of adequate health service."[59] Other peasants complained to the commission of being regularly terrorized and brutalized by colonial troops, and "some described the aldeamentos as a kind of death camp or concentration camp to isolate the people from FRELIMO's influence."[60]

In 1966 the colonial state began a similar forced resettlement program in Niassa Province; it was extended to Tete two years later. By the early 1970s the strategic hamlet program had been imposed throughout much of northern Mozambique. In Niassa 160,000 peasants had been relocated, and in Cabo Delgado the total was more than 270,000, nearly 50 percent of the African population in each province. In Tete Province, which after 1968 became the major combat zone, the Portuguese detained in strategic hamlets nearly 60 percent of the population, more than 250,000 people. In anticipation of further FRELIMO advances, the colonial regime began in 1971 to regroup Africans in the central provinces of Manica and Sofala as well as in Lourenço Marques, which was several hundred miles from the actual fighting.[61]

By most accounts, the strategic hamlets were no more successful in Mozambique than in Vietnam. FRELIMO cadres were able to organize cells in many, and their existence did not stem the flow of food, recruits, and strategic information to the liberation army. Portuguese propaganda bulletins conceded as much: "The enemy effort recently had been concentrated on impeding the grouping of further people into protected villages, especially in the Tete area, by seeking to win them over or forcing them to run away into the bush or over the frontier. As a result the situation has worsened in Tete."[62] Military communiqués, which were often issued in the wake of FRELIMO attacks, acknowledged the involvement of peasants living in the aldeamentos.[63]

Even less successful was the colonial strategy of establishing a network of predominantly European, paramilitary settler communities (colonatos) in zones of guerrilla activity. Influenced somewhat by the Israeli kibbutz, Lisbon envisioned resettling more than 1 million Portuguese by the year 2000, primarily along the banks of the Zambesi River. In the first phase Lisbon sought to recruit several thousand families, offering as inducements free passage, housing, agricultural equipment, and choice tracts of land appropriated from African peasants, who thereby became available to work on the European estates. Despite the fanfare, few Portuguese opted to become pioneers, and those who did failed to bring the technical skills and deep patriotic commitment necessary. By 1973 only a few hundred immigrants, primarily from Madeira, had resettled in these communities, and the absentee rate in some was more than 25 percent.[64]

Another central feature of Lisbon's counterinsurgency campaign was to pit ethnic groups against each other. Even before the armed struggle, the colonial state had employed this tactic, especially in the north, and once the war began, Portugal intensified its campaign to politicize tribal distinctions.

In Cabo Delgado Province Portuguese patrols distributed pamphlets proclaiming that "whites and blacks are friends but FRELIMO seeks to destroy this friendship," that FRELIMO was dominated by the Makonde tribe, which "is the enemy of the Makua tribe, and that therefore the Makuas should join forces with the Portuguese to fight against the Makondes."[65] A Mozambican of Makua descent who had been conscripted into the colonial army recounted: "In my region, which is inhabited by people of the Makua tribe, they say that the war is being fought by the Makonde, who want to oppress and dominate the Makuas. They had several times killed the people in one village and called the people of the neighboring village to go and see. They tell that this was done by the FRELIMO Makonde."[66] Colonial propaganda in Niassa Province fostered similar hostility between the Yao and Nyanja, who, together with the Makonde, purportedly dominated FRELIMO. The appeal to the Makua and Yao, both Muslim, was often couched in religious terms as well, contemptuously referring to the Makonde pagans and Protestant Nyanja and emphasizing FRELIMO's allegedly anti-Islamic policies, such as its refusal to recognize Muslim headmen and its opposition to polygamy. Other government broadcasts and pamphlets claimed that the Makonde, although numerically superior in FRELIMO, were being duped by southern Mozambicans of Tonga and Ronga descent who monopolized the leadership positions.

By demonstrating to the villagers the ethnic heterogeneity of the guerrilla bands, FRELIMO was able to defuse, at least partially, the divisive impact of these tactics. "In our unit," one militant declared, "I am with Ajawa, Nyanja, Makonde and people from Zambézia. I believe this is good. Before we did not think of ourselves as a single nation, FRELIMO has shown us that we are one people."[67] This public expression of solidarity was reinforced during intensive discussions in which peasants and soldiers recounted common experiences of colonial exploitation.

The escalating conflict also required a sharp increase in the number of colonial troops operating within the colony. In 1961 there were only 4,000 Portuguese soldiers, stationed primarily in the provincial capitals. By 1966 the size of the military had increased tenfold, and by the early 1970s more than 70,000 men were under arms. To alleviate manpower pressures created by the need to fight simultaneously colonial wars in Angola, Guinea-Bissau, and Mozambique, as well as by growing draft evasion in Portugal, in 1966 the colonial regime began a major campaign to Africanize the army. Africanization could also be used by Lisbon to support its propaganda that the war was nonracial in character. By the early 1970s between 10,000 and 20,000 black troops were fighting in the north, including an elite brigade of 4,000 volunteer paratroopers.[68]

In addition to enlarging the army, Lisbon allocated an increasing percentage of the national and colonial budgets to the war effort. The air force was substantially upgraded with fighters, helicopters, and large numbers of transport and reconnaissance planes, and new airfields capable of handling heavy planes were constructed throughout the country. Naval coastal facilities, especially in the north, were also improved, and in response to FRELIMO activity in Niassa Province, the Portuguese navy established a Maritime Defense Command to patrol Lake Nyasa and interdict insurgent forces and supplies. In addition, Lisbon undertook a massive road construction and paving program because the dirt roads of Cabo Delgado and Niassa hampered troop movement, especially in the rainy season, and left the colonial forces extremely vulnerable to the mines planted by FRELIMO. By the early 1970s two major roadways linking Portuguese strategic centers and towns in Cabo Delgado and Niassa had been completed, and construction had begun on a major north-south highway extending to the capital of Lourenço Marques in the extreme south.[69]

In June 1970, in a campaign known as Gordian Knot, Portugal attempted to wipe out FRELIMO bases in the liberated zones. More than 10,000 troops, including elite paratroop battalions, under the cover of Portugal's airpower, swooped down on FRELIMO liberated zones in the Makonde highlands and in northeastern Niassa. Despite an initial tactical advantage and short-term gains, the Portuguese were soon ensnarled in a protracted and costly engagement that proved unsuccessful.

As the war escalated, so did political repression. Opposition in any form—strikes, protest writing, public rallies—was not tolerated. One prominent Portuguese lawyer estimated that at least 10,000 opponents of the regime were arrested between 1967 and 1973.[70] Dissidents, black as well as white, were apprehended by the notorious secret police and sent to Machava Prison on the outskirts of Lourenço Marques, the penal camp at Ibo Island, or labor camps and jails in São Thomé. Many never returned. Those who did suffered repeated torture before their release. Arihdhi Mahanda, who survived Ibo Island, recalled: "I was imprisoned by PIDE and taken to Ibo Island where they beat and tortured me claiming that I had sold the country to foreigners coming from Tanzania. At Ibo 20 to 30 Mozambicans died each day. Others were repeatedly beaten until they could no longer use their arms or legs. Many died from jaundice and others who were very ill were only given sea water."[71]

The secret police did not limit its activity to known dissidents. It would pick up people for the slightest reason and would torture them to find out if they had any connection with the guerrillas. Some were hung upside down by their feet and beaten until they confessed. Others succumbed to electric shock torture on their genitals. Many people died under the torture.

During this period Lisbon turned increasingly to its NATO allies for diplomatic, military, and economic assistance. Portuguese officials maintained that Mozambique, Angola, and Guinea-Bissau were legitimate overseas provinces of Portugal, and they pointed with pride to the "multiracial paradise" they had created and the reforms they had introduced since 1961. Their most compelling argument, however, was that FRELIMO was a communist-backed terrorist organization controlled by the Soviet Union, which would ultimately benefit if Portugal was defeated. Foreign Minister Franco Nogueira proclaimed:

> Russia's naval penetration in the Indian Ocean will occupy a great deal of what is abandoned by Britain, and many bases and ports will be denied the West.
> We are in Africa because that is our right, our duty and our interest. But we are in Africa because that is also the general interest of the free world.
> If the bases and the islands and the ports and airports and the coastline were not in firm Portuguese hands, one can ask, in whose hands would they be? But in any case, those new masters would not offer to the West the guarantees which we, if we want to, will be in a position to offer.[72]

These claims of strategic need and racial harmony gained wide credibility in Western Europe and the United States. No less eminent a scholar and policymaker than U.S. Ambassador George Kennan concluded, "The situation in the great Portuguese territories of Angola and Mozambique differs fundamentally from that prevailing in South and Southwest Africa in that the central issue is not that of race. Neither the personal observation of a detached visitor nor the literature of unbiased scholars who address themselves to Portuguese-African affairs afford much confirmation for such allegations."[73]

To increase NATO support and enhance the state's financial ability to pursue the war, the Salazar regime made important economic concessions to Western capital. In 1965, for the first time, foreign enterprises without the participation of Portuguese capital were permitted to operate in Mozambique. Western companies, long frozen out of the colony, jumped at the opportunity to explore for oil and rare minerals and expressed an interest in its strategic metals, especially tantalite, and its rich iron and coal deposits.[74] The construction of Cahora Bassa Dam was the single most important new investment in the colony. ZAMCO, an international consortium of British, U.S., South African, French, West German, and Italian capital under the guidance of the Anglo-American Corporation, planned to invest $515 million to build the dam, which would be the fifth largest in the world and the largest in Africa. Cahora Bassa, it was hoped, would facilitate not only the extraction of minerals in Tete Province but also the settlement of 1 million Portuguese in the strategic Zambesi Valley.[75]

Despite rhetoric supporting the principle of self-determination, Portugal's NATO allies, led by the United States, increased their support for Lisbon's African policy. Even before the conflict broke out, the Western countries had begun to revamp and modernize Portugal's antiquated military. The United States provided fighter planes and bombers, helicopters, jet transports, B-52s, and chemical defoliants, and it trained more than 2,000 military personnel in counterinsurgency activity. West Germany, whose military assistance was probably the largest, sold more than 200 jet planes and napalm, and France offered armored cars, helicopters, warships, and ammunition, with loans backed by the government. The

NATO allies stipulated that the arms be used within the "NATO framework," but they acknowledged that they were powerless to prevent Lisbon from transferring the arms and munitions to Mozambique, Angola, and Guinea-Bissau. At the same time, they rejected overtures from FRELIMO for humanitarian as well as military assistance.[76]

The Salazar regime benefited significantly from the unyielding diplomatic support of the NATO countries. At the United Nations and elsewhere, Western representatives warned against "destructive criticism" of Portugal and urged that Lisbon be given more time to pursue its reformist policies. From 1964 onward Western representatives at the United Nations refused to support any resolution on the Portuguese colonies that moved beyond declaratory language about the right to self-determination.[77]

The Western countries also provided Lisbon with badly needed aid and loans, which helped to finance the war and to alleviate Portugal's economic crisis. Although many of the agreements still remain secret, the few documented cases suggest the scope of this assistance. In the early 1960s West Germany gave Portugal $90 million in direct financial aid; the United States supplied $110 million. Between 1967 and 1969 the French government guaranteed a $100 million loan to upgrade the Portuguese navy. These loans did not compare with the Nixon administration's $435 million commitment of Export-Import Bank money in 1971—a quid pro quo for the formal extension until 1974 of the lease of land on the Azores to the U.S. military. The significance attributed by the United States and its NATO allies to the perpetuation of the status quo, albeit with some superficial modifications, is reflected in the fact that this $435 million loan was more than the bank had provided to all of Africa from 1946 to 1970.[78]

FINAL VICTORY—INDEPENDENCE

Despite increased Western support, by 1972 the situation in Mozambique was desperate for the colonial regime. Lisbon's much-heralded Gordian Knot had failed. Armed with more sophisticated weapons, provided primarily by China and the Soviet Union, and enjoying increased popular support, FRELIMO had expanded the liberated zones in the north, consolidated gains in Tete, and for the first time was operating in the southern half of the country. FRELIMO's front in Manica and Sofala threatened not only the white settler highlands but also Beira, the country's second largest city. By the end of 1973 FRELIMO guerrilla forces had mined several trains going from Beira to Southern Rhodesia; raided settler-owned sugar, cotton, and sisal plantations; attacked inland towns; and interdicted traffic going from Beira to Tete and to Cahora Bassa Dam. These raids undercut the sense of security within the European community and provoked large-scale settler demonstrations in Lourenço Marques and Beira demanding more effective military control. Despite civilian complaints, the colonial army was unable to blunt FRELIMO's advance. By the end of the year groups of guerrillas had reached the Save River, only 400 miles (640 kilometers) from the capital of Lourenço Marques. In early 1974

Portuguese intelligence estimated that FRELIMO forces had jumped to more than 10,000 and acknowledged growing opposition to the war within the colonial army.[79]

Portugal also suffered a major propaganda reversal from publicity concerning the massacre of 400 villagers at Wiriyamu, just south of Tete. Based on eyewitness accounts collected by Spanish missionaries, the story published in the *London Times* focused international attention on Portuguese colonialism, generated widespread protest, embarrassed Portugal's Western allies, and brought FRELIMO concrete financial and moral support from the World Council of Churches.[80]

At the same time, opposition within Portugal to the war was intensifying. Leaders of the small but growing Portuguese industrial sector, which had strong links to international capital, expressed concern about the mounting national debt and the flight of vital Portuguese labor to avoid the draft.[81] Anxious to integrate the country into the European Economic Community, they began to question the efficacy of pursuing a war that could not be won. Younger army officers, many of whom had become radicalized by both the colonial wars and oppression at home, secretly organized the Armed Forces Movement. On April 24, 1974, they overthrew the authoritarian regime of Marcello Caetano, Salazar's hand-picked successor. Supported by workers and peasants in Portugal, they pledged a return to civil liberties at home and an end to the fighting in all the colonies.

The rapid chain of events within Portugal caught FRELIMO, which had anticipated a protracted guerrilla campaign gradually extending the liberated zones, by surprise. Nevertheless, it responded quickly to the new situation. On the battlefield, its forces continued their forward advance, opening up a new front in Zambézia Province in July 1974. FRELIMO cadres also intensified their activity, especially in the urban centers of Lourenço Marques and Beira, where the movement's presence had been minimal. In prolonged and difficult negotiations with the new Portuguese government FRELIMO unequivocally rejected attempts to impose in Mozambique a "neocolonial" solution, which would have also ensured a role for the anti-FRELIMO African organizations that had suddenly sprung up.[82] On September 7, 1974, it won from the Armed Forces Movement an agreement to transfer power to FRELIMO within the year.

The next day a white settler movement, Fico ("I stay"), attempted an abortive coup. Supported by some military commandos, it captured the radio and the newspaper in Lourenço Marques and blew up an arsenal on the outskirts of the city. Three days later a joint force of Portuguese and FRELIMO troops crushed the rebellion. A transitional government led by Joaquim Chissano was installed on September 20, 1974, composed of six FRELIMO and four Portuguese members. It served as a caretaker until independence.

During this interim period FRELIMO sought to take advantage of a groundswell of popular support to extend its political presence throughout the country and to create grassroot links with all sectors of the population. Many areas, particularly in southern Mozambique, had had little direct contact with FRELIMO during the liberation struggle. Therefore, they did not understand the movement's political and economic programs, nor had they had experience with democratic participation in the decision-making process—a prerequisite for mass mobilization.

To familiarize people with FRELIMO's goals and to provide them with a crash course in decision making, FRELIMO created the dynamizing groups. Each group was composed of individuals selected by their local communities or fellow workers because they enjoyed the personal confidence of their neighbors and colleagues and they appeared to have the best understanding of FRELIMO's policies. During the period of transition to independence the dynamizing groups performed multiple functions with varying degrees of success. They organized discussions of FRELIMO's ideology, encouraged individuals to assert themselves and participate in decision making, protected neighborhoods against vandalism, ended strikes, and explained to their communities the advantages of collective labor.[83]

The transitional government also began to grapple with the deep-rooted social problems inherited from the colonial period. It encouraged literacy programs, began a health campaign, and strengthened the Mozambique Women's Movement. Through public pronouncements and private meetings, Prime Minister Chissano also sought to assuage anxieties within the white community and to prevent a massive exodus that would deprive Mozambique of critical skilled labor and place new strains on the underdeveloped economy.

On June 25, 1975, Mozambique became free. At the independence celebration President Samora Machel warned that although the first phase in the struggle had been won, the young country still had to overcome illiteracy, disease, poverty, and economic dependence, which were the legacies of colonialism. In addressing these issues, the organizing skills, the emphasis on self-reliance and local initiative, and the revolutionary values developed in the liberated zones were to prove critical. At the same time, however, the new government's attempts to overcome these problems have created contradictory tendencies. In the chapters that follow the reader should be aware of the tensions between local initiative and bureaucratization, between self-reliance and statism, between experimentation and orthodoxy, and between grassroots democracy and vanguardism. How Mozambique's leaders ultimately resolve these tensions will shape the character of their revolutionary experiment.

6

The Making of a Mozambican Nation and a Socialist Polity

*The fight began five centuries ago, the fight began
with our ancestors*

*The fight began with arrow and spear, against guns against
cannons*

*The fight grew in slavery and in the chibalo in the forced
work*

*The fight grew in mountains and woods with guns in hands,
with flags of freedom.*

*The fight grew in cold and rain with our heroes, still sure
of independence*

*The fight grew under the People's sons, under FRELIMO leadership
and continues*

until Socialism.

—Hermínio Malate, "The Fight,"
in Chris Searle, *Beyond the Skin*
(London, 1979), p. 9

*The truth is that we understand fully what we do not want: oppression, exploitation,
humiliation. But as to what we do want and how to get it, our ideas are
necessarily still vague. They are born of practice, corrected by practice. . . . We
undoubtedly will run into setbacks. But it is from these setbacks that we will
learn.*

—Samora Machel,
A Nossa Luta (Maputo, 1975)

If FRELIMO's ideas were necessarily vague when the liberation
movement assumed power, the urgent problems that Mozambique faced
nevertheless demanded immediate attention and concrete solutions. FRE-
LIMO had captured the colonial state, and now it faced the more difficult
task of creating a nation. To a certain extent, all underdeveloped countries
experienced similar uncertainties at independence. Illiteracy, poverty, un-
familiarity with democratic processes, racial and ethnic cleavages, and the
threat of an autonomous bureaucracy have plagued all newly independent

109

President Samora Machel visiting Niassa Province (Credit: Ricardo Rangel)

countries of the Third World. Other problems, however, some already familiar to the liberation movement, were related specifically to the Mozambican experience. How was FRELIMO to create a sense of national unity and overcome the long history of ethnic and regional particularism that had been heightened by intense colonial propaganda? What was the most effective way to instill a sense of self-confidence and political consciousness among peasants and workers long oppressed by an autocratic police state? How could FRELIMO maintain the level of political mobilization and extend the base of popular support, while asking for continued sacrifices, when there was no longer a visible symbol of colonial oppression? That FRELIMO was not well entrenched in the southern half of the country, especially in the cities, further complicated matters, as did the unrealistically high expectation, especially among urban workers, that independence would bring instant relief from all suffering.

Beyond these immediate problems, the path toward socialism, which FRELIMO chose, raised both theoretical and practical dilemmas. How could the needs for vanguard leadership and for popular participation be reconciled to avoid the tendency for democracy to give way, under conditions of economic scarcity and the need for capital accumulation, to a new ruling class composed of state bureaucrats and party officials?[1] The insignificant size and disorganized state of the Mozambican working class and the shortage of trained cadres to staff both a vanguard party and the state apparatus would also hamper the transition from colonial-capitalism to socialism. Finally, FRELIMO's commitment to locate its socialist experiment within the Mozambican reality, rather than merely copying foreign forms, demanded a high degree of creativity.

That Mozambique has been under siege from either Rhodesia or South Africa for all but six months of its independence has distorted the political process in a number of ways. The need to maintain unity in the face of constant aggression compelled FRELIMO to ignore such potentially divisive issues as how to forge a national culture while still celebrating the diverse ethnic, linguistic, and historical traditions of the Mozambican people. Strategic needs also limited the extent to which controversial subjects, such as the abuse of power, were aired and publicly discussed. It is no coincidence that major reforms and public criticism of state and party officials occurred primarily during the first few months after independence and during the short interlude between the independence of Zimbabwe and the intensification of attacks by South African–controlled guerrillas.

The postindependence political history of Mozambique can be divided roughly into two periods. During the first year and a half FRELIMO focused almost exclusively on the twin tasks of national integration and political mobilization. This phase was a continuation of its efforts to restructure the political process, which had been begun but not completed during the armed struggle. The Third Party Congress, held in February 1977, launched the second stage, known in the lexicon of FRELIMO as the "Popular Democratic Revolution." At the congress FRELIMO adopted an explicitly Marxist-Leninist character. Specifically, the party committed itself to intensifying the class struggle, expanding the vanguard role of the party, developing new and responsive political institutions, and placing the strategic sectors of the economy under state control.

POLITICAL CHANGES UNTIL 1977: FORGING NATIONAL UNITY

The new government that assumed power on June 25, 1975, included the most senior members of the liberation movement. Of the nineteen new ministers, all but four had actually fought in the armed struggle (see Table 6.1). Others, such as Mário Machungo and Rui Balthazar dos Santos Alves, had worked clandestinely within the country for FRELIMO and had served as FRELIMO representatives in the transitional government.

The inextricably intertwined goals of forging national unity and mobilizing the masses were at the center of the government's postindependence political strategy, especially in those regions where the populace had not experienced life in the liberated zones. The war had demonstrated the necessity of political mobilization to transform people's consciousness and sense of identity. It also revealed that improving the quality of life, however marginally, and providing a vision and a hope for the future were important ingredients in winning the hearts and minds of the people.

These goals were embedded in the new Constitution, which codified the experiences of the liberated zones, modified to meet the needs of a sovereign government. In this respect, the Constitution was substantially different from those of most new African states, which were written by, and inherited from, the colonizers.[2]

The government's first major concern was to integrate diverse sectors

TABLE 6.1
First Government of the People's Republic of Mozambique

President of the Republic	Samora Moises Machel
Minister of Development and Planning	Marcelino dos Santos
Minister of Foreign Affairs	Joaquim Chissano
Minister of National Defense	Alberto Joaquim Chipande
Minister of Information	Jorge Rebelo
Minister of Labor	Mariano de Araujo Matsinhe
Minister in the Presidency	José Oscar Monteir
Minister of Agriculture	Joaquim de Carvalho
Minister of Education and Culture	Graça Machel
Minister of Health	Helder Martins
Minister of Industry and Commerce	Mário da Graça Machungo
Minister of Transports and Communications	José Luís Cabaço
Minister of Justice	Rui Baltazar dos Santos Alves
Minister of Public Works and Housing	Júlio Zamith Carrilho
Minister of Finance	Salomão Munguambe
Vice-Minister of National Defense and Chief of General Staff	Sebastião Marcos Mabote
Vice-Minister of Foreign Affairs	Armando Panguene
Vice-Minister of Interior	Daniel Saul Mbanze
Political National Commissar of the People's Armed Forces	Armando Emílio Guebuza

Source: Mozambique Revolution 61 (1975): 28.

of the population into a newly emerging nation. "We do not recognize tribes, regions, race or religious beliefs," declared President Machel at the Independence Day celebrations. "We only recognize Mozambicans who are equally exploited and equally desirous of freedom and revolution." He nevertheless acknowledged that such proclamations were not sufficient to jump over history. "To be united it is not enough to state that one is united. It is necessary to wage a constant battle against all divisive situations and tendencies."[3] Tribalism fanned by Portuguese propaganda, a lingering fear of "reverse-racism" within the white community, and the continued subordination of women complicated the processes of political mobilization and national integration.

These themes remained an important part of the government's campaign to mobilize and unify the Mozambican people. The president and other high-level officials made repeated trips from the capital, Maputo (formerly Lourenço Marques), located in the extreme southern part of the country, to every province, emphasizing each time that "the fulfillment of the giant task that lies ahead of us implies achieving and consolidating unity." They rejected any division of authority and responsibility among different racial and ethnic groups or any other artificial balancing act that would fragment rather than unify. Daily broadcasts and numerous newspaper articles reiterated the themes that "from the Rovuma to Maputo we are all Mozambicans" and that victory could be achieved only through

"Unity, Work, and Vigilance." Grassroots dynamizing groups organized in rural communities, factories, and urban neighborhoods attacked pejorative ethnic stereotypes and emphasized the value of national unity. Xiconhoca, a cartoon character and the archetype of the corrupt Mozambican, regularly appeared on posters and in magazines, schoolbooks, and newspapers. He quickly became known throughout the country as the negative role model, fostering tribalism, sexism, and exploitation (see Figure 6.1).

The ethnically heterogeneous composition of the FRELIMO Central Committee, as well as the presence of Mozambicans of all regions in high government positions, further discredited charges of "tribal favoritism." The insignificant role of ethnic politics and the absence of secessionist tendencies during this formative phase testified to FRELIMO's success—rare among African countries—in defusing the potentially divisive issue of tribalism.[4]

National unity also required that the new government address the vexing problem of racism and the nagging question of citizenship. The Constitution explicitly outlawed all acts creating divisions or privileged positions based on color, race, sex, ethnic origin, or class position. Rights of citizenship were unqualified by origin or skin color. The vigorous antiracialist campaigns continued after independence. Upon arriving in Mozambique, visitors were greeted in the airport by a conspicuously large poster depicting a black and white arm embracing, whose caption read, "Down with racism." This message was repeated daily on the radio, in the newspapers, and in wall drawings displayed throughout the principal cities and towns. Although not pandering to the concerns of the white community, FRELIMO did appoint several militants of Portuguese ancestry to prominent positions within the new government.

Such assurances, however, failed to assuage deep-seated fears within the white community, fears often rooted in perceived racial turmoil in other parts of the continent. As a businessman in the capital explained, "FRELIMO needs us now. But what about when black people are trained for our positions. Look at every other African country—Ghana, Nigeria, Tanzania, Kenya—they all promised multiracial societies. But how often do you see whites in governments there? And Africanization programs have led to nationalization of companies all over the continent. What kind of future do I have here?"[5] The flow of white emigrants and of a small number of mulattoes and blacks who had either collaborated with the colonial regime or who feared that FRELIMO's long-term socialist goals jeopardized their relatively privileged social position increased. Within a year after independence the white population had dwindled from more than 200,000 to about 20,000. Ironically, most of those whites who chose to stay and become Mozambicans continued to enjoy the privileges conferred by their relatively advanced education, technical skills, and family savings. To some degree, even the most deeply committed militants benefited from these privileges.

The new government also reiterated its long-standing support for the liberation of Mozambican women who, after all, were a majority of the population—a majority whose participation in the political life of the

114

FIGURE 6.1 Xiconhoca
Top right: Xiconhoca is a parasite. He refuses to work. He doesn't participate in
production. *Bottom:* Xiconhoca is a bureaucrat. He complicates the life of the people.
Top Left: Xiconhoca is an agent of the enemy. He guides the invaders. He collaborates
in aggression and the massacre of the people. *Source:* Edição do Departamento de
Trabalho Ideológico (FRELIMO), *Xiconhoca o Inimigo.*

country was critical for the advancement of the process of creating a new nation. Integrating women into society as equal citizens and socially productive members became the official policy, which the Mozambique Women's Movement (OMM) had the task of carrying out. Listen to President Machel as he addressed the controversial issue of the emancipation of women:

> The emancipation of women is not an act of charity, the result of humanitarian or compassionate attitude. The liberation of women is a fundamental necessity for the Revolution, the guarantee of its continuity and the precondition for its victory. The main objective of the Revolution is to destroy the system of exploitation and build a new society which releases the potential of human beings, reconciling them with labor and with nature. This is the context within which the question of women's emancipation arises.[6]

The broad principles he articulated at the founding conference of the Mozambique Women's Movement in 1973 were subsequently enshrined in the Mozambican Constitution: "In the People's Republic of Mozambique, women and men have equal rights and duties, this equality extending to the political, economic, social and cultural spheres."[7] There is, however, one important law that is inconsistent with the principles of gender equality embedded in the Constitution. The Nationalities Law, enacted the same day as the Constitution, discriminates against women by depriving them, but not men, of their Mozambican nationality if, after independence, they marry foreigners.[8]

In many respects combating the legacy of the past, be it racism or sexism, posed less of a problem than forging a new national culture with which all Mozambicans could identify. What was necessary was to recapture the Mozambican history that the colonial regime had violently repressed, to popularize and incorporate the progressive cultural contributions of diverse ethnic groups, and to instill in all Mozambicans the new revolutionary values born in the liberated zones. In short, FRELIMO stressed the rich and complex ways in which the people's culture influenced and was, in turn, influenced by the armed struggle. Officials believed that such a synthesis held the key to developing a unique Mozambican personality free from foreign domination. "Let art seek to combine old forms with new content, then giving rise to new form. Let painting, written literature, theater, and artistic handicraft be added to the traditional culture, dance, sculpture and singing. Let the creativity of some become that of all, man and woman, young and old, from the north to the south, so that the new revolutionary and Mozambican culture may be born to all."[9]

During the first year and a half after independence, however, economic problems and increasing attacks from Rhodesia consumed the government's attention, and the creation of a national culture receded into the background. Once Portuguese had been selected as the national language, because no indigenous language transcended ethnic groups or regions, public discussion of what the policy toward second languages should be never took place—despite its far-reaching implications for nation building and combating tribalist tendencies.

Nevertheless, there were some potentially significant, though tentative, cultural advances. The reorganization of the primary and secondary school curricula to emphasize the country's rich and varied heritage was the most important of these. No longer did teachers extol the heroic exploits of Henry the Navigator and the civilizing mission of the Catholic Church. As one high school teacher bitterly noted, "Our students could identify Tras Montes and the River Tejo 10,000 kilometers away in Portugal, but did not know the names of the rivers and mountains 10 kilometers from their village."[10] Beginning with pilot programs in 1977, the minister of education organized a national network of cultural centers in towns and cities to exhibit art from different regions and to present musical and theatrical performances. All over the country peasants, through song, dance, and poetry, celebrated their past and their hopes for the future. The poem of a young student in Nampula province was typical of the outpouring of popular arts.

> I greet you Mozambique. Country of my grandparents,
> of my parents, my country.
>
> Country of my childhood of my first school and my first
> study, of my first love, first dream and anxiety
> I greet you Mozambique, I greet you.
>
> Mozambique of the black man of the white man and of
> the mulatto. Mozambique old Mozambique
> new Mozambique eternal Mozambique with your
> history your legends, your mystery.
>
> Mozambique of the truth and of superstition,
> Mozambique of the huts and the modern houses of
> asphalted streets and virgin paths.
>
> Mozambique—you who suffered yesterday, and you who
> were colonized—Today you are liberated today you
> belong to the People.[11]

In a more structured way the National Institute of Culture undertook to study and popularize "traditional" music in order to create a national musical heritage, and in 1978 more than a half million Mozambicans participated in the first National Dance Festival.

No matter how explicit or evocative, however, poetry, posters, public pronouncements, and legal and philosophical principles stressing the unity of the Mozambican people had little transforming potential if they were not connected to broader, ongoing processes of mass mobilization and political education. This responsibility, in the first instance, fell largely to the dynamizing groups.

In many respects the dynamizing groups were a transitional institution in which were embedded elements of both participatory democracy and a vanguard party. They were committees of approximately a dozen FRE-LIMO sympathizers, democratically elected at public meetings in residential areas and the work place. In some cases state officials and FRELIMO representatives visited sites before the selection of dynamizing groups to explain the roles of these groups and to describe the attributes their members should possess. Manuel Armando Machay recalled their formation in Gaza:

> Members of the dynamizing groups were chosen in general assemblies of all the people. Members of the party arrived to hold a meeting and encourage people to organize and select dynamizing group members. They explained what was necessary, what the role of the dynamizing group was, what its fundamental characteristics would be. They indicated each dynamizing group cell should have a secretary, a deputy and should emphasize the mobilization of peasants. And that the people themselves must choose their representatives. . . . Some of the dynamizing group members were chosen because of their general attitude and conduct. They know how to speak to the people, and how to resolve problems. They distinguish themselves by carrying out the political line of FRELIMO.[12]

In other situations the meetings and subsequent elections were the exclusive result of grassroots initiatives in which workers and peasants emulated, however imperfectly, what was occurring in adjacent communities and work places. Protracted discussion and, on occasion, heated debate accompanied the elections, which, for most Mozambicans, represented their first participation in the democratic process. Residents of Communal Village Patrice Lumumba in Gaza spent four successive Sundays selecting individuals "in whom they had confidence, who had been responsive to their community during the colonial period."[13]

The vanguard quality of the dynamizing groups was reflected in their mandated task, which was "to raise the political consciousness of the masses." They were also expected to organize and mobilize fellow workers and residents in collective economic, social, and cultural activities. In turn, the dynamizing groups were loosely linked to the FRELIMO network and to state structures that provided them with broad political orientations.

Above all else, the dynamizing groups served as schools in which to learn democratic skills and class unity. Community meetings, organized by dynamizing groups on a regular basis, provided a forum for involving citizens in the study and debate of the critical issues facing Mozambique. Throughout the country, participants examined such diverse topics as the divisive effects of tribalism, the need for an alliance between workers and peasants, the problems of national reconstruction, the reasons for combating the oppression of women, the necessity for vigilance against agents of the Rhodesian government, and the value of collective actions. In addition, dynamizing group members explained to the populace important government directives and newly initiated national programs and discussed ways to mobilize them more effectively for collective activities.

FRELIMO militants encouraged active participation in the debates. Individuals who had been silent for so many years often refused to give up the floor until they had made their points and underscored them repeatedly. Although such presentations necessarily extended the meetings,

President Samora Machel (Credit: Forças Populares da Libertação de Moçambique)

which to foreigners often seemed tedious and undefined, they provided a unique opportunity for direct participation and instilled a new level of public awareness. Reflecting on this somewhat cumbersome process of grassroots political education, Marcelino dos Santos noted that "it created a new sense of confidence in the oppressed masses and it helped convince them that they had the capacity to transform Mozambique. . . . This is the very essence of People's Power."[14]

The local dynamizing groups also figured prominently in efforts to increase and collectivize production, considered a precondition for Mozambique's economic recovery. In rural areas they stressed not only that greater agricultural output was needed to feed the country's hungry but that this could be achieved most efficiently through the formation of communal villages, cooperatives, and state farms. To try to relieve peasant anxieties about giving up their private holdings, to overcome their confusion about the organization and operation of these collective ventures, and to assure them that participation was voluntary and would not jeopardize the right to maintain a small private plot for their own use, dynamizing groups held numerous public meetings.

In the fertile Chibutu region of Gaza Province, for example,

> The dynamizing group organized a mass mobilization program to take over land which Portuguese estate-owners had abandoned. We attended numerous meetings where the peasants discussed how this was to be done. Ultimately, thirty-five people agreed to organize a cooperative. Others who were used to working individually, chose not to participate. After many meetings the dynamizing group began to organize production. Ultimately, many who initially refused to join sought membership as the cooperative prospered.[15]

The tasks of mobilizing the small but strategic Mozambican working class and transforming relations of production within the industrial sector were even more difficult. By independence, most factories in the country had been abandoned, and many were in total disrepair. Nevertheless, dynamizing groups attempted, with varying degrees of success, to raise both morale and production. The elected representatives met with their fellow workers to discuss common grievances and to figure out how to increase output. They reminded the workers that the crisis was brought about by Mozambique's enemies—the same people who refused to pay them decent wages, denied them opportunities to work at skilled jobs, and took the profits out of the country. To combat this enemy, "the battle of production" had to be intensified. Typical was the exhortation by the leader of the dynamizing group in the country's only glass factory against worker apathy: "Since we are now producing for the country and for ourselves and no longer for the capitalist-colonialist who oppressed us," such apathy was counterproductive.[16]

At the neighborhood level, dynamizing groups also helped to combat the community's social problems. They called meetings to identify the most critical local problems and simultaneously to instill in their neighbors a sense of confidence that collectively these problems could be overcome.

Among the projects undertaken were community crime-watch programs, neighborhood clean-up campaigns, literacy classes, and day-care centers. Similarly, in rural areas suffering from a lack of basic commodities, these grassroots organizations, with the help of government loans, built and stocked consumer cooperatives.

Dynamizing groups varied not only in their precise structure and the specific tasks they undertook, but also in what they achieved. This is hardly surprising given their ad hoc nature, their broad range of responsibilities, the lack of political experience and self-confidence among the participants, and the absence of either government or party structures responsible for directly supervising their activities. Such a fluid situation also permitted abuses. According to one Western scholar residing in Mozambique at the time:

> The more articulate and educated members of the petty bourgeoisie were quick to present themselves as longstanding sympathizers. Within the colonial hierarchy, they occupied the junior grades but still enjoyed a social superiority in relation to the overwhelming proportion of black Mozambicans who were workers or peasants. The latter let them take over control of many [dynamizing groups] in part as a result of deference to their superior wealth, education and social standing.[17]

There were even cases of ex-PIDE officials who got themselves elected to the dynamizing group by espousing FRELIMO rhetoric. Once in power, they exploited their positions for personal gain. Although the state, responding to public outcry, removed a number of these opportunists, there were undoubtedly many other situations in which peasants and workers, long repressed, chose to remain silent.

Despite their uneven record, there is little doubt that dynamizing groups were an important instrument of national unity. As Michael Kaufman of the *New York Times* cautiously noted in late 1977: "If enthusiasm has waned in other places [in Africa], it is palpable here. The experience of Mozambique is only two years old and any instantaneous reading of revolutionary changes is subject to revisions. Still, there is evidence that the degree of mobilization and national purpose attained here is great and may be more durable than anything black Africa has known."[18]

Along with stressing popular participation, the new government moved to dismantle inhibiting and oppressive colonial structures and to replace them with new institutions that, it was hoped, would ultimately guarantee all citizens the basic necessities of life. In July 1975, hardly a month after independence, the state abolished private schools and nationalized the educational system, making free education available to all Mozambican citizens. Six months later it took over the medical profession, declared that proper health care was a right of citizenship rather than a privilege of race or class, and initiated a massive preventive medicine campaign in which health brigades traveled the countryside, where 90 percent of the population lived. Simultaneously, the government nationalized all houses not used by their owners as a family residence and relocated thousands of Mozambicans from substandard housing in the periurban shantytowns to the previously segregated city of cement.[19]

THE THIRD PARTY CONGRESS—BEGINNING THE TRANSITION TO SOCIALISM

Several months before the Third Party Congress, seven "theses"— a synthesis of FRELIMO's central ideological propositions—appeared throughout the country in daily newspapers, magazines, pamphlets, and on centrally placed bulletin boards (the *jornal do povo*, literally "people's newspaper"). These theses, treating such issues as the nature of class struggle, the leading role of the working classes in creating a new society, and the transformation of FRELIMO into a vanguard party,[20] served as basic texts for discussions led by dynamizing groups in work places and residential areas. Their wide distribution, lack of abstract formalism, and use of examples based on concrete situations familiar to most Mozambicans demonstrated FRELIMO's commitment to making socialism intelligible.

The Third Party Congress addressed three basic political questions: In whose interest should Mozambique be governed? What role should FRELIMO play? What should be the relationship between the party and the state? Although these issues are central for all societies pursuing a socialist path of development, the congress sought to strike a balance between Marxist orthodoxy and the specific class configuration and contemporary realities of Mozambican society.

The final congress report specifically identified the alliance of workers and peasants as constituting "the political base of People's Democratic Power": "Internally, the working class and the peasantry, which today hold political power in our Country, are determined to break with the heritage of dependence and misery. . . . The workers have long understood that this fight is inseparable from the fight against the system of exploitation of man by man, against capitalism, against imperialism."[21] While accepting the proposition that the working class is the "leading force" in society, the congress departed from conventional Marxist wisdom, often disdainful of peasants, and accorded a central role to the Mozambican peasantry, which was not only the most numerous stratum but "had already presented great proof of its engagements in the revolutionary transformation of our society."[22] To this alliance were added soldiers, progressive intellectuals, and "all social forces which by their class position, are open to the ideas of the socialist revolution in Mozambique."[23] FRELIMO's own rather ambiguous postindependence status was further clarified. "The Party's historic mission is to lead, organize, orient and educate the masses, thus transforming the popular mass movement into a powerful instrument for the destruction of capitalism and the construction of socialism."[24] Rather than being a mass party, it became a self-defined vanguard party whose ultimate objective was to organize the worker-peasant alliance to "crush the class enemy." The class enemy was defined as including the remnants of the colonial bourgeoisie, an aspiring national Mozambican bourgeoisie that sought to fill the vacuum created by the departure of the Portuguese, and thieves, murderers, and other criminals. Although relatively weak in 1977, its reputed ties to foreign imperialist powers made it a significant threat. Thus, class struggle had both an internal and an international dimension. Finally, the congress specified that the role of the party was to assume control over the state—a state built upon colonial structures that needed to be dismantled and revamped.

Immediately after the congress, FRELIMO took several steps to strengthen the party and to reconcile the tensions between vanguardism and popularly rooted socialism. In February 1978 FRELIMO began a national campaign to create party cells throughout the country as a means of expanding its political base and becoming firmly connected to the working class. Previously membership had been limited to about 15,000 men and women who had participated in the armed struggle. The "order of the day" was clear:

> We must resolutely engage in creating Party organizations in the factories, cooperatives, offices, military and para-military bodies, within the state apparatus, in the villages and communities, in all work places and residential areas. . . . We must create Party organizations everywhere people work or live, from the Rovuma to the Maputo; we must bring into the ranks of the Party an ever-growing number of vanguard workers; we must dynamize the process of training cadres for the Party; such are the central tasks as regards the creation and consolidation of our Party.[25]

Directions were specifically given to recruit women, who were underrepresented in the party.

To minimize the abuses that had sometimes accompanied the selection of dynamizing group members, the population as a whole, guided by FRELIMO organizing brigades, was to participate in the election process. Party members visited communal villages, work places, and residential areas where they held public meetings to explain what type of person would be suitable for party membership. They emphasized the need for vigilance and urged the people to speak out against those who had collaborated with the colonial regime or had engaged in antisocial behavior, ranging from polygamy to thievery.

People who had declared themselves candidates were subjected to intense public scrutiny. Their fellow workers and neighbors gathered at FRELIMO-organized meetings to discuss and evaluate their political qualifications and personal behavior. For many candidates, these discussions were traumatic. One party member recounted his sense of anguish:

> For a person with my educational background, becoming a Party member was a psychologically wrenching experience. I was educated in a religious school. There, you only tell your sins to the priest, and he is the only one who can absolve you. In becoming a Party member you are confronted with an entirely different process. Here you are not talking to one person but to everyone.
> Throughout one's religious education you get the idea that only you or your closest relatives should know your weaknesses. This is your morality.

Then suddenly you are involved in a process where you must show how you have defended the interests of the majority. And you find that it is not enough merely to defend these interests, but you must demonstrate that you are strong enough morally, politically and ideologically to continue this struggle.

You have to speak to the people to prove that you are with them and you have to expose your entire life to demonstrate your commitment. And that is what is psychologically wrenching.[26]

He went on to outline his experience.

The first step was to present myself to the militants of the dynamizing group. All 24 candidates were called one by one to present their autobiographies. You had to be honest; you could hide none of your problems because if you did, someone would come forward and expose you. Then the party analyzed all the biographies. The candidates were not involved in this step.

The next stage was to be presented to all the workers at my workplace. There were 180 workers present. This was the most anxiety-producing part. People were honestly appraising all the candidates not just you. Even someone just observing this process could not help but feel the tension.

Finally, all the candidates in Information [Ministry] were presented to a larger gathering of several hundred who worked in the same field. First the names of all who had been rejected were read, and the workers were asked to comment. No one said anything. Then the names of those for whom the decision was to be deferred were read, and comments were solicited. No one said anything. Lastly the candidates who had been accepted were called to the podium, and the workers were urged to comment. A number of questions were raised about the behavior of several of the prospective candidates, but in the end we were all accepted provisionally. The Party Secretary for Ideology told all those assembled that the candidates would not receive Party cards for a year and a half. During this period our behavior would be carefully watched, and only if we acted properly would we be finally admitted into the Party.[27]

This form of popular participation, however, presupposed that the workers and peasants had sufficient self-confidence and class-consciousness to denounce their superiors at work as well as their friends and neighbors. Although this did not occur everywhere,[28] the process usually generated substantial political discussion in which collaborators were identified and unworthy candidates rejected. At CIFEL, Mozambique's only steel mill, an old, barefoot man from the scrap yard came forward to criticize factory administrators and members of the dynamizing groups. In the end, according to a British *cooperante* (expatriate) employed there, "Six of the twelve candidates proposed for the Party were finally accepted by the Brigade and formed a provisional cell. But this happened only after each had stood before countless meetings of his fellow workers in his section and in the factory, in which every aspect of his life and his attitudes was critically examined."[29] Several janitors at the university criticized the arrogant and condescending attitude of a prominent department head, who was a candidate. At the Central Hospital, after some prodding from

TABLE 6.2
Party Members in Selected Communal Villages, 1979

Village	District	Party Members			Percentage of Women
		Total	Men	Women	
Nampula Province:					
Namachila	Nampula	13	10	3	23.1
25 de Setembro	Meconta	23	21	2	8.7
Samora Machel	Nampula	25	20	5	20.0
Muatala	Muecate	14	10	4	28.6
Napala	Muecate	23	17	6	26.1
Gaza Province:					
3 de Fevereiro	Gaza	54	2	32	59.3
Samora Machel	Guija	500ᵃ			more than 50.0
7 de Abril	Guija	92			more than 50.0
Chaimite	Chibuto	66			more than 50.0
25 de Junho	Chibuto	300ᵃ			more than 50.0
Terceiro Congresso	Massingir	32	20	12	37.5
Paulo Samuel Kankhambe	Massingir	145			more than 50.0

ᵃEstimate of number of candidates for party membership

Source: Interviews in Nampula, January 1979 and May 1979; interviews in Gaza, February 1979 and June 1979

the FRELIMO convener, workers denounced several of their colleagues for drinking excessively and for not performing their tasks responsibly.[30] Armed with these comments, the party brigades interviewed additional workers, colleagues, and friends of the candidates before making the final decision on admission.

By 1980, FRELIMO had become firmly implanted throughout the country. Although precise figures are not available, high officials placed the number of candidates and members in 1982 at more than 100,000.[32]* Regional data suggest that women, prodded by the OMM, overcame centuries of passivity and a sense of their own worthlessness and became candidates in substantial numbers. This was especially true in the rural areas of Gaza and Cabo Delgado provinces and in the factories of Maputo. As Table 6.2 indicates, their numbers were appreciably smaller in Nampula, where Islamic influence remained powerful.

To avoid any ambiguity, in the late 1970s the dynamizing groups, envisioned from the outset only as transitional institutions, were stripped of their political functions and eliminated in the countryside and the work place, where the local political assemblies and the production councils assumed many of their remaining duties. They continue to operate, however, in urban areas as liaisons between the residents and the municipal

---

*The 1983 FRELIMO Congress gave an exact number of 110,323 candidates and members, of whom 53.5 percent were peasants and 18.9 percent were workers.

assemblies, and they still perform important educational and mobilizing functions there.

To ensure that the party would, in fact, defend the interests of workers and peasants required continual vigilance against abuses of power and any tendencies by party officials to become a new privileged class. The evidence suggests that FRELIMO's leaders were acutely aware of this potential problem, which could depoliticize the masses and rob the revolution of its vitality and popular support. Since independence a number of party officials have, in fact, been removed from their positions and publicly exposed for improper conduct. In 1978 the Central Committee expelled four leading members and long-time militants, three of whom were found guilty of "abuses of power, immorality, disrespect for women and indiscipline."[32] In 1982 João Pelembe was removed for corruption from the Central Committee, where he was ranked fourteenth, and from his state position as governor of Gaza.[33] During this four-year period several other prominent party members, including the president's sister-in-law, suffered similar fates.[34]

However important, merely cleansing the party from time to time would not necessarily make it the leading force in society, in fact as well as in theory, and give it a tangible presence throughout the country. As Jorge Rebelo, the party secretary for ideology, acknowledged in 1980, the work of the party organizing brigades had been of uneven quality. Lacking direction from the national secretariat, many cells did not function effectively. In a speech to secretaries of the party cells, he warned that there had been "a noticeable decrease in dynamic actions by the Party structures."[35] Characteristically, the Central Committee, in its final resolution of July 1980, took responsibility for these broad failures and "criticized itself for neglecting to pay due attention to strengthening Party machinery. The Central Committee members paid more attention to the state machinery than to the Party machinery. [This] . . . was an incorrect attitude because it is by strengthening the Party machinery and the Party's leading role that the task of destroying the old state machinery and building a new socialist state can be carried out."[36]

To remedy this situation, two prominent ministers and senior members of FRELIMO, Marcelino dos Santos and Jorge Rebelo, were relieved of their state functions in April 1981 so that they could devote their energies to strengthening the party.[37] In addition, FRELIMO announced plans to improve the literacy and political education of party cadres, to intensify the campaign against corruption within FRELIMO and the state apparatus, and to root the party more firmly in its popular base. There have already been some successes. By 1982, FRELIMO had a full-time staff at its headquarters in Maputo, full-time personnel coordinating its mobilizing activities in the provinces, and a newspaper and a theoretical journal.

Nevertheless, serious problems, which threatened both to isolate FRELIMO from its worker and peasant constituents and to undercut its ability to organize and direct society, persisted. A highly self-critical national conference on the party's ideological work concluded that it had little contact with large sectors of the country and that unhealthy bureaucratic, formalistic, and elitist tendencies had surfaced within FRELIMO.[38] A 1981 Central Committee communiqué was even more explicit:

> [There is] in the midst of the Party, an erratic conception of party discipline. Large numbers of members and party cadres confuse party discipline with militaristic discipline. In struggling to create discipline in the Party, their preoccupation is more in terms of formal questions than questions of whether the tasks are fulfilled or not or the degrees of contact with the masses. Many party cadres consciously isolate themselves from the masses, living in closed circles; [and] decline invitations to participate in popular meetings or in celebrations organized by the people. Impregnated by the bourgeois spirit of *structure* they erroneously believe that their contact with the masses makes them lose a pretended respectability. For these kinds of party members, to be chief, be responsible, necessarily implies to live far from the masses and be feared by them.[39]

The communiqué pointed to the inherent tension between vanguardism and popular democracy and reiterated the need to combat tendencies by party cadres to use their positions for personal gain. At the end of the year Rebelo announced plans to reverse this situation. Harking back to a long-standing FRELIMO tradition, he indicated that strengthening local cells was FRELIMO's most urgent task because "the essence of the party's work is at the grass roots."[40] Specifically, he emphasized that party cells had to gain a clearer idea of their role as forums for serious discussion and debate. In the same spirit, the party journal *Voz da Revolução* announced in early 1982 that orientation courses for cell leaders would no longer emphasize abstract and rigidly theoretical issues but would focus on the kinds of daily problems the cells would have to tackle in the work place and the community.[41] The decision in March 1982 to postpone the Fourth Party Congress until the following year to allow "for massive political mobilization on a national scale" was yet another indication that more attention had to be given to reinforcing the bonds between FRELIMO and the workers and peasants in whose name it governs.

These problems made it that much more important for the party to strengthen its ties to the "mass democratic organizations"—the Mozambique Women's Movement, the Mozambique Youth Movement (OJM), and the Production Councils—which not only facilitated the flow of party doctrine downward but could enable FRELIMO, in principle, to "learn from the people." The extent to which the OMM, the OJM, and the Production Councils were able to mobilize their respective constituents also had far-reaching consequences for the party, as these organizations provided one of the main avenues through which nonparty members could participate in the political life of the country.

Of the three major mass democratic organizations, the oldest and most active is the Mozambique Women's Movement. At its second conference in November 1976, the OMM defined as its highest priority the incorporation of large masses of Mozambican women, who were overwhelmingly rural, into the political and economic life of the country. Its strategy was to establish branches in every work place and residential area so that it could combat the reactionary institutions and ideologies that reduced women to passivity and subordination. It also sought to make the male-dominated party leadership sensitive to gender inequality and to the serious problems Mozambican women confront in their daily lives.

Although understaffed and undertrained, the OMM, aided by FRELIMO and the state, began to spread its message to women throughout Mozambique. In the countryside it worked to persuade women to join communal villages and to participate in all aspects of communal life, including the village's direction. Many fathers and husbands, humiliated under colonialism, saw independence as an opportunity to reassert their authority over the private sphere in general and the household in particular, and they opposed women's involvement in communal affairs. In the newly formed communal villages the OMM held regular meetings to attack such stereotypes as "women's work" and "male superiority" and such traditional institutions as initiation rites, child marriages, bride-price, and polygamy, which reinforced women's sense of inferiority.[42]

By early 1978 a number of communal villages in Gaza had women in a majority of the elected positions. The selection of Virginia Chamblisse as president of the agricultural cooperative of Communal Village 25 de Junho in Gaza is a case in point. Throughout the colonial period she, like many other peasants, had worked on a European estate. With independence she emerged as an outspoken defender of FRELIMO. She played an important role in organizing one of the first informal cooperatives, and during the floods in February 1977, she continued to work the land, often alone, and became a source of inspiration to her neighbors. As a result, when the communal village was formally organized, she was the logical choice for president. The male treasurer of the communal village, when asked his reaction to her selection, responded: "We are satisfied. Our president is a good leader and defends our interests. She has proven her leadership capacity which many men don't have. Today we understand that women have the same abilities as men."[43]

Compared with most other African nations, Mozambique has made great strides in combating the institutionalized oppression of women. By 1980 the OMM was firmly established throughout the country. Mozambique also has considerable legislation mandating gender equality. Women have become increasingly involved in the political process (see Tables 6.2 and 6.3), and they have made small, but potentially significant, breakthroughs in the economic sectors where, for the first time, women are being trained and employed as tractor drivers, construction workers, factory workers, police officers, and administrators, all occupations traditionally reserved for men. Nevertheless, the sexual division of labor that legitimates the subordination of women is still very much in place, and male resistance to OMM campaigns to end child marriage and polygamy continues to be very strong in parts of the country.[44]

The Mozambique Youth Movement, created after the Third Party Congress, is responsible for identifying the particular needs and problems of Mozambicans between the ages of eighteen and thirty-five and raising their political consciousness. As part of its effort to help create "the new

TABLE 6.3
Women Workers and Party Members in Selected Production Units, 1979

Factory	Sector	Province	Women Workers(%)	Party Members	Women Party Members(%)	Women Party Leaders
Belita	Clothing	Sofala	26.8	72	18.1	1
Favezal	Clothing	Zambezia	8.6	4	0.0	0
Emma	Textiles	Manica	16.1	77	19.5	0
Facobol	Shoes	Maputo	31.6	28	35.7	1
Sociedade Ultra-marina Tobacaria	Tobacco	Maputo	8.3	20	5.0	1
Caju de Moçambique						
Chamanculo	Cashew	Maputo	82.5	130	86.2	5
Machava 1	Cashew	Maputo	67.1	44	36.4	?
Machava 2	Cashew	Maputo	62.6	68	45.6	0
Manjacaze	Cashew	Gaza	52.9	63	17.5	?
Machamba Estatal Umbeluzi	State farm	Maputo		96	10.4	2

Sources: Questionnaires of Ministry of Industry and Energy, July 1979; interview with "responsibles" of Umbeluzi State Farm, March 14, 1979.

Mozambican," the OJM initiated a major urban campaign against prostitution, theft, and "bourgeois habits"—legacies of the colonial system that are deeply embedded in urban youth and are exacerbated by high unemployment. It also organized a number of rural projects to demonstrate the value of collective labor and the contributions young people can make to the process of national reconstruction. That the OJM is even more understaffed, undertrained, and underfinanced than the OMM has seriously hampered its mobilizing potential, especially in the rural areas.[45]

Whereas the OMM and the OJM are gender and age specific, the Production Councils exist to mobilize Mozambique's small and disorganized proletariat and to ensure that "workers can participate in an active, collective and conscious way in the discussion and resolution of their problems, especially in relation to production and productivity."[46] Formed in 1976, but extended beyond Maputo only after the Third Party Congress, production councils had been organized in all major factories throughout the country by 1981. Eventually, they are to be transformed into national trade unions, but their degree of autonomy from the state and the party, reputedly a subject of intense debate within the Central Committee, remains publicly undefined.

Another way FRELIMO sought to ensure greater popular participation was by dismantling the colonial administrative apparatus and creating new democratic institutions. Between September and December 1977, all adult Mozambicans, except those who had formerly worked for the Portuguese secret police or for other colonial organizations that terrorized the populace, voted in elections for representatives to local and municipal people's assemblies. They chose more than 22,000 men and women to serve as deputies in 894 local assemblies.[47] One American reporter, visiting Mozambique at the time of the elections, filed the following account: "Every-

Candidates nominated for a local assembly (Credit: *Tempo*)

where there were meetings of peasants on state farms, of workers, of school children, to discuss the election of village and district assemblies. As singular as all this was, what was even more striking to a visitor was the absence of men in uniform and men with guns. . . . This effort in the countryside appeared to stem from pride and not coercion."[48]

Several days before the actual vote, notices went to all communities urging people to participate. In more remote areas people had to travel for one or two days to the site of the election, which began with songs and dances, celebrating rights that had long been denied. "It was a festive occasion," one observer noted, "the women wearing bright-colored cloth, the men in their best pants and shoes if they had them.[49]

After initial festivities, district electoral officials reminded voters to assess critically the qualifications of those nominated and not to be afraid to identify individuals who had collaborated with the colonial regime and were thereby ineligible for office. Officials then announced the list of candidates proposed by the dynamizing groups and bluntly asked the local population, "Does anyone have anything to say against this person?"

Popular reactions varied from one area to another, but the debates were often heated and sometimes antagonistic, as former collaborators were identified. At Communal Village Marien Ngouabi in Gaza Province, for example, Armando Ndimande had been nominated by the dynamizing group of which he was a member. Immediately, a villager stepped forward and read a letter that described how Ndimande had exploited the peasants while serving as foreman on a Portuguese banana plantation. Another man revealed that Ndimande had stolen bananas from his mother and had assaulted her sexually. The accused acknowledged these acts and asked to be forgiven. The voters were not moved and unanimously rejected his selection.[50] In the locality of Gazimbe in Niassa Province, two officials of the dynamizing group as well as another nominee were turned down after their involvement with the secret police became known, and in the province of Zambézia peasants eliminated 655 nominees, most of whom had served as labor recruiters during the colonial period.[51]

By the time the local elections had been completed, more than 2,200 candidates had been rejected. They included more than 700 "chiefs" and other "traditional authorities" who had sought to maintain their grip over their former subjects as well as hundreds of people whose behavior had not inspired confidence in their local communities. The largest number of rejected aspirants were former members of the secret police and other collaborators.[52]

Whatever the deficiencies of the elections, they revealed democratic vitality at the local level and popular scrutiny from which even members of dynamizing groups and the OMM were not immune. Not only were the nominees selected by popularly elected dynamizing groups, but the final judgment was left to members of the local community. The national rejection rate of 10 percent—in some areas it ran as high as 15 to 20 percent—of the proposed candidates demonstrated the direct and central role played by the voters. The local elections served as a school for political education and consciousness-raising and ensured the effective representation of the Mozambican people in the political process.

Representatives at the district and provincial levels were selected indirectly from the ranks of the lower assemblies and from a relatively small number of soldiers chosen by the region's military units. Thus, delegates to the local assemblies selected representatives to the district assemblies, who elected those to serve in the provincial legislatures. At each level candidates were seriously screened, and a small number of those nominated were deemed unfit to serve. Of the 3,500 candidates to the district assemblies, 200 failed to qualify; the rejection rate was slightly higher among those seeking provincial office.[53] After the provincial assemblies were chosen, the Central Committee of FRELIMO nominated 226 men and women to serve in the Popular Assembly—the country's highest legislative body. Their appointment was approved by each of the elected provincial structures in December 1977.

The social composition of the assemblies attests to FRELIMO's commitment to create popular democratic structures. At all levels, peasants and workers, traditionally exploited and voiceless, held a majority of the seats. Interestingly, their numerical predominance was greatest in the Popular Assembly, whose members were nominated directly by the FRELIMO Central Committee—60 percent of the deputies were peasants and workers and another 6 percent came from mass democratic organizations. Moreover, most of the representatives from the armed forces, who constituted 15 percent of the deputies, came from peasant backgrounds (see Table 6.4). Women, historically denied access to the political process, were

TABLE 6.4
Results of the National Elections Held Between September and December 1977

	Local Assemblies	District Assemblies	Municipal Assemblies	Provincial Assemblies	Popular Assemblies
Number of assemblies	894	112	10	10	226
Deputies elected	22,230	3,390	460	734	
Men	15,939(71.7%)	2,583(76.19%)	364(79.13%)	626(85.3%)	198(87.61%)
Women	6,291(28.3%)	807(23.81%)	96(20.87%)	108(14.7%)	28(12.39%)
Workers		878(20.0%)	179(38.91%)	193(26.3%)	71(31.42%)
Peasants		1,288(37.99%)	49(10.65%)	163(22.2%)	65(28.76%)
State workers		541(15.96%)	114(24.78%)	192(26.16%)	25(11.06%)
Members of Popular Forces (military)		581(17.14%)	71(15.43%)	121(16.49%)	35(15.49%)
Representatives of Mass Organization		302(8.91%)	47(10.23%)	65(8.85%)	13(5.75%)
Others		206	26	11	17(7.52%)
Candidates rejected	2,182				

Percentages of men and women add up to 100 percent, as do those of the class positions (the remaining categories of deputies).

Source: <u>Tempo</u> 378 (1978): 53-54

also represented in appreciable numbers, although still well below their percentage of the population. At the local level, 6,300 women (about 30 percent of the total membership) served as deputies, and their representation was only slightly lower in the district bodies. New elections are planned for 1983, at which time the franchise and the right to serve in the assemblies will be extended to all who had been barred for collaborating with the colonial regime.

But the ultimate question is the extent to which the assemblies have played a meaningful role in the political life of the country. At the lower levels, where the issues debated and decided are of a local nature, there has been a substantial amount of discussion, although FRELIMO officials have expressed some concern about the quality of the debates. To upgrade them, deputies, many of whom could not read or write, received priority for admission to literacy programs, and by 1980 most had acquired at least minimal skills.[54] Although conceding that local autonomy exists, many foreign observers contend that the Popular Assembly appointed directly by the Central Committee has done little more than rubber-stamp party policies. We observed the working of the Assembly in December 1979 and again in September 1982; it would appear to be neither a rubber stamp nor a forum for the rancorous debate, caucusing, and behind-the-scenes dealings characteristic of Western legislatures.

Although deputy initiative appeared minimal—the five major pieces of legislation on the 1979 agenda were all passed unanimously—the decision-making process is far more complex than it appeared. As one delegate informed us, what we observed during these two days was merely the end of a long deliberative process. Some legislation had already been substantially modified as a result of debates in subordinate legislative assemblies, work places, communal villages, party meetings, and various government organs.[55] Moreover, deputies with whom we spoke at both sessions of the Assembly emphasized that the closed-door work sessions were characterized by animated discussion and debate in which almost all the deputies participated, even though several who knew no Portuguese had to rely completely on interpreters.[56] Another admitted that, although the highly technical budget proposal was beyond the comprehension of most of the deputies, the work sessions produced criticisms that were openly discussed in the later plenary sessions. The ultimate test of the democratic nature of the Popular Assembly is whether it and the assemblies at the lower levels will represent and serve the interests of the Mozambican people. This will turn on their ability, in private deliberations and public pronouncements, to criticize party and state failings and to help shape future policies.

In addition to creating the assemblies, the Third Party Congress mandated that the legal system be revamped in accordance with the Constitution and FRELIMO's broad socialist principles. This was easier said than done, given the absence of lawyers, judges, and other trained personnel who could draft a new legal code. That the Portuguese codes were cumbersome, procedurally complicated, and extremely legalistic further hindered initial efforts to write the new code. In the absence of new codes

The Popular Assembly—Mozambique's highest legislature (Credit: Ricardo Rangel)

A local peoples' tribunal in southern Mozambique (Credit: *Tempo*)

and legal structures, the practices of informal justice established in the liberated zones and modified during the transitional period continued to operate through the dynamizing groups, which assumed most legal functions at the local level. Only at the end of 1978 did the Justice Ministry create a national court system to replace the moribund and dysfunctional colonial apparatus.[57]

The jurisdiction of the people's tribunals corresponds to the administrative structures established in the Constitution—provinces, districts, and localities. The provincial courts hear more serious crimes and larger civil disputes, whereas the district courts handle crimes that carry a penalty of two years' imprisonment or less and civil disputes involving smaller amounts. The tribunals at the locality and communal village level deal only with minor offenses.

This new system offered the overwhelming majority of Mozambicans their first opportunity to have cases tried in a court of their peers rather than by capricious colonial adminstrators or collaborating chiefs. By 1981, more than 300 people's tribunals had been established in the major urban centers and in some district seats, localities, and communal villages in each province[58] (see Table 6.5).

The court system is guided by the broad principles of popular justice that FRELIMO first formulated in the liberated zones. Every court includes some lay judges elected by their fellow workers and neighbors. The formalistic procedures of the colonial past were drastically simplified because the lay judges could not comprehend them and because there were no private attorneys to capitalize on procedural errors. Thus, procedures have become more intelligible even without a new procedural code. Judges reach decisions based on common sense and general notions of justice outlined in the Constitution. Similarly, much of the formalism and paperwork has disappeared, as litigants do not know what paper must be filed by what date or in what form. The president of the court, a trained jurist—or, at the district level, a person with a few months of legal training—assists the litigants with some of this and ignores the remainder.

Substantive changes also occurred without code revision. According to the senior judge of Maputo Province, for example, there was a substantial reduction in the penalty imposed for property crimes unaccompanied by personal injury; and in Tete Province the courts acted vigorously to punish people who engaged in the lethal practice of using the poison ordeal to identify witches—something the colonial courts generally ignored. Although it is still illegal to perform or have an abortion, since independence the police, the medical profession, and the judges have exercised discretion in deciding which perpetrators to prosecute. The courts are also committed to rehabilitating convicted criminals through work programs and political education, rather than merely incarcerating them. As of August 1980, there were only 3,800 Mozambicans in jail out of a population of more than 12 million.[59]

At the local level and in the communal villages the tribunals are composed entirely of lay judges selected either by the local legislative assembly, if it has already been established, or by the community at large. Orientation sessions, organized by the FRELIMO party cell, resembled those that occurred in the liberated zones, and the cadres stressed the importance of electing women judges. Although women remain a minority, their presence on the courts is part of a long-standing FRELIMO commitment to give women a legal personality, to guarantee equality before the law, and to ensure that the perspective of women is considered in judicial deliberations.

The local tribunals sit once a week and are open to the public. Indeed, in many communal villages all adults attend. The tribunals hear a wide range of minor disputes and petty crimes. Despite substantial regional variation in the mix of cases, which reflects both local cultural traditions and contemporary social and economic realities, interviews conducted throughout the country suggest that domestic issues predominate. Of the twenty-six cases adjudicated at Communal Village Musira in Cabo Delgado province during the second half of 1979, for example, thirteen dealt with divorce and the related issue of polygamy and five with robbery; the remaining eight included accusations of poison ordeal, prostitution, conflict over property, and claims of debt.[60]

More serious crimes and complicated civil matters are resolved at the district and provincial levels, at which the presiding judge, appointed by the state, must have some higher education and formal legal training. At the district level, the appointed judge is required to have a sixth-grade education and to have completed a six-month legal course, whereas the lay judges elected by the legislative assembly need no formal training.

The provincial people's tribunals are more specialized and more professional. In Maputo Province, for example, the court is divided into

TABLE 6.5
Distribution of People's Tribunals, 1981

Province	Provincial Level	District Level	Locality	Communal Villages	Urban
Maputo	1	1	7	-	9
Gaza	1	2	7	14	2
Inhambane	1	1	19	9	1
Sofala	1	1	14	1	7
Zambezia	1	2	26	-	-
Manica	1	1	19	5	2
Tete	1	1	17	-	3
Nampula	1	9	30	25	4
Niassa	1	1	8	-	-
Cabo Delgado	1	2	8	16	4

Source: Justiça Popular 3 (April/August 1981): 10.

three civil sections, five criminal sections, a children's section, and a police section dealing primarily with road accidents. Each section is composed of one appointed judge and at least five judges elected by the provincial assembly. Before the election, justice brigades and FRELIMO party officials went to each candidate's work place and neighborhood to solicit information from those who knew him or her best. The elected judges come from all sectors—factory workers, clerks, teachers, nurses, and peasants (see Table 6.6). Whatever their backgrounds, all elected judges have other full-time jobs and annually take two-month paid leaves of absence to sit on the court. Each year they serve in a different section of the court in order to obtain the widest possible exposure.[61]

TABLE 6.6
Composition of the Elected Judiciary of the Provincial
Court of Maputo, 1980

	Men	Women
State functionaries	5	1
Members of the mass democratic organizations	5	25
Workers	70	12
Total	80	38

Source: Ministry of Justice, 1980.

All trials at the district and provincial levels are open to the public, and the accused has the right to be represented by either a public defender or a lay person of his or her choice.[62] The public defenders must have at least a sixth-grade education and have completed a six-month training program similar to that of a district judge, although law students or trained lawyers occasionally perform this function. A presumption of innocence, vigorous questioning of the witnesses by several of the judges, and intense debate between the public defender and the state prosecutor characterized the trials we observed. The purpose of these criminal proceedings, according to the judges, was not just to try the defendant for an isolated act but to locate the social and economic context within which the crime occurred, evaluate its seriousness, prevent it from recurring, and determine how best to reeducate and reintegrate the convicted.[63]

Fragmentary court records, our own observations, and discussions with various officials in the Ministry of Justice make clear that the rigid and severe punishments enshrined in the colonial penal code, although still officially authorized, have uniformly if informally been modified by the decisions of the provincial and district courts. Periodic meetings between Justice Ministry officials, their provincial counterparts, and judges have produced a consensus that adapts the range of penalties for each crime to the new priorities and values of the socialist society in the making. Mitigating and aggravating factors, including the motivation of the guilty party, recidivism, physical violence, restitution, cooperation by the accused, and confession are given considerable weight. Although confessions occur in about 75 percent of the cases, that alone is not sufficient to prove guilt. A member of the party or a person in a position of authority who committed a crime is likely to be punished more severely—a tradition that originated in the liberated zones.

Notwithstanding the considerable achievements of the people's tribunals in democratizing justice, they continue to be plagued by the legacy of colonialism. Both parties and witnesses, because illiterate or only minimally competent in Portuguese, often have difficulty comprehending questions from the bench and responding coherently. Moreover, their demeanor and reticence clearly reflect the anxiety associated with memories of the colonial courtroom. The substantial educational gap between presiding and lay judges confers too much authority on the former, further distorting the judicial process and frustrating the real meaning of popular justice. Finally, the small number of trained judges, public defenders, and prosecutors delays trials. As of August 1980, more than two-thirds of the 3,800 people held in Mozambican jails were still awaiting trial.[64]

One of the most important dimensions of the evolving legal system has been penal reform. Of particular significance was the decision to close down the antiquated colonial jails and move the prisoners to rural penal centers that emphasize rehabilitation through education and collective labor, both of which were difficult to pursue in prisons. By 1980 eleven centers existed, into which 1,000 inmates had been transferred, and several of the worst jails had been closed. The opening of additional centers will permit the transfer of most prisoners, although those considered particularly dangerous are likely to be kept in traditional settings. At the same time, the highly publicized reeducation camps were being phased out, and by 1982 most of the prisoners, some of whom had been arbitrarily detained, had been freed and reintegrated into Mozambican society.[65]

Rural penal centers had no cells, no barbed wire, and no dogs to confine or intimidate the prisoners. Each had only a handful of guards, none of whom was normally armed. The penal center in Sofala, with more than 1,000 prisoners, had four; the one in Manica, with slightly fewer inmates, had two. The prisoners divided their day between collective labor, often in fields outside the formal confines of the center, and classes in which they received literacy training and studied Mozambican history and FRELIMO ideology.

Revamping the legal system was part of the broader campaign to dismantle repressive colonial institutions and improve the quality of life for all Mozambicans. Despite the acute shortage of capital, the state has annually channeled about 30 percent of the national budget into education, health, and housing. Only the military, faced with increasing attacks first from Rhodesia and then from South African–backed guerrillas, received allocations on a similar scale (see Table 6.7).

From independence the government emphasized the transforming potential of education. It immediately launched vigorous national and local campaigns to enroll all children in school. At public meetings in rural villages and urban townships dynamizing groups and representatives of the OMM proclaimed that "all children have a right and obligation to attend school." They focused their attention on young girls whose parents, in the past, had kept them at home to utilize their labor while preparing them for early marriages. The success of this campaign is reflected in the

TABLE 6.7
State Budget, 1981-1982 ($ million)

	1980	1981	1982
Health, education	132	151	176
Defense	132	155	176
Economic sectors	49	38	64
Other state expenditures	85	38	64
Price subsidies	25	25	25
Debt service, reserve	39	51	38
Total	472	519	594
Expected deficit	56	74	80

Sources: Compiled from official government figures; and Iain Christie and Joseph Hanlon, "Mozambique," in Africa Contemporary Record, 1982 (London, forthcoming).

fact that between 1974 and 1981 the number of children attending primary school increased from 700,000 to 1,376,000, almost half of whom were girls, while secondary school enrollments went from 20,000 to more than 135,000. Moreover, the rate of illiteracy dropped from 95 to 75 percent during the first five years of independence, and among Mozambicans aged ten to twenty-four, it declined to less than 60 percent[66] (see Table 6.8).

Equally important strides were made in the health sector, the restructuring of which posed far greater problems than those associated with reorganizing education. Of the 550 doctors in the country in 1973, only 87 remained at independence. The state moved decisively to remedy this situation. By 1977 it had recruited more than 500 medical workers from more than twenty different countries and the preventive medicine campaign had "taken off." Despite serious transportation problems, the scattered rural population, and Rhodesian attacks, the national vaccination campaign against measles, tetanus, and smallpox, which was completed in 1979, reached more than 90 percent of the population. According to the World Health Organization, this was one of the most successful efforts in Africa.[67] At the same time, the nationalization of medicine made medical services virtually free. Although health statistics are not generally available, the 20 percent decline in infant mortality during the first five years of independence suggests the degree to which Mozambique's new health program is working.[68]

Sweeping changes also occurred in the aftermath of the nationalization of rental housing. By 1978 more than 160,000 Mozambicans living in substandard housing or in shantytowns had been relocated into high-quality urban residences that had previously been reserved for Europeans, and the rents, pegged to income and size of dwelling, averaged between 10 and 20 percent of family income for all Mozambicans.[69]

To be sure, these new social programs generated problems of their own. The jump in the number of students taxed Mozambique's educational resources. Shortages of teachers, books, and supplies inevitably reduced

TABLE 6.8
Educational System, 1981

	Number of Matriculated Students	Number of Teachers
Primary school	1,376,865	18,751
Secondary school	135,956	3,784
Pre-university and university	3,886	157
Literacy programs	309,669	
Adult education	143,833	

Source: Comissão Nacional do Plano, Moçambique: Informação Estatística 1980/81 (Maputo, 1982), p. 72.

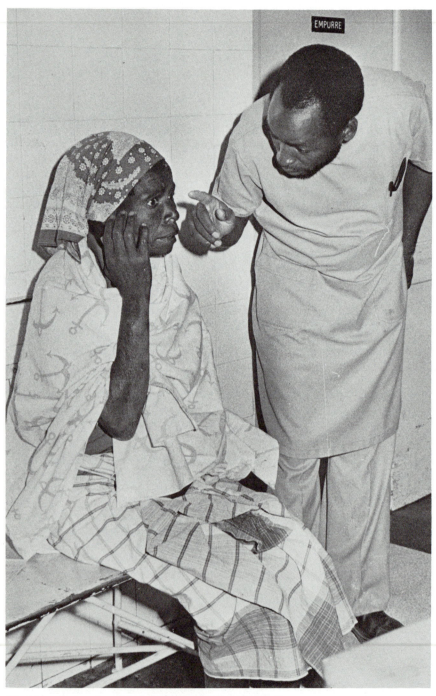

Health care for the elderly (Credit: Ricardo Rangel)

Teaching the young (Credit: Ricardo Rangel)

the quality of education. Despite the recent introduction of a new, integrated educational system, which makes primary education compulsory for all children, by 1990 2 million children will still lack access to a complete primary education.[70] For all the advances in health care delivery, the newly built rural infirmaries were often inadequately staffed and supplied, and the effort to introduce "barefoot doctors" has not worked well.[71] Nationalizing housing also provided a new opportunity for the state bureaucracy to engage in corruption, and officials in the State Housing Authority (APIE) became notorious for allocating the best houses to their families and friends.

The abuses of APIE highlighted the threat to the revolution posed by the state bureaucracy. As in other parts of Africa, it vigorously protected its autonomous, privileged position and frustrated major social transformations. As early as 1976 FRELIMO announced its intention to dismantle the colonial state machinery, but faced with a shortage of trained personnel, the leadership, fearing the paralysis of the civil service, deferred the wholesale removal of ex-colonial bureaucrats. Instead, it tried "to win them over to the correct political line, to reintegrate them into the heart of the broad masses, to transform them into true workers of public administration in the service of the people."[72] Despite numerous meetings, compulsory political study sessions, and a campaign to identify those civil servants who had actually collaborated with the colonial regime, bureaucratism intensified as a result of the continued reliance on archaic Portuguese practices, the arrogance of many functionaries, and a greater state involvement in the economy. In July 1980 the Popular Assembly reached an alarming conclusion. "Taking a close look at the situation of our country five years after independence, we noted that the state apparatus we had at our disposal was threatening our power, the power of the workers and peasants."[73]

With peace in Zimbabwe FRELIMO launched a political and organizational offensive against the state bureaucracy. At a furious pace President Machel and senior party officials, surrounded by throngs of journalists, made dozens of surprise visits to state enterprises and government agencies, where they encountered evidence of corruption and indiscipline. The most serious abuses were found at Maputo port, the national airlines, the State Housing Authority, and the People's Shops. Those in charge were summarily removed and, in some cases, subsequently arrested.[74]

In 1981 FRELIMO extended the political offensive to the state security sector in order to weed out undisciplined and corrupt police officials and members of the security apparatus, of the armed forces, and of the people's militia. In an angry public speech, broadcast on national radio, President Machel acknowledged that these forces had been "infiltrated by elements who violate the constitution, the principles of the FRELIMO party, and the law of the land through arbitrary imprisonment, beatings and torture."[75] He conceded that FRELIMO had committed a serious error by failing to dismantle the colonial police force. "We did not have enough courage to accept a temporary vacuum while we created a police of our own. We preferred to use the colonial police force because they were trained. But to do what? They were only trained to oppress, brutalize, and humiliate the people. And they exercised a profound and malicious influence on the inexperienced young men who joined the police force."[76] Machel reserved his harshest criticism for security. "Our security is not achieved by secret methods and intimidation, but by mobilizing popular vigilance. We don't want any secret police. We don't need them."[77] He then exhorted citizens to come forward and report abuses of power, promising that all accusations would be "rigorously investigated and the guilty punished." To underscore this point, he turned to the ministers of the interior, security, and defense, who were sitting on the podium, and warned them that they would be held personally responsible if they did not take immediate action.

Shortly thereafter, state authorities removed a number of guards and security officials for abusing prisoners. In the most celebrated cases, the director of Machava Prison, the country's largest, was dismissed from his position in response to prisoner complaints that they were being mistreated, and the director of the reeducation camp at Ruarua, in northern Mozambique, was arrested on similar charges. By 1982, more than 400 police and security officials had been dismissed after recurring complaints of police brutality.

This campaign continued throughout 1981, although some observers questioned how long ministers, high party officials, and the president himself could maintain the intensity and whether it was the most useful allocation of their time and energy. To such queries, Machel responded: "When you get hold of the lion's tail, you don't let go. If you do, he'll kill you. And when the lion has gotten tired, you pick up a knife and kill it. We have already gotten hold of the lion's tail. And we're going to the end."[78] His comments suggested that the offensive was likely to remain a permanent central feature of political life in Mozambique.

The struggle to subdue the embattled lion symbolizes Mozambique as it moves through the throes of transition. To be sure, many problems have not as yet been overcome. The ability of the bureaucracy to stifle change, corruption and abuses of power by state functionaries and party officials, the low level of literacy, and the lack of familiarity with democratic institutions all pose serious problems. Above all else, there is the constant tension between vanguardism and popular democracy. Nevertheless, for the first time, workers, peasants, and indeed, all Mozambicans are participating in the political process. Elections have been held throughout the country, and the campaign against corruption and the betrayal of the public trust is a central and highly visible theme in Mozambique's political life. Moreover, the highest levels of the government and the party have been remarkably free from corruption and intrigue. In a continent where coups and secessionist tendencies are the norm, Mozambique is notable for its stability. Of the nineteen ministers in the first government, fourteen are still a part of the cabinet, and two others have assumed full-time positions in the party (see Table 6.9). Apart from a brief mutiny in 1975,

TABLE 6.9
Council of Ministers, 1982

President of the Republic	Samora Moises Machel
Minister of Foreign Affairs	Joaquim Chissano
Minister of National Defense	Lt. Gen. Alberto Joaquim Chipande
Resident Minister of Sofala Province	Armando Emilío Guebuza
Minister of the Interior	Mariano de Araujo Matsinhe
Chief of the General Staff and Deputy Minister of Defense	Lt. Gen. Sebastião Marcos Mabote
Minister of Security	Jacinto Soares Veloso
Minister of Planning	Mário da Graça Machungo
Minister of the Presidency	José Oscar Monteiro
Minister of Finance	Rui Balthazar dos Santos Alves
Minister of Education and Culture	Graça Machel
Minister of Information	José Luis Cabaço
Minister of Public Works and Housing	Júlio Zamith Carrilho
Minister of Foreign Trade	Salomão Munguambe
Minister of Agriculture	Sérgio Vieira
Minister of Justice	Teodata Hunguana
Minister of Industry and Energy	António Lima Rodrigues Branco
Minister of Health	Pascoal Manuel Mocumbi
Minister of Ports and Surface Transport	Luis Maria Alcántara Santo
Minister of Posts, Telecommunications and Civil Aviation	Rui Lousa
Minister of Internal Trade	Manuel Jorge Aranda da Silva
Minister Governor of the Bank of Mozambique	Prakash Ratilal

Source: Agência de Informação de Moçambique, Information Bulletin 66 (1981): 12.

there have been neither serious challenges to the government nor even organized expressions of discontent. Ultimately, however, the decisive factor for ensuring political stability may be the ability of the state to revitalize and restructure the economy to meet the very real material needs of the Mozambican people.

7

Transforming the Economy

Few newly independent nations have inherited as many far-reaching and deeply embedded economic problems as Mozambique. Four hundred years of Portuguese rule and more than a half century of colonial-capitalist penetration had left the country's economy underdeveloped and distorted. Witness the low level of agricultural productivity, the underutilization of the land, the dependence on food imported from South Africa, the high rate of African unemployment, the retarded industrial sector built on the use of unskilled labor, and the negative balance of trade since 1957. By 1970 the value of imports was twice that of exports, and the trade deficit had ballooned to $50 million. A 17 percent decline in the gross national product between 1970 and 1975 reveals the precarious state of the economy at the time of independence (see Table 7.1).

Structures, attitudes, and economic distortions created by four hundred years of exploitation cannot be transformed overnight, no matter how dedicated the leadership and mobilized the people. In theory, FRELIMO's capture of the colonial state gave it the means to address these problems and to begin a major economic transformation based on broad socialist principles. But before the party and the government could do so, they had to overcome staggering difficulties, which paralyzed the economy.

Between 1974 and 1977 the Portuguese community shrank from 250,000 to approximately 20,000.[1] This exodus created an acute shortage of technicians and professionals, as the Portuguese, by virtue of their privileged racial and class position, had been the only group with access to higher education during the colonial period. Gone were the engineers, mechanics, accountants, and agronomists who had managed the economy. At independence there were only six economists and not one geologist in the entire country,[2] and the strategic port and railroad sector had lost more than 7,000 skilled and semiskilled workers. Gone, too, were the inland Portuguese and Goan merchants who had controlled the system of rural marketing. Bitter about their lost privileges, unwilling to believe that FRELIMO would follow a nonracial policy, and insecure about the prospects of living in a socialist country, departing settlers destroyed whatever they could not take with them—factories, farm equipment, trucks, machinery, cattle. In an effort to end this sabotage and keep abandoned enterprises functioning, the transitional government enacted Law No. 16/

TABLE 7.1
Gross National Product, 1970 and 1975 (\$ million)[a]

	1970	1975	Changes in %
Agriculture	5,824	5,813	0
Industry	5,546	4,660	-16
Service	16,757	12,848	-23
Total	28,127	23,321	-17

[a]Calculated at 29 escudos to the dollar

Source: Jens Erik Torp, Industrial Planning and Development in Mozambique (Uppsala, 1979), p. 31. Reprinted with permission.

75, which gave it the power to establish administrative commissions to run abandoned and mismanaged companies.

Nevertheless, production in key sectors of the economy continued to decline. The fragmentary data available for this period suggest extensive dislocation. Sugar production dropped from 279,000 tons in 1974 to 159,000 tons in 1977, and cashew output fell by 44 percent in the same period. Cement and coal production also declined. By 1976 cement output was less than one-half the 1974 level, having dropped from 465,094 to 215,6633 tons.[3]

Natural calamities placed additional strains on the fragile rural economy. A drought in the north in 1976 further reduced the normally low level of food production, and massive flooding in the south the following year left hundreds of thousands homeless and devastated the fertile Limpopo Valley, a major food-producing center. To feed its people, Mozambique had to increase substantially its imports of food, thereby exacerbating the balance-of-payments deficit (see Table 7.2).

Mozambique's economy suffered another major setback in 1976 when the government decided to enforce the United Nations sanctions against the minority regime in Rhodesia, one of the country's three most important trading partners. The lucrative Rhodesian tourist trade had already come to a halt, but by closing its border with Rhodesia, Mozambique also lost between \$105 and \$165 million per year in port fees, freight charges, and remittances of migrant workers. Another \$300 million worth of property and equipment was destroyed during subsequent Rhodesian attacks. These figures, of course, do not include the cost of feeding the Zimbabwean refugees, who by 1977 numbered more than 100,000.[4]

The FRELIMO Central Committee Report to the Third Party Congress in February 1977 sketched the broad outlines of its strategy for reversing this downward trend and transforming the economy along socialist lines.

TABLE 7.2
Balance of Payments, 1973-1981 ($ million)

	1973	1974	1975	1976	1977	1978	1979	1980	1981
Merchandise Trade									
Imports	394	404	299	259	352	537	580	790	720
Exports	191	261	144	132	161	167	260	281	394
Balance	-202	-144	-155	-127	-191	-370	-320	-509	-326
Invisible Items[a]									
Payments	71	80	92	109	99	78	74	96	114
Receipts	163	200	255	277	220	204	206	245	249
Balance	+ 92	+120	+163	+168	+121	+126	+132	+149	+185
Overall Balance	-110	- 24	+ 8	+ 41	- 70	-244	-188	-360	-191

[a]Foreign assistance is included in invisible receipts. Not included is capital taken out by departing Portuguese of over $200 million in the period 1974-1977 or profits from gold sales of about $100 million per year through 1977.

Source: United Nations, General Assembly, A/34/377, August 16, 1979, p. 7; United Nations, General Assembly, A/36/267/S/14627, August 21, 1981, p. 10; Iain Christie and Joseph Hanlon, "Mozambique," in Africa Contemporary Record, 1982 (London, forthcoming).

Our strategy for development rests on agricultural production. The communal villages are the fundamental lever for liberating the people in the rural areas. Industry is the dynamizing factor for economic development. The construction of heavy industry constitutes the decisive factor for our total independence. . . . The building of socialism demands that the economy be centrally planned and directed by the State. Planned management is one of its basic characteristics. It falls to our State to create a structure able to organize, direct and develop the economy, planning and rationally distributing the productive forces throughout the country. It falls to the State to guarantee the full use of human and material resources at the regional level, linking centers of production and consumption, and therefore developing the rural areas and the towns in a balanced way. In this context, the State also creates the material conditions to guarantee the right of all citizens to work.[5]

Embedded in the strategy itself were a number of unresolved issues. At one and the same time FRELIMO had to shore up the existing economy to prevent total economic collapse and create the preconditions for transforming it along socialist lines. It also had to grapple with the problems of "statism" and overbureaucratization, which, in other countries, have thwarted local initiative and self-reliance.

The report, based on the fragmentary statistical data available,[6] set production quotas for strategic sectors of the agricultural and industrial economy so that output by 1980 would equal or surpass that of the best year of the colonial period. Most sectors, however, failed to meet these quotas. Although total production increased by 19 percent during the 1975–1980 period, state officials acknowledged that the economy still suffered from extreme distortions and that serious obstacles to development remained.[7] The fact that both agricultural and industrial production declined in 1982 after several years of uneven growth underscores the precarious position of the economy.

RESTRUCTURING THE RURAL ECONOMY

As 90 percent of the population lived dispersed throughout rural areas at independence and cultivated less than 5 acres (2 hectares) of land with extremely rudimentary tools, agricultural transformations were central to FRELIMO's long-range economic program. "The socialization of the countryside" was to be based on the organization of communal villages, with agricultural cooperatives serving as their economic base, and the creation of productive state farms out of the large abandoned plantations and settler estates.[8] FRELIMO believed that the integrated development of these two strategic rural sectors would stimulate economic recovery and heighten rural class-consciousness. State farms, with their sophisticated technological base, were expected to develop new agricultural techniques, breed high-yield seeds, and train agricultural personnel, all of which would be available to help adjacent communal villages increase their productivity.

Creating a network of state farms from estates formerly belonging to European farmers and foreign investors received the state's highest priority. Following the Europeans' exodus, the state took over almost 2,000 abandoned estates. In southern Mozambique, for example, a smallholder scheme involving 1,500 Portuguese families in the Limpopo Valley became one large production unit, the Limpopo Agro-Industrial Complex (CAIL), with a permanent work force of 2,700 and up to 20,000 seasonal workers. To the north in Zambésia, twenty-two private tea plantations were forged into EMOCHA, whose 35,000 acres (14,000 hectares) make it the largest tea company in Africa.[9] As of 1982 more than 325,000 (130,000 hectares) of choice land belonged to the state farm sector, and it is projected that by the end of the decade it will contain more than 2.5 million acres (1 million hectares) and employ at least 2 million workers.

Three factors precipitated state intervention. First was the increasing shortage of food—a structural problem built into the colonial-capitalist system, which had intensified after 1971.[10] Peasant and settler output, even before independence, had been insufficient to meet the country's consumption needs. The collapse of the European agricultural sector, which served the growing urban population, merely exacerbated these shortages, forcing the government to use scarce foreign exchange to purchase food. In 1977 and 1978 alone more than 350,000 tons of grain were imported. Nationalization and rapid mechanization seemed the quickest way to overcome these shortages and revitalize the cash-crop sector,[11] and the government hoped that the savings from decreasing food imports would partially pay for imported equipment. Second was the need to keep all agricultural operations running, even if they were unprofitable, in order to avoid massive unemployment, which would have had both economic and political ramifications. To have allowed the estates to remain paralyzed would have left between 150,000 and 200,000 agricultural workers idle. Third was the belief that the creation of state farms would facilitate the mobilization of part of Mozambique's small working class, thereby advancing the process of socialization of labor in the countryside.

Beyond the immediate concerns, state farms were considered the key to rapid economic development. The mix of high technology and economies of scale would permit Mozambique to increase greatly its agricultural exports and would also provide raw materials for its nascent industries. Cotton, sugar, rice, citrus fruits, copra, sisal, and tea received the highest priority.

The two major vehicles for increasing output were an expansion of land under cultivation and rapid mechanization. In 1977 the minister of agriculture allocated $40 million for heavy equipment, including 1,200 tractors, 50 to 100 combines, and irrigation pumps and equipment. The following year the ministry spent approximately $25 million of the $38.5 million budgeted for agricultural development on heavy agricultural equip-ment for the state farms.[12] At the same time, it initiated seed and soil testing, introduced agricultural training and literacy classes, and assigned an increasing number of agronomists from socialist countries to work with Mozambicans coordinating production on state farms.

By all accounts these policies ended rural paralysis, prevented massive unemployment, and produced modest gains in agricultural production (see Table 7.3). In 1979 production on tea and copra state farms surpassed the

TABLE 7.3
Estimated Crop Production, 1976-1981 (in tons)

	1976	1977	1978	1979	1980	1981
Rice	45,000	65,000	45,000	47,000	42,600	34,000
Cotton	18,000	18,000	22,000	15,000	22,300	40,400
Tea	13,000	17,000	15,000	16,000	18,000	--
Copra	**	**	**	10,000	26,800	28,400
Citrus fruits	**	**	**	**	37,300	36,700
Sugar cane	240,000	220,000	160,000	214,000	170,000	177,700

**No information

Sources: Speech of President Samora Machel to the 5th Session of the
People's Assembly, December 12, 1979; interview with Arnaldo Ribeiro on
August 28, 1980; BERI, FORCE Report on Mozambique (Washington, 1981), p.
14; and Comissão Nacional do Plano, Moçambique: Informação Estatística
1980/81 (Maputo, 1982), p. 47.

colonial levels FRELIMO had targeted as goals for 1980. And 1981 saw
a 12 percent increase in total agricultural production, a growth rate
significantly higher than in any other year since independence.[13] In 1981,
56 percent of all marketed agricultural produce, representing 15 percent
of total agricultural output, came from the state farm sector, which included
only 4 percent of the land under cultivation.[14]

Despite the absolute gains, productivity on state farms remained
relatively low. The tendency was to raise production through increased
land utilization rather than by improving the output per hectare. Thus,
CAIL output during 1981 was only 1.1 tons of rice per acre (2.8 tons per
hectare), and even on more efficient state farms in Cabo Delgado Province
the rice output was only 1.6 tons per acre (4 tons per hectare). By
comparison, yields in Spain were 2.6 tons and in China were more than
3.6 tons per acre (6.7 tons and 9 tons per hectare), with similar or lower
levels of technical input. Because output was generally below projected
levels, Mozambique was not able to decrease its food imports, and thus
there were no savings that could be used to pay for the imported equipment,
as had been projected. In fact, due to recurring droughts, population
growth, and heightened consumer demand as a result of better wages,
Mozambique increased its food imports each year.[15] By 1980 food imports
represented more than 50 percent of all imported consumer goods.[16]
Moreover, the state farm sector, despite the substantial investments and
attention it received, annually lost money. In many cases, most noticeably
rice, it probably would have cost Mozambique less had it imported the
food rather than investing in the machinery to produce it.

Several factors contributed to the low productivity and unprofitability
of this sector. Most serious was an overreliance on equipment that was

Heavy equipment for state farms (Credit: Allen Isaacman)

not always appropriate and was inefficiently utilized. The most highly publicized failure of high technology occurred at CAIL, although its problems characterized the entire sector. Imported combines were unable to harvest the type of rice planted in 1978, and more than 30,000 volunteers had to be mobilized to pick the crop by hand. Furthermore, its largely illiterate workers lacked the necessary experience and training to operate this sophisticated machinery, there were few mechanics to repair the machines, and an ever-increasing demand for spare parts taxed Mozambique's limited foreign exchange reserves. As a result, a substantial number of tractors and combine harvesters fell into disrepair, and 130 of CAIL's 200 tractors did not operate during the 1979-1980 rice campaign. Because tractors and other heavy equipment were generally needed for only two or three months a year, after which they were either left idle or used to transport workers, they were an inefficient allocation of capital.

Of almost equal significance was the largely seasonal, unstable, and untrained rural labor force—a legacy of the colonial period. Dependency on seasonal labor was most acute on the larger estates, such as CAIL and EMOCHA, which in 1980 employed 10,000 and 24,000 such workers respectively. Even on smaller state farms, such as Matama in Niassa, 25 percent of the 800 workers were seasonal, and at Inhassune in Inhambane the figure was 75 percent. This seasonality was due to the monocultural character of most state farms and the tendency to plant only once a year, both of which created sharp fluctuations in labor requirements.[17] Rather than having well-organized and stable brigades that specialized in a particular aspect of the labor process, brigade membership on most state farms varied daily, frustrating the development of group cohesion and class-consciousness, limiting productivity, and undermining training programs. This problem has not been treated with the seriousness it deserves.

Finally, the tendency to aggregate small farms and plantations into unmanageably large state entities made it impossible for the administrators even to tackle the problems associated with the inefficient utilization of material and human resources.

By 1980 it had become increasingly clear that FRELIMO had succumbed to the temptation to see mechanization as an easy solution to rural problems and had ignored the need for a politically mobilized labor force. The highly publicized failures at CAIL, one of the main beneficiaries of the mechanization program, forced the party to reevaluate its policy to take into consideration these other factors. Although the government continued to invest the bulk of the money budgeted for agriculture in the state farm sector, the ten-year plan for the 1980s required rationalization of the sector and increased profitability. State farms that were unmanageably large were broken down into smaller units. The government also attacked the monocultural nature of production. All state farms were required to introduce new crops whose growing seasons were complementary to that of their main product, and most expanded into cattle, pork, and chicken production. This diversification permitted them to use their machinery more efficiently and to cut down the large fluctuation in labor requirements. It also has increased the amount of food available to Mozambique's citizens, as much of the diversification has been into grains and vegetables.

To resolve the low level of political mobilization among state farm workers, production councils, which had proved successful in the urban industrial setting (see pp. 165–166), were extended to this sector in 1980. Through involvement in the production councils, rural workers participated in decision making and gained some control over their conditions of employment. Although still at an early phase, the rural production councils will, FRELIMO hopes, organize training programs, raise the consciousness of rural workers, and link them to the urban working class through the developing trade union movement.

By 1982 some of these principles had already been put into practice, with positive results. Strategic state farms in Cabo Delgado and Niassa provinces were producing 2.4 tons of corn per acre (6 tons per hectare), the highest yield in the country. Rice production on CAIL, down dramatically in 1981, rebounded to more than 40 million tons. In Angónia, in Tete Province, the state farm was growing corn, vegetables, potatoes, and temperate-climate fruits and had recently introduced soybeans. Aside from these large state farm complexes, smaller farms of from 1,250 to 2,500 acres (500 to 1,000 hectares) are planned for each province to resolve its specific food problems. It is projected that by 1990 the ten large complexes will comprise 1 million hectares and will furnish 75 percent of the agricultural products, 78 percent of the meat, 83 percent of the milk, and 56 percent of the eggs produced by the state sector.[18]

The other structural prerequisite for socializing the countryside was the formation of the communal villages. First developed in the liberated zones, these villages would be expanded throughout Mozambique by convincing peasants to leave their scattered homesteads and move into large rural communities. The new revolutionary institutions to be located

there—party cells, schools, health services, the mass democratic organizations, a variety of craft and consumer cooperatives, and above all else,
agricultural cooperatives in which villagers would spend a portion of their
day working collectively producing cash crops for sale—would transform
relations of production, raise peasants' political consciousness, and improve
the quality of their lives. The communal villages would also be the
battleground on which the reactionary ideas of colonialism and traditional
society would be vanquished. The Report of the FRELIMO Central Committee to the Third Party Congress, held in 1977, elaborated this theme:

> The Revolution demands that we extend the experience of the liberated areas
> to the entire country. The organization of the peasants into rural communities
> is essential for the development of collective life in the countryside and for
> the creation of the necessary conditions for socialized agriculture. . . . It is
> in these, through collective production, that the workers' ideological battle
> grows stronger. The villages permit a rapid growth in revolutionary class
> consciousness and the consequent freeing of the workers' immense creative
> capacity. The organization of the people into Communal Villages makes it
> possible for us to achieve self-sufficiency in food relatively quickly, and also
> enables us to satisfy health, educational and cultural needs.[19]

These advances, in turn, would lead to the stabilization of the work force
and alleviate growing pressure to migrate to the cities.

Several factors facilitated the formation of communal villages in the
first years after independence. In Niassa, Cabo Delgado, and Tete provinces,
the colonial regime had already resettled almost 1 million peasants into
large strategic hamlets on which the structures of the communal village
could be superimposed. The thousands of refugees who returned from
Tanzania and Malawi were settled from the start in embryonic communal
villages in the northern provinces of Niassa and Cabo Delgado. The 1977
floods in the south also quickened this residential transformation. They
sent peasants who previously had been reluctant to leave their isolated
homesteads and ancestral homelands fleeing to the highland areas of Gaza
and Maputo provinces, where government officials provided them with
food and clothing and encouraged them to organize communal villages.
There were also indications that in matrilineal areas, especially in Nampula
Province, men joined newly formed communal villages to break the control
exerted by their wives' lineages over family matters.[20]

To overcome anxieties and misinformation, and to demonstrate the
advantages of communal life to the peasantry, FRELIMO initiated a massive
educational campaign. Locally elected dynamizing groups studied FRELIMO
documents describing the potential benefits of cooperative agriculture,
learned about the experience in the liberated zones, and then met regularly
with community members to discuss the merits of communal life. Government and party officials periodically participated in these discussions,
either to help resolve disputes or to describe specific plans for the region.
They emphasized how communal villages would expedite efforts to build
roads, electrical lines, wells, irrigation systems, schools, and health clinics.
Sometimes they offered low-interest loans or promised machinery or

Working in a communal village (Credit: Ricardo Rangel)

technical assistance on the layout of the village and the construction of new houses.[21]

Initial reactions varied considerably. Many peasants were confused and anxious about the organization and operation of communal villages. "Traditionally each one of us had our own field where we cultivated food to feed our family. Then . . . the administrator told us that it was no longer good to cultivate individual fields. It was better to join forces and establish collective farms on the abandoned European estates. However, in the beginning we did not accept the idea. We thought the administration was trying to trick us, and make us work for the government."[22] Those most opposed were relatively privileged members of rural society, such as chiefs and African capitalist farmers who, through collaboration with the colonial regime, had acquired substantial holdings and exploited local African labor. Opposition was particularly strong in the coastal regions, where African farmers owned large numbers of cashew and coconut trees yielding annual incomes of several hundred dollars. Other peasants objected because communal villages were to be the site of the struggle against reactionary ideas and values, especially the exploitation of women.[23] Most, however, were enthusiastic about communal villages, despite a lack of familiarity with the concept. Noted Julião Tang, founding member of Communal Village Rumba-tsa-tsa in Manica: "I lived near here before and worked mostly on my own. I got the idea of coming here from a meeting on the need to build and live in communal villages and to live collectively. After the meeting we began to get organized because we realized we would be better off living and working together, and it was the only way to satisfy our needs. The peasants who live in this area organized themselves to clear the land and the *shambas* [fields] were opened in May last year."[24]

By the end of 1977 there were more than 100 communal villages, varying in size from 50 families at Meponda in Niassa Province to the more than 11,000 families at Julius Nyerere in Gaza. Five years later, the National Commission on Communal Villages reported that almost 2 million peasants, close to 20 percent of the total population, were in communal villages in various phases of development (see Table 7.4).[25] Sixty percent of the communal village members were concentrated in Gaza and in Cabo Delgado provinces, which together had only 16 percent of the nation's population. Zambézia and Nampula, the two most populous provinces, had the lowest relative peasant participation. Mozambican officials predict that by 1990 more than 5 million Mozambicans will be incorporated into this collective network.[26]

Although large numbers of peasants have, at the government's urging, voluntarily moved into communal villages, there has been little progress in socializing the basic relations of production. At a 1980 Conference on Agricultural Cooperatives, peasant cooperative leaders spoke out frankly and critically about the problems they were facing, forcing state officials to acknowledge that "deep-seated and far-reaching problems" had surfaced "which severely impeded the advance of the cooperative movement."[27] Although FRELIMO had intended to establish agricultural cooperatives, based on collective labor, around which peasants would later build housing and organize communal villages, the progression of events was usually the reverse. Because refugees returning from Malawi and Tanzania and victims of the floods needed to resettle immediately, constructing living

TABLE 7.4
Number of Communal Villages and Cooperatives as of May 31, 1982

Province	Number of Comm. Villages	Population of Comm. Villages	% of Rural Population	Number of Agricultural Cooperatives	Number of Pilot Cooperatives
Maputo	22	17,873	3.64	8	4
Gaza	139	298,812	30.15	32	6
Inhambane	47	73,352	7.36	13	3
Sofala	88	106,139	9.47	28	5
Manica	111	143,541	22.39	32	4
Tete	40	84,558	10.18	23	4
Zambezia	39	49,220	4.97	22	5
Nampula	260	154,186	6.42	32	4
Cabo Delgado	543	815,551	86.77	18	4
Niassa	63	63,215	12.30	21	5
Total	1,352	1,806,447[a]	19.12	229	44

[a]Newspaper reports place the number at 1.2 million. See Notícias (Maputo), August 28, 1982.

Source: National Commission of Communal Villages.

quarters with adjacent family gardens received the highest priority, and collective fields came only later, if at all. To make matters worse, under-trained and overworked officials often selected inappropriate sites for the collective field. Village members sometimes had to spend several hours a day merely getting to and from it; in other instances the poor quality of the soil or lack of sufficient water impeded production.

Another problem was the lack of real incentive for most peasants to work collectively. Land was readily available and membership in the communal village was not contingent upon joining its agricultural coop-erative. Most peasants feared giving up their known methods of farming, which seemed more secure than the uncertainties of new forms of collective agriculture, and the failure of the collective fields to generate large profits reinforced conservative tendencies.

The colonial legacy placed additional burdens on the embryonic agricultural cooperatives. Planning and bookkeeping were required to organize the distribution of tasks, to acquire the necessary seeds, to make arrangements for marketing the produce, and to divide the profits in accordance with the number of days each member worked. Illiterate and unorganized peasants, however, rarely had the skills or self-confidence to undertake such tasks, and there were only a handful of agronomists, bookkeepers, and technicians throughout the country who could assist them. The destruction of the rural marketing and transportation systems meant that some products spoiled during shipment, other commodities never reached their intended markets, and there was a sharp decline in the availability of consumer goods in the countryside. Similarly, the abrupt departure of European farmers required the state to invest most of its scarce resources in reorganizing and modernizing the abandoned plan-tations, leaving very little for the cooperative sector.[28]

To stimulate production on the cooperatives and increase their appeal to the peasants, the state had promised fertilizers, seeds, tractors, and other technical inputs. Often, however, these failed to be provided. Increased demand for tractors, coupled with a shortage of parts and trained mechanics and callous bureaucratic inefficiency at the state tractor firm MECANAGRO, resulted in long delays at the critical planting season. When the tractors failed to appear, activity on many cooperatives ceased, as the peasant members were no longer willing to clear by hand. At the 1980 Conference on Cooperatives, peasant leaders complained that they had not received promised fertilizers, seeds, tractors, and other technical inputs and that, when such assistance did arrive, it was often too late.[29]

These problems severely limited the appeal of agricultural cooperatives. No matter how committed the founding core members and no matter how high their level of class-consciousness, without tangible economic benefits they could not attract new adherents or even maintain existing popular support. As of 1982 the overwhelming majority of peasants living in communal villages were practicing solely family farming, and only 229 of the 1,352 communal villages even had agricultural cooperatives. Estimates from 1981 placed the number of cooperative members at a mere 70,000. Cooperatives cultivated only 1 percent of the land and contributed 0.3

percent of production; the family sector farmed 94 percent of the cultivated land and produced 80 percent of the total agricultural output.[30]

Even politically mobilized peasants were not prepared to allocate much of their time to collective farming. Most spent as many or more hours on their family plots as they did on the collective field. Of the 216 cooperative members at Communal Village Eduardo Mondlane in Gaza, for example, only twelve members worked collectively 200 days each in 1978; 77 percent of the members worked less than 139 days in the cooperative field; and 35 percent worked 50 days or less.[31] In Communal Village Chicuedo in Inhambane, where all the adults were members of the cooperative, they agreed to work collectively three days a week, but only for two hours a day.[32] Wage employment opportunities, such as working on a state farm or in the South African mines, compounded the labor problem by siphoning off the labor of many younger men, leaving the women and elderly to work in the cooperative fields.

At the 1980 conference, participants made a number of proposals to increase productivity and strengthen collective agricultural labor in the communal villages—provide basic technical and bookkeeping training to members of the executive committee of the cooperative, integrate the cooperatives into a restructured rural marketing system, commit the state farm sector to a higher level of technical and material assistance, and develop middle-level technology, especially ox-drawn ploughs. At the same time, images of the liberation struggle were evoked to encourage peasants to become more self-reliant and assertive and to use the resources at their disposal. The lack of funds allocated for this process, however, and the realization that peasants would join cooperatives only if they could see the superiority of cooperative to family farming required the National Commission on Communal Villages to focus its limited resources on a small number of "pilot" villages. In 1982 a specially appointed commission chaired by Marcelino dos Santos, the party's secretary for economic development, chose forty-four of the most advanced cooperatives spread throughout the country to be the recipients of state planning and technical input on a scale that heretofore had been impossible (see Table 7.4). In addition, the state committed funds to develop the economic and social infrastructure—such as irrigation, housing, schools, and health posts—that would make these communal villages more attractive places in which to live and work. The remaining communal villages were made the responsibility of local state authorities and of neighboring state farms, whose own production targets included the output of these satellite agricultural cooperatives.

Although FRELIMO has always identified communal villages as a priority, it has provided little assistance to them and has made the political decision to allocate scarce resources elsewhere. Unless capital is transferred from the state farm or the industrial sector, a subject likely to be debated at the Fourth Party Conference in April 1983, the socialization of the peasant sector will continue to face serious problems.

The communal village system has, however, been far more successful in changing social relations. In communal villages the inequalities of the colonial-capitalist system have given way, at varying speeds, to new social relations and patterns of behavior. Peasants have begun to recognize that it is both their right and their responsibility collectively to assume greater control over their own destinies. The popular election of communal village authorities and of deputies to the people's assemblies and the heated debates that often accompanied the selection of new party members testify to the peasants' political mobilization and increased consciousness. Communal villages have also been at the forefront of the struggle against traditional and colonial ideas that have kept women and children subordinate. The battles to get rid of initiation rites, child marriages, polygamy, and bride-price have made their greatest advances in communal villages. Involving women as full and equal members in all aspects of communal village life has also made significant, although uneven progress. The tyranny of illiteracy and obscurantism has been attacked in village schools and literacy classes, and the newly organized health clinics have become an important instrument in the campaign to reduce parasitic and infectious diseases.

The relatively small numbers of rural Mozambicans involved in the state farm and cooperative sectors meant that most continued to farm tiny family plots. In 1981, as already noted, family farms accounted for 94 percent of the land under cultivation and 80 percent of total production—including the bulk of marketed food crops and beef, all the cashews, most of the sunflower seeds, and one-half of the cotton. Thus, the family sector was critical of FRELIMO's promise to eradicate hunger in Mozambique.

Nevertheless, until 1981 the state provided virtually no support to this sector and in some cases even discriminated against it. Thus, for example, credit, which was available to cooperatives and even to the large private farmers, was withheld from family farmers growing the same crops.[33] This policy, in conjunction with low prices and the sharp decrease in available consumer goods after 1978,[34] caused many to drop out of the cash economy or to sell their produce only on the black market.

In a sharp reversal of policy, the ten-year plan for the 1980s recognized the importance, at least in the short term, of the family sector and promised greater state support. Although the ultimate goal remained the socialization of the countryside, immediate food requirements and the unevenness of rural transformation prompted the government to raise prices, to provide fertilizer and pesticides, to promise technical assistance and price supports, and above all else, to make consumer goods more available in rural areas. As one government planner candidly noted,

> The most important thing is to provide consumer goods. Even if prices are high, if there is nothing to buy, peasants will not sell their crops. It isn't sufficient for us to flood the market only once. Peasants must see these goods all the time. After all, peasants sell their crops little by little, and they will only sell this year's surplus when they are convinced that next year's harvest will be good. Therefore, shops must always have such items as cloth, sugar, soap, oil and bicycles to stimulate future production.[35]

THE PROBLEMS OF DISTRIBUTION

Problems associated with distribution have been as difficult to resolve as those in the productive sectors. The large-scale departure at independence of Portuguese and Asian merchants, who controlled the commercial and transportation systems, effectively paralyzed marketing of both agricultural and manufactured goods. The shortage of working vehicles, and the fact that railroad lines and paved roads connected the ports of Mozambique with South Africa and Rhodesia and not with the Mozambican hinterland, made things worse. And the few European and Asian merchants who remained in the rural areas doubled or even tripled prices and then hoarded scarce products to drive prices up even higher.[36]

To attempt to solve these problems, the state organized two new distribution systems. It funded and staffed a national network of state-run retail outlets and warehouses, modeled on the People's Shops in the liberated areas. It also urged citizens to form neighborhood- and community-based consumer cooperatives, reflecting its belief in self-reliance and local initiative. Through these complementary distribution systems FRELIMO hoped to make basic commodities widely available at the lowest possible prices.[37]

From the outset, the People's Shops suffered from a lack of skilled personnel to run them, mismanagement at the warehouse level, an insufficient number of transport vehicles, and substantial corruption and hoarding. Because the stores rarely had adequate supplies of basic consumer goods, peasants had no incentive to produce badly needed cash crops and foodstuffs for the cities. In 1979 the People's Assembly, Mozambique's highest legislative body, ratified the Private Commerce Law, which encouraged individual merchants to take over from the state in all aspects of petty commerce. In a major policy address in March 1980, President Machel promised that the state would create the conditions to support private traders and that special incentives would be offered to the 10,000 Mozambicans in South Africa, Swaziland, and Zimbabwe who had expressed an interest in returning home and entering this sector. Although very few returning Mozambicans have gone into trade, the government dismantled the People's Shops, on the grounds that they were inefficient and that the state had to channel all its energies into managing the strategic sectors of the economy, and sold them to private individuals or to consumer cooperatives. From then on the policy became to encourage cooperatives in the urban areas and private commerce in rural zones.

Consumer cooperatives, especially those located in urban centers, have proved much more effective. Beginning in 1976 the government held seminars throughout the country in which participants selected by their villages and neighborhoods learned how to organize cooperatives. It also offered loans to consumer groups whose membership fees did not cover initial capital expenses and supplied otherwise unavailable basic commodities from state warehouses. Cooperatives varied in size from small rural shops in communal villages serving 100 families or fewer to the consumer cooperatives of the Polana neighborhood in Maputo, whose 800 families operated several stores, each with a slightly different selection of products to accommodate its diverse urban membership.

The consumer cooperatives were designed to overcome problems of hoarding and price gouging, and they have been reasonably successful. During the serious shortages in February 1977 members of the cooperatives voluntarily adhered to a quota system for scarce commodities. Cooperatives were also instrumental in the government's system of rationing basic commodities, begun in Maputo in 1980 and later extended to other urban centers. Under the program, all families were assigned to a cooperative or a private store at which they received monthly allotments of oil, grains, sugar, soap, and detergents. The equitable allocation of these goods helped to reduce hoarding, speculation, and long lines of people waiting patiently to enter the shops. In Maputo membership in consumer cooperatives jumped from 75,000 in 1977 to 500,000 in 1982, more than 50 percent of the city's population. Nationally, more than 2.3 million Mozambicans had joined consumer cooperatives by 1982, and party officials hailed this as "one of the main forms of struggle in the field of trade."[38]

The state took two other steps to reduce food shortages in the cities. To increase the supply, it encouraged urban residents who were not productively employed to cultivate food on abandoned truck farms located in the periurban areas of Maputo. As an incentive the state provided farm implements and seeds, and local dynamizing groups mobilized residents to form cooperatives. By 1982 there were between 40 and 50 cooperatives with more than 3,000 members and an even larger number of individual farmers, all of whom were permitted to sell produce either at their fields or in market stalls reserved for their use. As a result, vegetables for Maputo's growing population became more available and black market activity declined.

The ever-increasing influx of people into urban centers, however, threatened to undercut the advances that had been made in providing basic consumer goods. To alleviate this pressure and cut down the demand for food and social services, in mid-1982 the government issued residence cards to all urban dwellers in Maputo. These cards entitled their holders to a monthly supply of basic foodstuffs and to the use of basic urban services, such as schools and hospitals. These complementary strategies are being extended to Mozambique's other urban centers.[39]

Despite such achievements, transportation problems continued to hamper the distribution of basic commodities. The movement of agricultural products from areas of surplus to those in need, difficult in the best of times, was virtually impossible during the rainy season. At CAIL, for example, more than 4,000 tons of vegetables spoiled in 1977 because of inability to get them to the urban markets. To overcome these difficulties, the government imported several thousand trucks and embarked on a crash program to construct all-weather dirt roads to link food-producing centers with the rail networks and main highways. Nevertheless, stepped-up attacks on the transportation network by the South African–backed National Resistance Movement (see Chapter 8) have virtually cut off commodity distribution in parts of central and southern Mozambique. Moreover, the absence of consumer goods in rural shops discouraged farmers from selling their surpluses to the state, thereby hampering the entire program of economic recovery. In the long run, more roads, new bridges, additional fleets of trucks, internal security, and more consumer goods will be necessary to overcome the distribution problems—all of which require substantial capital investment.

REVIVING AND RESTRUCTURING THE INDUSTRIAL SECTOR

Lisbon's colonial strategy of blocking industrial development to ensure markets for Portuguese manufactured goods meant that FRELIMO inherited an underdeveloped and distorted industrial sector. In 1975 industrial output accounted for 15 percent of the gross national product, and there were almost no basic transforming industries (see Table 7.1). Almost 70 percent of the factories were located in Maputo and Beira, and they used raw materials to produce primarily consumer commodities for the Portuguese settler community. The other salient feature of the industrial sector was the small, largely illiterate, untrained, and disorganized African working class, numbering approximately 150,000, most of whom were restricted to menial positions by the informal color bar. Years of political intimidation, cultural and racial denigration, and exclusion of Africans from the state-controlled labor movement had precluded the development of a coherent sense of class-consciousness.

Many of the same factors that compelled FRELIMO to reorganize agriculture necessitated state intervention in industry. Abandoned factories, sabotaged machinery, illegal transfers of hard currency, destruction of vital records, and the exodus of skilled labor threatened to paralyze existing production and create large-scale unemployment. Even before independence the transitional government had appointed administrative councils to oversee the operation of firms plagued by gross irregularities or theft or those whose owners had abandoned them. To achieve the potentially contradictory objectives of preventing the total collapse of the industrial sector while laying the basis for its diversification and transformation, the state took over the administration of mismanaged firms, nationalized strategic industries, sought to attract foreign investment primarily through joint ventures, and created worker-based production councils.

The increasing rate of economic sabotage after 1975 necessitated state intervention in all industrial sectors.[40] The most celebrated case involved the British-owned Sena Sugar Estates. In 1978 its debts to the Bank of Mozambique were more than $45 million (15 percent of the country's national budget), and production was one-fourth the 1974 level. When Sena Sugar announced plans to go into bankruptcy, the government intervened and appointed an administrative commission to ensure that its factories and plantations would continue to function and that the 12,000 workers would not lose their source of income.[41]

In December 1977 the Council of Ministers nationalized and placed directly under its control strategic sectors of the economy that were

The coal mine at Moatize (Credit: *Tempo*)

considered vital to national sovereignty and the transition to a socialist economy. These included the country's only coal mine, which was a source of substantial foreign currency; the petroleum-processing industry; Mozambique's principal banks; and all insurance companies. Unlike situations in which mismanagement had led to state intervention, compensation, guaranteed in the Constitution, was promised to nationalized firms. As part of its strategy of consolidating control over vital sectors, the state also assumed responsibility for the processing, transporting, and marketing of cashew nuts, cotton, sugar, copra, and rice, considered key cash crops. By 1981, as a result of nationalization and intervention, more than 75 percent of industrial production was state controlled.[42]

State intervention and nationalization served two interrelated goals—keeping the industrial sector operating and laying the basis for a planned economy. State participation also made it easier to compile vital statistical data, such as the composition of the labor force, location of industries, and output per sector, which were necessary for long-term planning.

Armed with this data, the National Planning Commission in 1979 produced Mozambique's first central state plan (1979-1980) and has since defined the priority areas for the 1980s. The plan stressed the short-term need to strengthen consumer industries and the long-term requirement to develop transforming industries to reduce the country's dependency on foreign imports and allow it to expand its exports. The plan also called for decentralization and the placement of industries near sources of energy, transport, and raw materials. In 1981 FRELIMO decided that the revitalization of consumer and agriculture-related industries should receive the highest immediate priority. Increased imports of raw materials for the clothing, shoe, household utensil, and agricultural implement industries were authorized to respond to the need to stimulate agricultural production. Long-term priority projects include constructing textile plants in each of the country's ten provinces and erecting an aluminum smelting plant in Tete, a paper and wood-processing complex in Manica, and an iron and steel mill in the central part of the country, using gas from Pande in Inhambane Province.[43]

Developing an industrial base, however, is a costly proposition—an estimated $600 million for the paper mills and steel factory alone—that requires massive foreign investment. Mozambique's leaders have sought investment capital from a wide variety of sources, both in the West and in the socialist countries. This policy is based on their assessment that the socialist countries were either unable or unwilling to provide the necessary capital, that Western countries had greater available investment capital and technological superiority in certain strategic sectors, and that the potential advantages of entering into agreements with capitalist countries and multinational corporations outweighed the necessary risks. "We are open to mutually advantageous cooperation with firms from other countries," announced the Council of Ministers in 1979. "As a socialist country we do not fear [such] cooperation. . . . We need technology. We need finance."[44]

Although they were anxious to attract foreign capital, Mozambique's leaders refused to jeopardize the nation's economic sovereignty in the

CIFEL—Mozambique's only steel factory (Credit: *Notícias*)

process. Foreign investments would be approved only if they furthered Mozambique's economic plan, ensured an appropriate transfer of technology, guaranteed the training of Mozambican workers, and permitted nationalization at the end of a specified time written into the initial contract.[45] President Machel emphasized these points at a meeting organized by Business International (a consulting firm that advises multinational corporations on foreign investments) for prospective Western investors that took place in Maputo in February 1980. "We do not intend to become perpetual suppliers of raw materials. We intend to develop our industry and agriculture. We intend to participate in the international division of labor in a position of equality."[46] Consistent with this position, Mozambique rejected offers by both Western investors and Eastern bloc countries to mine its highly prized pegmatites because they did not include commitments to construction of processing plants and supporting infrastructures. Despite these stringent requirements, since 1980 Mozambique has signed important agreements with Swedish, Italian, French, Belgian, Portuguese, British, Norwegian, and West German firms and with East Germany, Romania, the Soviet Union, China, and Bulgaria (see Chapter 8). In terms of overall capital, Sweden and then Italy and France are the largest investors.

State intervention, nationalization, economic planning, and control of foreign investments could create the possibility of a fundamental socialist transformation of the economy, FRELIMO leaders believed, only if the work place was also democratized and socialized. Although the sweeping industrial labor reforms announced in October 1976 were designed to allow "workers to participate in an active, collective and conscious way in the discussion and resolution of their problems, especially in relation to production and productivity,"[47] the immediate reasons for their promulgation were the widespread economic sabotage and worker indiscipline that plagued the industrial sector.

Because most factories were located in the southern part of the country, where FRELIMO's influence during the war had been minimal, workers had had little or no contact with the liberation movement. Thus, they had unrealistic expectations about the meaning of independence, they did not understand their role in industrial development, and they could not see why they had to continue to work with whites or to obey factory supervisors, both symbols of colonial oppression. To combat low productivity, widespread absenteeism, worker indiscipline, and the effects of the flight of most Portuguese technicians, Production Councils, composed of workers selected by their peers, were created in all industrial establishments.[48]

The Production Councils—one for each department of employees within a factory—were responsible for organizing and mobilizing the work force and instilling in the workers a sense of self-confidence and responsibility, tasks made more difficult by the alienating effect of a long history of labor exploitation. Their immediate objective was to investigate causes of low output and, where possible, to suggest measures to enable the factory to meet production targets. Weekly meetings of the workers also focused on improving conditions of employment, creating objective criteria for promotion, organizing worker-training programs, and planning cultural events. The Production Councils met regularly with the state administrators or private owners and with the FRELIMO cells to discuss and plan all aspects of factory life, including the establishment of production targets. They also intervened in disputes among workers and between workers and management, and they were involved in all promotion and dismissal decisions.[49] Nevertheless, all decisions ultimately affecting production remained the domain of the state-appointed director or the private owner. Other disagreements between the three structures were channeled to the party or to the secretary of state for labor for resolution.[50]

By 1979, 150,000 Mozambican workers in such diverse industries as textiles, energy, mining, and transportation were organized in Production Councils. Since then, all workers, except those in the most remote and marginal firms, have selected Production Councils (see Table 7.5).

The Production Councils, which, it is hoped, will soon be transformed into labor unions, have been an important instrument for democratizing the work place. The regular meetings provided workers with the first opportunity to exercise some collective control over the means of production. In factories like the SOVESTE textile factory and PROTAL, the nation's largest cheese plant, their suggestions increased output and improved

TABLE 7.5
Workers Organized in Production Councils, 1979

Province	Number of Workers	Number of Production Councils
Maputo	59,287	236
Gaza	12,462	--
Inhambane	10,663	11
Manica	10,763	--
Tete	2,765	13
Zambezia	21,798	85
Cabo Delgado	2,207	14

Sources: Comissão Nacional de Implementação dos Conselhos de Produção, Sede Nacional dos Conselhos de Produção, "Numero total dos CPs, seus membros, e trabalhadores existentes em cada ramo de actividade a o nivel nacional," December 12, 1979.

working conditions.[51] According to the Greek owner of PROTAL: "The production councils have been very helpful in mobilizing the company's labor force and instilling in it a sense of discipline and responsibility, which makes all the time we spend together worthwhile."[52] This involvement also fostered a new sense of self-confidence and collective identity. In the words of a worker employed at a wood factory near Inhambane, "Our life has changed markedly in relationship to the colonial era; in that time a worker was merely a servant who lacked and feared the factory owner. Now we respect one another. We live together and work out our problems together and there are none who are privileged."[53]

This progress, however, was not uniform. Many Production Councils were unable, or unwilling, to assume their responsibilities. Problems with management, including intimidation and refusal to give the Production Councils access to even the basic data about the firm, occurred with regularity in the period immediately after the councils were organized.[54] The Production Council at CIFEL, the state-owned steel plant, was inactive for other reasons: "The twenty-four man production council . . . seemed overwhelmed with the enormity of the tasks it faced. And one felt any suggestion like organizing a stock-taking or drawing together the priority orders so that a rational program could be drawn up for the mill . . . only seemed to increase the burden on them."[55] In many factories the lack of a clearly defined division of authority between the Production Council and the party cell further complicated worker mobilization.

As these examples suggest, creating new structures was a necessary, but not a sufficient, precondition for democratizing the work place and altering fundamental relations of production. State and party intervention was necessary to make the structures work and to prevent abuses of power, whether from the remnants of the colonial bourgeoisie or from state

Women in nontraditional forms of employment: welding (Credit: Ricardo Rangel)

bureaucrats and self-defined militants, who often controlled the dynamizing groups. To remedy these problems FRELIMO initiated its political offensive against bureaucratic tyranny in 1980, and party cells were organized to replace dynamizing groups in all factories throughout the country.

By 1978, state intervention, nationalization, and worker mobilization had halted industrial decline. Production increased by 20 percent, 10 percent, and 7 percent in the next three years, although in 1981 it was still well below the projected increase of 34 percent.[56] Over the same period, absenteeism dropped by more than 20 percent.[57] In 1981 industry's relations with the state were reorganized. Administrative commissions were abolished, and state enterprises were established in each industrial sector to coordinate the production of the state and private firms operating within it.[58]

Nevertheless, Mozambique's industrial sector remained both small and distorted, with a continued absence of transforming industries. A key economic document accompanying the ten-year plan described the situation in 1980 in the following gloomy terms:

> During the first five years the essence of the economic structure created by colonialism has remained unchanged. This translates into extreme foreign dependency characterized by

• an inability to transform primary material, either national or imported, into finished goods;
• a narrow industrial sector capable only of producing consumer goods;
• an excessive dependence on foreign markets, especially for petroleum, metals, chemical products, machinery and parts.[59]

Thus, despite a 40 percent increase in the real value of exports from 1975 to 1980, the high cost and excessive dependence on imports, which increased 60 percent in value, and the low prices paid for Mozambican commodities, primarily agricultural products, intensified the balance-of-payments problem (see Tables 7.2 and 7.6).[60] Whereas a ton of Mozambican sugar had had roughly the value of a ton of steel in 1975, in 1982 it took 4 tons of sugar to purchase 1 ton of steel. Similarly, a truck in 1975 cost approximately 5.3 tons of cotton; in 1982 it cost 13 tons of cotton.[61] Over roughly the same period petroleum prices increased fourfold, and in 1980 Mozambique spent about $235 million on petroleum imports—more than one-half the total value of exports.[62]

The balance-of-payments problem worsened drastically in 1977. A combination of three factors was responsible—the trade patterns discussed

TABLE 7.6
Value of Principal Exports and Imports, 1976, 1980, and 1981
($ million)

	1976[a]	1980[b]	1981[c]
Principal Exports			
Tea	6.6	35.6	34.6
Sugar and molasses	17.6[d]	50.9	45.2
Cashew nuts and by-products	37.2	67.5	60.0
Cotton	17.6	22.8	28.0
Shrimp and other shellfish	12.3	34.7	57.9
Principal Imports			
Equipment		146.7	142.2
Parts		60.3	170.9
Primary materials		331.1	335.3
Consumer goods		186.9	151.2

[a]Calculated at 29 meticais to a dollar
[b]Calculated at 32 meticais to a dollar
[c]Calculated at 35 meticais to a dollar
[d]Sugar only

Source: Comissão Nacional do Plano, Moçambique: Informação Estatística 1980-81 (Maputo, 1982), p. 62.

earlier, a sharp decline in invisible income from port and rail receipts due to both sanctions against Rhodesia and South Africa's decision to reduce its use of the Maputo port, and Pretoria's slashing by two-thirds the number of Mozambicans working in South African mines.[63] This balance-of-payments crisis forced Mozambique to cut its importation of raw materials, spare parts, and machinery needed for industrial revitalization. Rationalization of imports and the substitution of local raw materials wherever possible led to an increase in production in 1981, which, although well below the projected figure, was achieved without a concomitant rise in imported raw materials. The shortage of imported raw materials also meant that many factories continued to be underutilized (see Table 7.7), a pattern that was not altered in 1982.[64]

The 1978 balance-of-payments crisis made it apparent that Mozambique would be unable to finance even minimal industrial development through internal capital accumulation. Not only did Mozambique make overtures to Western investors, but first Iran and then Libya and Algeria agreed to subsidize a portion of the price of the oil each country sent to Mozambique, thereby helping to alleviate the balance-of-payments problem. At the same time Mozambique signed a number of long-term barter agreements with socialist countries. By 1979 approximately 15 percent of its commerce was with Eastern European countries, and the percentage has since risen. Mozambique acquired heavy equipment, trucks, tools, and badly needed spare parts in exchange for future deliveries of cashew nuts, citrus fruits, coal, cotton, sisal, and shrimp. These agreements, which transformed Mozambique's annual deficit from the exchanges into long-term, low-interest loans, enabled it to acquire badly needed capital equip-

TABLE 7.7
Estimated Industrial Capacity Utilization, 1979

Industry	Estimated Capacity Utilization (%)
Agro-industries	25-65
Leather tanning	45
Footwear	33
Cotton goods, woven	60
Cotton goods, knitted	18
Synthetic woven goods	40
Garments	40
Jute bags	45
Paper	20
Salt	60

Source: United Nations, General Assembly, A/36/267/S/14627, August 21, 1981, p. 6.

ment.[65] Mozambique also negotiated smaller-scale barter agreements with Tanzania, Zimbabwe, and Angola, and they are an important feature of the emerging Southern African economic bloc, the Southern African Development Coordination Conference (see Chapter 8).

Seven years after independence Mozambique's economic situation remained uncertain and somewhat contradictory. The legacy of colonialism still weighed heavily, as did the country's vulnerable position in the world economy. On the other hand, some important advances had been made. The precipitous economic decline, begun earlier but intensified in the immediate postindependence period, had been arrested and production in many sectors had risen through 1981, although not enough to meet the country's needs. As one development specialist concluded, "The continued problems should not overshadow FRELIMO's dramatic successes. With virtually no trained people, the economy has not only been kept running, but is now growing. Farms, ministry departments, schools and provincial governments are being managed by people in their twenties. They are often dedicated and frequently successful."[66] The framework for a restructured and planned socialist economy had been created, but debate continued over its specific character, over the allocation of scarce resources for state farms versus agricultural cooperatives and for consumer versus capital goods, and over the degree to which private enterprise in industry and agriculture should be encouraged, especially in the short run.

The economy is likely to be the central terrain of struggle during the 1980s—a decade FRELIMO has termed critical in the war against poverty, dependency, and underdevelopment. Mozambique's ability to achieve economic recovery and transformation may well depend on its capacity to find a niche in an increasingly hostile and complex world system—the subject of the next chapter. Just as external factors profoundly shaped the country's history during the colonial period, so international forces, especially escalating South African attacks, will continue to be critical in shaping Mozambique's future development.

8

Independent Mozambique in the Wider World

Africans must learn to use Marxism, but Marxism must not be allowed to use Africans!

—President Samora Machel, quoted in John Saul,
The State and Revolution in Eastern Africa
(New York, 1979), p. 443

The Sino-Soviet race for influence in Africa has taken a dramatic turn with the Soviets gaining a new edge in Mozambique, a vital strategic base for operations in Eastern and Southern Africa. Mozambique's new ties with the Soviets, marking a major ideological shift for the newly independent nation, could have broad ramifications for Southern Africa, particularly with the Soviets already influential in Angola.

—Robin Wright, *Washington Post*,
April 6, 1976

"Soviet satellite." "Moscow-dominated." The images most commonly evoked in the Western press tell us more about the Cold War perspective of journalists and global analysts than about Mozambique's foreign policy. To be sure, Mozambique and the USSR have signed bilateral economic and military agreements, and Moscow has replaced Peking as Mozambique's principal arms supplier. At the same time, however, FRELIMO supported the Zimbabwe African National Union (ZANU) rather than Moscow's ally, the Zimbabwe African People's Union (ZAPU), in the Zimbabwean struggle; concluded major agreements with Britain, France, and Italy; and is now receiving military assistance from Portugal.

Such examples suggest the shortcomings of the Cold War analysis, which fails to comprehend the fiercely nationalist roots of FRELIMO's foreign policy and its commitment to avoid all new forms of dependency. As Mozambican leader Marcelino dos Santos stressed, "We did not fight for fifteen years to free ourselves to become the pawn of yet another foreign power."[1]

The need for autonomy, nonalignment, and a special relationship with the socialist countries are all principles derived from the concrete experience of the armed struggle. It was, after all, nonaligned nations,

171

especially Egypt, Algeria, Zambia, and Tanzania, that provided FRELIMO guerrillas with their first arms and training. And as the conflict intensified, socialist countries, primarily China and the Soviet Union, became the major source of financial aid, weapons, and diplomatic support while the NATO alliance provided massive assistance to the Portuguese colonial regime. This configuration of international alliances helped to radicalize FRELIMO and shape its view of the international arena—an arena in which progressive Third World countries, aided by socialist nations, supported the struggle against colonialism, racism, and oppression while the West, with the exception of the Scandinavian states, helped to perpetuate the status quo. Having identified its allies, the liberation movement still insisted upon the right to pursue an autonomous and nonaligned policy, free from external pressure, in order to maximize its options and meet authentic Mozambican objectives. Thus, throughout the war, it refused to become embroiled in the Sino-Soviet split, even though each country pressured FRELIMO to endorse its position. "Our fight for national independence," emphasized FRELIMO, "requires a strong defense of our foreign policy and the complete respect of the principles of equality and non-intervention in our internal affairs with countries and other organizations."[2]

These foreign policy principles, culled from the war of liberation and enshrined in the Constitution, were reiterated at FRELIMO's 1976 Third Party Congress. The final communiqué stressed Mozambique's commitment to "strengthening the world anti-imperialist front and the struggle against colonialism, racism, neo-colonialism and imperialism" and the principle of independence in the conduct of foreign affairs. The congress also called for deeper ties to the socialist countries, identified for the first time as Mozambique's "natural allies," reaffirmed the nation's links to the Organization of African Unity (OAU) and the nonaligned movement, and expressed a willingness to establish mutually beneficial relations with all states regardless of their social and economic systems.[3]

In practice, Mozambique has operated in four distinct international arenas. As a rule of thumb, whatever country opposed the South African apartheid regime was considered a friend, no matter what its social system and ideological proclivity. Predictably, policymakers assigned the highest priority to reinforcing relations with neighboring front-line states in order to reduce South African–Rhodesian military and economic hegemony. As a member of the Organization of African Unity and the larger nonaligned movement, Mozambique joined with states it considered "progressive" in attacking Western imperialism and defending the proposition that nonalignment should not be equated with neutrality. It also reinforced its links with the socialist bloc while attempting to expand economic ties and improve diplomatic relations with the West, thereby diversifying policy options. Although for purposes of analysis Mozambique's involvement in each sphere will be examined separately, in reality they are interrelated, and the available options and policies implemented were often conditioned by considerations that transcended events in a particular international arena. Moreover, the overarching principles of autonomy, nonalignment, and ties to natural allies sometimes conflicted, further complicating the direction of foreign policy.

MOZAMBIQUE AS A FRONT-LINE STATE

Since independence, Mozambican policymakers have emphasized the need to forge a strong political and economic alliance with neighboring independent countries and Southern African liberation movements. FRE-LIMO had concluded during its liberation struggle that Mozambique's ultimate independence required the destruction of South African–Rhodesian regional domination,[4] and it vigorously endorsed the formation of an alliance of front-line states (Zambia, Tanzania, Botswana, and Mozambique) in 1974. This alliance, which Angola joined two years later, committed the member nations to help Zimbabwean nationalists to free Rhodesia and to aid the African National Congress (ANC) of South Africa and the South West African People's Organization (SWAPO).

Shortly after the front-line alliance was created, FRELIMO opened its 750-mile (1,200-kilometer) frontier with Rhodesia to the insurgents, invited ZANU and ZAPU to establish joint military bases, transferred a substantial quantity of modern weapons to ZANU forces based in Mozambique, and resettled more than 150,000 Zimbabweans in refugee camps. For at least a year, Mozambican reconnaissance forces operated inside Rhodesia with Zimbabwean guerrillas. Machel's government also tried to bridge the gap between the two nationalist movements by encouraging the formation of the Patriotic Front, a tentative alliance of ZANU and ZAPU. At the same time, Machel urged Robert Mugabe, president of ZANU, not to let the struggle degenerate into a race war that would ultimately precipitate the flight of white settlers and create the type of economic problems that existed in Mozambique. Mozambican diplomats also took every opportunity at meetings of the Organization of African Unity, of the nonaligned nations, and of the United Nations to generate international support for the Zimbabwean liberation movements, and they privately pressed socialist allies, especially the Soviet Union and Cuba, to abandon their long-standing opposition to ZANU and to provide it with badly needed heavy arms and equipment.[5]

On the economic front, Mozambique supported the United Nations boycott of the Rhodesian government by closing its borders with Rhodesia and denying Salisbury the use of its principal international outlet, the port of Beira. This action ultimately cost Mozambique more than $500 million in rail and transit fees—hard currency desperately needed for capital goods—and the diversion of sorely needed food to impoverished refugees placed an additional strain on the beleaguered economy.[6]

Since the victory of the Patriotic Front and the election of Robert Mugabe as president of Zimbabwe in March 1980, the two nations have consolidated and deepened bilateral relations.[7] The most immediate effects of Zimbabwean independence were the removal of a hostile regime from Mozambique's borders, the coordination of military activity against South African–backed guerrillas operating along the Zimbabwean-Mozambican frontier, and a renewal of Zimbabwean trade through the ports of Beira and Maputo.

Mozambique's direct involvement in the campaigns against the South African regime and its illegal occupation of Namibia has been more limited. In part, this reflects the country's inherited economic dependence on South Africa and Mozambique's extremely vulnerable military position, evidenced by the ease with which South African forces penetrated the outskirts of Maputo in 1981; by the assassination of ANC member Ruth First, a well-known South African sociologist, journalist, and political activist, at the Eduardo Mondlane University the following year; and by continued South African violation of Mozambican air space. In the first half of 1982 alone Mozambique reported more than thirty violations. Both Maputo and CAIL, the major agro-industrial complex in the Limpopo Valley, are within easy striking distance of Pretoria's forces, and despite a Soviet-installed air defense system, Mozambique would be hard-pressed to defend these strategic positions against South African Mirage jets and helicopter-borne troops.

These constraints have forced Mozambique to eschew any direct military confrontation with its powerful neighbor, whose military budget for 1981-1982 was estimated at $2.75 billion (as compared with Mozambique's allocation of $150 million) and whose arsenal includes some of the most advanced weapon systems in the world.[8] At the Tenth Session of the Central Committee, held in August 1982, Samora Machel was quite adamant on this point.

> The South African regime, a few days ago, alleged that Mozambique threatens it by concentrating sophisticated arms on its frontier. What are the arms to which they refer? Neither economically, nor militarily do we represent a threat to anyone. No reasonable person can think that an underdeveloped country as poor as us, still bloodied from the wounds of war, can pose a threat to the sovereignty, the territorial integrity, the stability of another state, particularly one as powerful as South Africa. In fact, the only thing that the regime can fear is our example.[9]

FRELIMO officials also dismissed as premature and unrealistic an economic boycott of South Africa. Such a boycott would cost Mozambique well over $100 million per year in lost port revenues and loss of income to thousands of Mozambicans working in the South African mines. As Marcelino dos Santos, the second-ranking member of FRELIMO, emphasized, "We did not create a revolution to heighten the level of impoverishment and suffering of the Mozambican people."[10] High government officials have not, however, ruled out participation in a United Nations–sponsored boycott at some future date when Mozambique has become less dependent on the South African economy and when the struggle of the African National Congress has intensified. Mozambique reluctantly refused to allow the ANC to establish guerrilla bases on its territory for fear this would give South Africa a pretext to launch a major invasion.[11] Armando Guebuza, resident minister of war-torn Sofala Province, assured

British reporters in June 1981 that "how long this situation persists depends on how the situation in all Southern Africa evolves . . . a lot depends on the West."[12] Clearly, Mozambique wants to avoid a direct confrontation with South Africa, which, FRELIMO fears, would have devastating economic consequences and lead to an internationalization of the Southern African conflict redefined in Cold War terms—an interpretation the South African regime has long sought to promote.

For the moment, therefore, Mozambican aid to the ANC is largely political. The ANC has offices in Maputo; Oliver Tambo, the ANC leader, is accorded full honors as a head of state; and Mozambique has given sanctuary and support to a number of South African refugees as well as exiled members of the South African Congress of Trade Unions. Mozambican diplomats at the OAU, at nonaligned nations conferences, and in the United Nations also press the ANC's claim that it is the sole legitimate representative of the South African people, and they have repeatedly denounced Western support of the racist regime in Pretoria. At a front-line summit in March 1982, the Mozambican delegation urged greater economic and military aid for the ANC and called for an intensified campaign to isolate South Africa.[13] Although the substantial escalation of ANC military operations in the Transvaal and other areas adjacent to Mozambique suggests that FRELIMO might be allowing guerrillas operating in small bands to pass through its territory, this is officially denied. Instead, Mozambican leaders stress that the success of the revolution in South Africa depends on the ability of the ANC to organize popular support internally and that, until then, the role of Mozambique and other front-line nations can be only peripheral.[14]

Maputo also supports the struggle of the South West African Peoples Organization, although its distance from Namibia precludes much practical assistance. Nevertheless, Mozambican diplomats are credited with playing an important role in pressuring the West to persuade South Africa to comply with United Nations Resolution 435. This resolution affirms the principle of majority rule and calls for an internationally supervised national referendum. Such an agreement, observers contend, would guarantee a SWAPO victory and eradicate South African domination.

On the economic front, Mozambique has sought to strengthen its relations with its independent neighbors. In July 1979, at the Arusha Conference, the Mozambican delegation played a significant role in enlarging the political alliance of front-line states into an integrated regional alliance, the Southern African Development Coordination Conference (SADCC), which included newly independent Zimbabwe, Swaziland, Lesotho, and Malawi plus Mozambique, Angola, Zambia, and Tanzania.[15] SADCC's long-term objectives, if realized, will help not only Mozambique but the other member states to reduce their structural dependence on South Africa.

SADCC identified five priority areas—developing regional transport and telecommunications systems, improving agriculture, providing manpower training, increasing port traffic-handling capacities, and determining long-term energy needs. Immediate priority was given to strengthening the transportation and communications networks without which all forms of regional cooperation would be impractical. Of the $800 million pledged to SADCC in 1980[16] $650 million was spent on transportation projects, primarily in Mozambique. Deepening the ports of Beira, Maputo, and Nacala and increasing their capacities, which could reduce the dependence of landlocked Swaziland, Botswana, Zimbabwe, Malawi, and Zambia on South African ports, was viewed by SADCC members as critical. For Mozambique, the prospect of a sharp increase in the use of its ports in the near future is considered vital to its economic recovery. Additional rail and port fees would help to alleviate the nation's shortage of foreign exchange and development capital. Anticipating a substantial increase in traffic, the government spent one-third of its total investment budget on upgrading railroad lines and ports in 1979, and large allocations to this area continue. Roll on–roll off terminals at the three major ports, facilities to handle container ships, and a new terminal in Beira from which 800,000 tons of crude oil can annually be pumped to Zimbabwe have already been completed, and a 9-million-ton coal storage facility at Maputo, mostly for Swazi coal, is planned.[17]

Preliminary indications are that through the SADCC transportation network international commerce is gradually being redirected away from South African ports. Zimbabwe, for example, which was totally dependent on South African ports before independence, exported 30 million tons through Maputo in 1980 and 203 million tons in 1981 as well as an additional 166 million tons through the adjacent port of Matola. Exports to Beira, although a fraction of what they were before the 1976 international boycott, nevertheless jumped from 15 million to 60 million tons in the same period.[18] For Mozambique the port duties and transportation fees from Zimbabwean commerce have already replaced those from South Africa as the country's principal source of invisible income.[19] With ties to Swaziland, Botswana, and Malawi expected to increase, the beginnings of a regional transportation system have been made.[20]

Mozambique's attempts to restructure Southern Africa's economic and political relations have been costly. Before the regime of Iain Smith fell, Rhodesian forces had launched more than 350 military assaults against Mozambique. These raids were initially designed to intimidate unarmed Zimbabwean civilians and guerrillas, but by the end of 1978, Salisbury's purpose had become to disrupt Mozambique's fragile economy, create popular discontent, and demonstrate to FRELIMO the futility of continued support for the Patriotic Front. Rhodesian forces blew up the strategic railroad bridge on the Beira-Moatize line, thereby preventing the export of coal for several weeks, destroyed agricultural projects in the fertile Manica highlands, and attacked the Limpopo Valley agro-industrial complex 250 miles (400 kilometers) inside Mozambique. The final cost to Mozambique was more than half a billion dollars—including lost revenue, destroyed transport and agricultural equipment, and damage to dams and bridges.[21]

The Rhodesian Special Branch, according to its former chief, Ken Flowers, also organized the Mozambique National Resistance (MNR) as an anti-FRELIMO fifth column to work inside Mozambique.[22] From 1976 onward, Rhodesian security officials, working with their South African counterparts, recruited Portuguese settlers and mercenaries, black and white secret police agents, and former African members of the elite special forces of the colonial army who had fled to Rhodesia after Mozambican independence. Three former agents of the Portuguese secret police (PIDE) figured prominently in the formation of the MNR. The principal figure was Orlando Cristina. A prominent PIDE official, he became the secretary general of the MNR. Evo Fernandes, who had infiltrated the antifascist student movement in Lisbon during the 1950s and subsequently had worked for the colonial police while covertly in the employ of PIDE, was appointed the MNR spokesperson in Europe. Casimiro Monteiro, a professional assassin implicated in the 1965 murder of Portuguese opposition leader Humberto Delgado and probably involved in the murder of FRELIMO's first president, Eduardo Mondlane, took over as liaison with South African security. To this initial group were added ex-FRELIMO guerrillas who had been expelled for corruption or had left because of unfulfilled personal ambitions. Andre Matzangaissa and Afonso Dhlakama, two former FRELIMO soldiers, received prominent positions in the MNR to give it visible black leadership.[23]

The Rhodesian government provided the MNR with arms and bases along the Mozambican border and with logistics support. In retaliation for Mozambique's imposition of United Nations–backed sanctions against Rhodesia, it sent MNR bands repeatedly into Mozambique to burn villages, plunder agricultural cooperatives, attack railroad lines and road traffic, disrupt commerce, and raid reeducation camps, from which the MNR recruited additional members. These bands also collected valuable intelligence data on ZANU forces in Mozambique and intimidated Zimbabwean refugees.

In return for its assistance, Rhodesian security demanded MNR subservience—as is clear from MNR documents found stuffed down a latrine when the Mozambican army captured the MNR's Garagua base in Manica Province. In the words of Dhlakama, "We were oppressed by the Rhodesians and the leaders of our movement were not allowed to make any of the decisions. . . . We worked for the English, neither I nor the deceased Andre could plan any military operations. It was the English who determined the areas to attack and where to recruit."[24]

With the signing of the Lancaster House Agreement in late 1979, guaranteeing the end of minority rule in Rhodesia, the Mozambican government, feeling confident that it had the situation firmly under control, began to turn its energy toward national reconstruction after nearly five years of war. It was during this period that SADCC programs were crystallized and several important economic agreements were signed. The popular militias were also disbanded in many frontier regions. Machel's government failed to anticipate, however, that the remnants of the MNR would transfer their base of operations to South Africa, and it underestimated the amount of military and logistic support South Africa would provide.

Whereas the Rhodesian government used the MNR to collect information on Zimbabwean nationalist operations and to intimidate refugees who had fled to Mozambique, South Africa saw the roving bands as instruments of havoc to paralyze SADCC. At a meeting between Dhlakama and Colonel Van Niekerk of South African security on October 25, 1980, at a military base in the Transvaal, Van Niekerk ordered the MNR to extend its operations from central to southern Mozambique—to "interdict rail traffic from Malverne-Gwelo [southern Mozambique], to establish bases inside Mozambique adjacent to the South African border, open a new military front in Maputo province."[25] The South African strategy was clear. By extending its activity to the strategic southern provinces, the MNR would discourage Zimbabwe and Botswana from exporting their commodities through Maputo, which was drawing substantial traffic away from South African ports. To accomplish these objectives, South African officials agreed to provide large supplies of war material, including rockets, mortars, small arms, and advisers, "who will not only teach, but also participate in attacks."[26]

In 1981 the MNR blew up the Beira-Umtali pipeline, cut the railway between Zimbabwe and Beira, disrupted traffic along the Maputo-Beira highway, and claimed credit for destroying the marker buoys in the port of Beira. The following year it intensified its activity in the southern provinces, attacking bridges, railroad lines, and development projects. In a particularly devastating blow, the MNR attacked the Maputo-Zimbabwean railroad line in July 1982, cutting service for fifty days.[27] Many Zimbabwean companies dominated by South African capital used this uncertainty to justify continuous use of the port of Durban, despite the appreciably lower cost of shipping through Maputo.

By the middle of 1982, Western diplomats in Maputo estimated the MNR numbers at about 5,000. Most MNR recruits seem to have been coerced into joining.[28] Nevertheless, Mozambique's serious economic problems made MNR recruitment that much easier. Droughts (which the MNR attributed to the alienated ancestors), the Mozambican government's failure to provide sufficient support for the family farming sector, and the lack of consumer goods in parts of Manica, Sofala, and Inhambane provinces provided fertile ground for MNR overtures. So did the MNR's manipulation of tribal divisions and appeals to Shona chiefs, spirit mediums, and "traditional" Shona values. Whatever the initial attraction of these appeals, widespread plundering and increasing terrorism quickly dissipated support for the MNR and alienated the rural population,[29] which, above all else, wanted to be left alone.

Early in 1982 the Mozambican government turned its attention to combating the escalating MNR threat. It quickly acknowledged the need for a new military and political strategy, one that would incorporate aspects of guerrilla warfare and peasant mobilization that FRELIMO had previously used successfully. To regain the confidence and support of peasants living in the war zones, in May 1982 FRELIMO reactivated more than 1,500 former guerrillas, many of whom were organized in counterinsurgency forces, whose job was to harass the MNR deep in the bush. It also strengthened the rural militia. As of August 1982, about 40 percent of the adult rural population in Sofala was armed, and in the capital the newly formed militia boasted more than 30,000 men and women.[30]

Nevertheless, combating the MNR is just the first skirmish in a lengthy struggle with the group's backer—the apartheid regime of South Africa. That regime has invested a great deal, and is likely to invest even more, to ensure that the SADCC nations remain in a perpetual state of economic dependency.

MOZAMBIQUE IN THE ORGANIZATION OF AFRICAN UNITY AND THE NONALIGNED MOVEMENT

Mozambique has used the OAU and the nonaligned movement as international arenas in which to generate support for Southern African liberation struggles and to articulate broader anti-imperialist positions. Evoking the anticolonial tradition of Nehru, Tito, Nkrumah, and Nasser, Mozambique has consistently joined with progressive members of both organizations to condemn Western imperialism and neocolonialism. At the same time Mozambican diplomats have called for closer Third World ties to the socialist countries, even though some of Mozambique's closest African allies, including Tanzania, Zimbabwe, and Guinea-Bissau, are skeptical of the long-term objectives of the Eastern bloc countries. During an emotional debate on Southern Africa at the 1978 OAU meeting in Khartoum, Mozambique reminded member states: "It is not by chance that the weaponry of the liberation movements, the armaments which defend the dignity of Africa, generally comes from the socialist countries. Just as it is not by chance that it is the NATO members who supplied the arms which Portugal attacked us with and which are used by South Africa and Rhodesia to attack. Africa."[31]

Mozambique's nonaligned posture rests on two deeply held principles that, to many analysts, appear difficult to reconcile. On the one hand, Foreign Ministry officials insist that nonalignment demands autonomy from all foreign powers. On the other, as their OAU statement suggests, they reject as specious the equation of nonalignment with neutrality and the formation of a "third force" hostile to both power blocs. Addressing the 1979 Nonaligned Conference in Havana, President Machel was unequivocal on this point.

> Non-alignment is a specific strategy of our peoples to guarantee independence and peace in the face of the cold war imposed by imperialism. It is to affirm that non-alignment is an anti-imperialist strategy for the total liberation of our people. . . .
>
> It is important to emphasize these basic features because imperialism is trying directly or through its mouthpieces in our Movement, to dilute and confuse the realities in an attempt to transform non-alignment into a position equidistant between imperialism and the anti-imperialist struggle—a third force, rival to the blocs. . . . To dilute and confuse in an attempt to convince us that the enemy of non-alignment is the rivalry between certain countries, and finally, that imperialism is not our permanent enemy.
>
> It is precisely with the appearance of socialist countries that the correlation of force changed in our favor. This is an indisputable fact of history. Imperialism

was no longer able to concentrate all of its forces against us. Our peoples began to have weapons to neutralize and defeat the armed aggression of which they were victims. . . .

The socialist countries are natural allies of our peoples. There must be no confusion. They constitute a secure rear guard for the triumph of our liberation struggle and for the defense of our economic independence, the foundation on which non-alignment is built.[32]

This radical redefinition of nonalignment informs all substantive foreign policy positions Mozambique has taken. The government in Maputo has vigorously criticized Western intervention, supported guerrilla movements fighting colonial or neocolonial regimes, and voted with governments it defines as progressive. Thus, Mozambique has attacked United States–Pretoria ties, French intervention in Zaire and Chad, and British support for the Rhodesian regime, although in the Falklands crisis, Maputo remained conspicuously silent even though most socialist countries and radical nonaligned nations condemned Great Britain. Consistent with its self-proclaimed "internationalist" commitment, Mozambique has supported the Palestine Liberation Organization (PLO), the guerrillas of El Salvador, and the Sandinistas in Nicaragua, with whom extremely close relations subsequently developed, and has been the leading international defender of the Front for the Independence of East Timor (FREITLIN), which has been waging a war against the Indonesian occupation of East Timor since the late 1960s. It has also embraced the cause of Polisario, and along with Algeria and Libya, advocates immediate Western Saharan independence. At a recent OAU meeting, Mozambique, raising the specter of "reverse racism," chided its members:

It is regrettable to note that since 1976, since the Port Louis summit, our organization has not managed to firmly condemn Moroccan colonialism. What difficulty do we have in adopting a just position in this case? How can we accept that after eighteen years of effective struggle against colonialism the OAU failed to identify a colonial situation? Might it be because this time it involves an African country? . . . If we are lenient with colonialism because the colonizer is an African country, we must not be surprised or indignant should someone propose the admission of racist South Africa which occupied and colonized Namibia.[33]

Maputo's most controversial international position has been its muted support for Soviet intervention in Afghanistan. Only two other African countries—Angola and Ethiopia—voted against the United Nations resolution deploring the Soviet action; a number of Mozambique's closest allies—including Guinea-Bissau, Zambia, Algeria, and Congo (Brazzaville)—abstained; and Tanzania voted in favor of the motion. Foreign Ministry officials took the position that Afghanistan, a sovereign nation, had the right to seek assistance from whatever source it chose and suggested an analogy with the Angolan government's decision to invite Cuban troops to help protect it against a South African invasion.[34] Privately, some Mozambicans close to the situation suggested that Mozambique's decision may have been affected by contemporaneous South African troop movements along its border and into Zimbabwe together with intelligence reports of a likely preemptive strike against ZANU troops in southern Mozambique.[35] After all, it is the USSR on which Mozambique depends for its air defense system, and in the final analysis, support from the socialist countries represents the only possible counterbalance to South African might. Endorsement of the Vietnam-backed Heng Samrin government in Kampuchea was also interpreted by some foreign observers as a further indication that Mozambique found it increasingly difficult to avoid a pro-Soviet line, even at the expense of its long-time Chinese allies, who staunchly supported the ousted Pol Pot regime.

Mozambique's ideological affinity with more militant Third World nations provided a basis for economic cooperation with such countries as Iraq, Libya, Algeria, and India. Iraq, Mozambique's principal supplier of oil, agreed in 1978 to provide petroleum at below the world price. A bilateral agreement with India signed in 1982 called for $14 million in credit, technical assistance to upgrade Mozambican railroads, and a joint aluminum project in which Mozambique would smelt Indian-supplied bauxite using power from Cahora Bassa Dam.[36]

MOZAMBIQUE AND THE SOCIALIST COUNTRIES

A long history of support, a shared ideology, and increasing military and economic links have deepened Mozambique's ties to the socialist countries. The signing of a twenty-year Treaty of Friendship with the Soviet Union in 1977 and Maputo's decision three years later to open an embassy in Moscow, only its second outside the African continent,[37] underscored the high priority Mozambique placed on relations with its "natural allies." Although its ties to the socialist countries, especially to the USSR and East Germany, have grown, the relationships are complex, punctuated by periodic disagreements on questions of vital interest to the young nation.

Since the days of the armed struggle, Mozambique has received extensive military aid from the Soviet Union and other socialist countries. Shortly after independence the USSR replaced China as Mozambique's principal supplier of war material—a SAM air defense system to protect the capital and other strategic locations, tanks, artillery, MiG-17 jets, and military training. Although these Soviet weapons are costly and outdated, a fact not lost on Mozambican leaders,[38] they nevertheless represent the main line of defense against South Africa. East Germany has provided military equipment and a radar and telecommunications system and has helped to reorganize the country's security forces; Hungary and Bulgaria have made more modest contributions, often as gifts. It is estimated that there are a few hundred military advisers from Cuba, although the overwhelming majority of Cubans in Mozambique are employed in economic sectors, especially agriculture and planning.[39]

The South African attack on the suburbs of Maputo in January 1981 revealed the potential significance of Mozambique's security ties to the

Soviet Union. Within days of the incursion, the USSR had sent two warships into the port of Maputo, and the Soviet ambassador had warned of military reprisals "if anyone attacks us or our friends."[40] Because of increased South African support for the MNR, Moscow agreed in May 1982 to upgrade substantially the quantity and quality of weapons it provides to Mozambique.[41] Thus, a continued escalation of the conflict in Southern Africa may ultimately increase Mozambique's dependence on the USSR and reduce its freedom of action in the international arena. It most certainly will require using an increasing proportion of scarce resources to pay for arms.

Economic support from the socialist nations in the form of direct aid and capital investment has been far less significant than their military assistance. Nevertheless, through barter agreements Mozambique has acquired heavy industrial equipment, trucks, tools, and badly needed spare parts in exchange for deliveries of cashew nuts, citrus fruits, coal, cotton, sisal, shrimp, and fish. Details of the financing are secret, but the agreements transform Mozambique's annual deficits from these exchanges into long-term, hard-currency loans at rates somewhat below international levels. This strategy, beneficial to the Eastern European countries as well,[42] has enabled Mozambique to acquire badly needed capital goods without having to utilize its limited hard currency, has provided it with new markets, and has helped Mozambique to reduce, if not reverse, its dependency on South Africa. Whereas in 1975 trade with the Warsaw nations was negligible, in 1979 it accounted for approximately 15 percent of Mozambican commerce, and by 1982 East Germany had become Mozambique's fourth largest trading partner. During the same period imports from South Africa declined significantly.[43]

Since 1980 the USSR and East Germany have increased nonmilitary aid to Mozambique, which was negligible up to that point. Both have helped to fund mineral exploration, Mozambique's fledgling textile industry, and some heavy industry, including a truck and tractor assembly plant. In celebration of the fifth anniversary of the Mozambican-Soviet Friendship Treaty, Moscow provided Mozambique with a $55 million loan and a large floating dock, which permitted domestic ship repair for the first time in Mozambique's history and promised to save the country much-needed hard currency.[44]

Technical assistance from the socialist countries is quite substantial in comparison to direct financial support. Bulgarian agronomists play a critical role in the state farm sector, Soviet technicians are helping to build agricultural workshops in Beira and Nampula as well as a factory in Beira to produce farm implements, East German mineral engineers are involved in coal production and geological exploration, and Cuban technicians have helped to resuscitate the sugar and chemical industries. In addition, the socialist countries provide a large contingent of doctors, planners, and teachers and offer thousands of Mozambicans scholarships abroad.[45] As of 1982 more than 900 students were studying in East Germany and 1,200 were in Cuba, with which Mozambique has developed an increasingly close relationship.[46]

The ideological affinity, friendship treaties, and material assistance notwithstanding, Mozambique's foreign policy does not mirror that of the Soviet Union or, for that matter, that of any other socialist country. Mozambican leaders insist that foreign policy be guided by national interests. The U.S. ambassador to Mozambique, Willard DePree, confirmed its commitment to pursuing authentic, self-defined objectives. "Sure, FRELIMO's Marxist, but they keep their distance from Moscow. They're very independent, pro–Third World."[47]

President Machel's plea for the demilitarization of the Indian Ocean, first made at the 1976 Conference of Nonaligned Nations in Sri Lanka and repeated with regularity, is aimed at both the Soviet naval presence and that of the United States. One Foreign Ministry official put it quite bluntly: "If the United States and the Soviet Union want to fight, they can fight in their own house."[48] Mozambique has refused to provide Moscow with a requested naval base that would have increased the Soviet Union's military capabilities in this strategic zone, and at a diplomatic reception at the Soviet Embassy in Maputo at the end of 1975, Foreign Minister Joaquim Chissano is reported to have publicly chided the Soviet ambassador for pressuring Mozambique on this issue, which Maputo considers an infringement on its national sovereignty.[49] Three years later, when South African–inspired rumors surfaced that Mozambique had acceded to Soviet demands, President Machel personally invited Western diplomats to fly over the Bazaruto Islands, location of the reputed Soviet base, to see for themselves that the islands were uninhabited. Several senior members of the Western diplomatic corps subsequently suggested that Mozambique's refusal to permit the establishment of the naval base helps to explain the relatively modest Soviet military assistance in comparison to that given to Ethiopia and South Yemen.

Mozambique and Eastern European nations have been at odds on several African issues, most notably the Zimbabwean struggle. Whereas FRELIMO developed close ties to ZANU, whose military tenacity it came to respect, the Warsaw countries strongly preferred ZAPU and rejected Mozambican appeals for Soviet military assistance to ZANU because of the latter's historical ties to China. Machel's government also played an active mediating role in the British-orchestrated Lancaster House Agreement, to which the socialist countries were not a party, after concluding that the Zimbabwean liberation forces would win any fairly conducted election. Similarly, Mozambican diplomats have since 1978 supported United Nations Resolution 432 calling for an election in Namibia, even though Soviet support stems only from 1981. In the same year a joint communiqué following the visit of a high-level Soviet delegation to Maputo made no reference to the Polisario struggle in the Western Sahara, leading some observers to conclude that differences on this issue had surfaced in private discussions. Regarding Ethiopia, where the USSR and Cuba backed the Marxist government against Eritrean rebels, Mozambican newspapers and state radio have been sympathetic toward the Eritrean People's Liberation Front (EPLF), while calling for a negotiated settlement of the crisis. In late 1982 the Mozambican foreign minister indicated that his country could support a progressive, independent Eritrean nation if an agreement for such a solution was reached through negotiations.[50]

Tensions have also periodically surfaced over perceived socialist paternalism. Mozambican officials acknowledged privately that they were angered when the Soviets rejected their request to build a steel mill on the ground that it was not appropriate for Mozambique's level of socialist development. The reluctance of Eastern European ideologues to accord FRELIMO vanguard status as a mature Marxist-Leninist party, and their concerns that "the progress of socialist-oriented countries is obstructed by serious obstacles of an objective and subjective nature,"[51] undoubtedly inspired President Machel's acerbic comment that "some people seem to think that the development of Marxism ended in October 1917."[52] Mozambican officials could hardly have been pleased with the Soviet Union's support of a coup attempt against their long-time ally, Angolan President Agostinho Neto, in 1977,[53] or the reported decision of the socialist Council for Mutual Economic Assistance (COMECON) in 1981 to turn down, at least for the moment, Maputo's bid for full membership.[54] The Mozambican government made no statement in support of the Polish crackdown against Solidarity, and there were reports of its dissatisfaction with the way the East Germans had trained the security police, more than 400 of whom were replaced for abuse of power during the 1981 campaign to weed out corrupt and authoritarian state officials.[55]

Mozambique has also refused to take sides in the Sino-Soviet split. In an evenhanded 1978 commentary, FRELIMO's Central Committee deplored the division in the "international Communist movement as highly prejudicial to the development of the common struggle benefitting the maneuvers and actions of imperialism."[56] While explicitly criticizing China's misguided Angola policy and its invasion of Vietnam, the FRELIMO leadership nevertheless affirmed that "we will never forget those who supported us when times were hard." Despite continued disagreement over specific issues, the People's Republic of China has provided important assistance in health, agriculture, and the military sphere and has agreed to finance partial construction of the largest textile factory in northern Mozambique. In the middle of 1982 Mozambique and China signed a far-reaching commercial agreement that was a pointed reminder of Mozambique's autonomy within the socialist camp.[57]

MOZAMBICAN RELATIONS WITH THE WEST

Mozambique's relations with the West, as with the socialist countries, cannot be reduced to one-dimensional clichés. In some respects, because of Mozambique's attempts to balance historical commitments and contemporary needs, they are more complex, multifaceted, and fluid than those with its "natural allies." Mozambican leaders have also always carefully distinguished among Western nations as well as between particular governments and their people.

Predictably, relations with the NATO countries were severely strained at the time of independence. To show its displeasure over NATO support for Portugal during the independence struggle, Mozambique invited neither the United States nor West Germany to its independence celebrations, and their consulates were both closed down. Other NATO countries, although present, were treated perfunctorily. In striking contrast, FRELIMO publicly hailed the presence of progressive groups from the NATO countries that had supported its cause during the armed struggle, separating the "people" in the West from their imperialist governments. Mozambican leaders also reaffirmed their appreciation for the humanitarian assistance given by the Scandinavian countries during the armed struggle and called for expanded and deepened relations with them.

Mozambique's relations with the West remained unchanged through 1977. Military and economic links between the NATO countries and South Africa, the presence of Western mercenaries in the Rhodesian army, an anti-Mozambican media campaign in the Western press, and a ban by the U.S. Congress on economic assistance to Mozambique heightened animosity toward the advanced capitalist countries. On the other hand, Mozambique welcomed hundreds of *cooperantes* from Western Europe, the United States, and Canada, who came to Mozambique to help fill the void created by the flight of Portuguese technicians, doctors, teachers, and engineers. For their part, the Nordic countries responded to Mozambique's appeal for aid with a $55 million grant for agricultural development—the single largest grant they gave to any Third World country—and Sweden's additional bilateral assistance made it the most important donor to Mozambique.[58]

By 1978, Maputo had become interested in establishing better relations with the United States and its allies. FRELIMO pronouncements began to emphasize that "on the basis of strict equality, absolute respect for sovereignty and territorial integrity, non-interference in internal affairs and reciprocity of benefits, we are ready to develop friendly and cooperative relations with all states, irrespective of their social systems."[59] At a meeting between President Machel and then President Carter in New York, the Mozambican leader offered "to wipe the slate clean" and forget the long history of U.S. support for the Portuguese colonial regime. In an interview somewhat later, he reiterated his hope for improved bilateral relations and acknowledged that President Carter, in sharp contrast to his predecessors, had "tried to initiate a new American policy toward Africa, which for once, would disassociate the United States from the injustices of colonialism, racism and apartheid."[60] That this desire to improve relations was not propaganda purely for external consumption is reflected in a long interview Machel gave to *Tempo*, the country's only national magazine.

> We have found out that economic relations between our countries [Mozambique and the United States] have plenty of room to develop to our mutual advantage. Politically, both sides are interested in finding ways to ease tension in the Indian Ocean, both sides are trying equally to find the way to put an end to colonialism, racism and apartheid in Southern Africa. We are interested in developing relations of cooperation—understand me clearly, political, economic, cultural, scientific, technological and commercial cooperation with all countries including the U.S.[61]

Several factors seem to have contributed to Mozambique's "opening to the West." A growing recognition that the West's positions on the illegal Rhodesian regime and the South African occupation of Namibia were not necessarily incompatible with those of Mozambique helped to create a framework for improved relations. Mozambique also hoped to expand its extensive commercial ties with Western countries; diversification of its international network would avoid dependency on any one bloc. Undoubtedly, the most significant factor, however, was the realization that the socialist countries were either unable or unwilling to provide capital and advanced technology on the scale Mozambique needed to achieve its ambitious, billion-dollar development projects (see Chapter 7). That only the advanced capitalist countries had this capacity supported the government's decision that the potential long-term benefits of such economic relationships outweighed the risks posed by multinational corporations. Greater Western investment, it was hoped, would also encourage NATO members to pressure South Africa into limiting the activities of the MNR.

Since 1978 Mozambique has sought increased economic cooperation with the West. In quick succession Maputo signed a $40 million loan agreement with Great Britain, negotiated a $15 million aid package with the Netherlands, and despite a congressional ban on bilateral, nonhumanitarian aid to Mozambique, received a U.S.-guaranteed Export-Import Bank loan to purchase General Electric locomotives manufactured in Brazil. Among the major new accords entered into between 1980 and 1982 were a ten-year agricultural and industrial agreement with Italy, worth more than $140 million; a $450 million French loan to help fund a truck factory and cotton project; a $170 million railway rehabilitation pact with Canada, Portugal, and France; and assistance from Greece and the Netherlands in rehabilitating the port of Beira. In 1981 Mozambique and Sweden signed a trade agreement giving the two countries most-favored-nation status in their bilateral commerce. Other bilateral agreements with Western European countries promise funds to be used in the second phase of the construction of the huge Cahora Bassa Dam, in extending electricity lines to northern Mozambique, and in constructing textile factories in each of the nation's provinces. The funding of the textile mill at Mocuba by a consortium of French, Italian, and Romanian capital suggests that Mozambique is eager to transcend the East-West divide in order to achieve its development goals. Several major companies have also signed oil and gas exploration contracts. Despite these agreements, Mozambique still does not have sufficient foreign capital to implement many of its major development projects. Government officials believe that multinational corporations will remain reluctant to make firm commitments until the security problems posed by the MNR are resolved; they also fear that the Reagan administration has orchestrated an undeclared economic boycott.[62]

In addition to the economic agreements signed with Western countries, Mozambique accepted an offer of military assistance from Portugal to help thwart MNR attacks and South African incursions. As part of a broader agreement signed on April 27, 1982, Portugal's military pledge, in the aftermath of President António Ramalho Eanes's successful visit to Mo-

zambique six months earlier, signaled a dramatic improvement in Mozambique's relations with the former colonial power and marked the first
time that it had turned to the West for any military assistance. Although
the details of the agreement have not been spelled out, it reportedly
included both war material and training for Mozambican officers in
Portugal.[63] In June a shipment of Portuguese rifles and uniforms arrived,
which the government immediately distributed to the militia.

Asked by a Mozambican journalist if this agreement with a NATO
country would not compromise Mozambique's socialist integrity, the minister of defense, Alberto Chipande, responded:

> We are not going to be prevented from cooperating with the Portuguese
> merely because we are a socialist country. They left infrastructure and
> equipment here that could be used for military objectives. . . . Portugal left
> war material, various boats [about twenty] on Lake Niassa and communications
> equipment. This material is deteriorating and in some cases is no longer
> functioning because of a lack of spare parts. . . . We cannot permit military
> equipment to rot because we are a socialist country. We cannot spend millions
> and millions of dollars merely because we do not want to buy a part from
> a country that is a member of NATO.[64]

In addition, the Portuguese military possesses maps and other strategic
information collected during the armed struggle that would be invaluable
to Mozambique. For its part, Lisbon was anxious that its citizens working
in Mozambique, who have been the target of MNR attacks, be protected;
Portuguese officials also saw this as a stepping-stone toward rebuilding
economic and cultural relations with their former colony.

The "opening to the West" added a new dimension to Mozambique's
foreign policy but in no way altered its basic international alignment.
Moreover, while relations with the West generally have improved, relations
with the United States have deteriorated markedly due to the Reagan
administration's tough, anticommunist, pro–South Africa posture. The
February 1981 exposure of Central Intelligence Agency (CIA) activity in
Mozambique, including charges that agents passed on information that
facilitated the South African attack on the Maputo suburbs, resulted in
the expulsion of several U.S. Embassy officials.[65] When pressed on the
expulsion, the Mozambican foreign minister, Joaquim Chissano, emphasized
that "while my government is aware and disapproves of all foreign
intelligence branches operating in Mozambique, when their covert activity
jeopardizes national security, the government must take the appropriate
actions. We would do the same if it were Soviet intelligence."[66] The Reagan
administration subsequently refused to replace the U.S. ambassador, who
had departed several months earlier. This action further worsened bilateral
relations, as did continued U.S. refusal to allow Mozambique to purchase
Boeing 707s and badly needed agricultural equipment.[67]

Mozambican officials criticized Western efforts to woo Mozambique
away from the socialist camp or to infringe on its sovereignty as sharply
as it did the tactics used by the Soviets to get a naval base. In the most
celebrated case, Mozambique publicly rejected a $10 million grant and

the gift of a ground satellite station (which would have modernized its archaic telecommunications system) from West Germany because the agreement contained a clause supporting the claim that West Berlin is a state of West Germany. As West Germany did not insist on such clauses in agreements signed with the Soviet Union and with Eastern European countries, Mozambique refused to let itself be bullied merely because it was a Third World nation.[68] Faced with serious strategic and economic problems in 1982, however, Mozambique reluctantly signed the "Berlin clause" as part of a commercial agreement with West Germany, although Mozambican officials maintained that the modified wording left the legal status of West Berlin open to a variety of interpretations.[69] The agreement is not likely to please East Germany, but it opened the way for increased economic agreements with the Bonn government, and in August 1982 a high-level Mozambican delegation visited West Germany seeking aid for its ports and transportation system.

At the same time, Mozambique rebuffed suggestions that it apply for loans from the Western-controlled International Monetary Fund and the World Bank. The demands they make on recipient nations as a condition for assistance would, it believed, compromise its economic autonomy. It has also been reluctant to sign the Lomé agreement, which would link Mozambique to the European Economic Community (EEC). Instead, Mozambican officials have indicated that they will continue to emphasize bilateral agreements with Western countries. They have not, however, ruled out the possibility of eventually entering into a formal relationship with the EEC countries, perhaps at the same time they join COMECON, in a status yet to be defined.

Seven years after independence Mozambique's leaders are still grappling with the complex problems of formulating an autonomous foreign policy that best serves its interests. To be sure, key features—autonomy, nonalignment, and a special relationship to the socialist countries—continue to define the ideological framework for specific policies. Strengthening its security capabilities, diversifying economic relations, and reducing South Africa's regional stranglehold remain the nation's highest priorities. A comprehensive strategy to achieve these goals does not, as yet, seem to exist. On the one hand, there are signs that Mozambique is being drawn into a closer relationship with the socialist countries. On the other, there is the deeply held belief that the country can most effectively pursue authentic Mozambican objectives by diversifying its international relations while maintaining its socialist identity. The extent to which Mozambique will be able to reconcile these two global strategies and forge a coherent, nonaligned, socialist alternative will have great bearing on the future course of its history.

Appendix

Report from the Commission for Economic and Social Directives: FRELIMO Fourth Party Congress, 1983

Comrade President, comrade delegates, invited comrades and friends:

We have been designated to present the Economic and Social Directives to the Fourth Congress. In doing this, it is with deep feeling that we say to all of you: many thanks for the honour given to us.

The Economic and Social Directives of the Fourth Congress come within the main lines of development included in the Report of the Central Committee. In this respect they provide a detailing of these main lines through definition of growth rates and overall and sectorial tasks for the economy of the People's Republic of Mozambique.

We want to stress that the general directives laid down in 1977 in the Economic and Social Directives of the Third Congress remain in force, since as Third Congress Directives they cover a broad period of our growth. They remain valid in the same way as do the objectives laid down in the Long-term Plan (PPI) for the elimination of underdevelopment, although the current demands of the fight against the enemy lead us to adopt less-rapid growth rates and to postpone implementation of some expected new investment.

The Economic and Social Directives we are now presenting define short- and medium-term actions to overcome current difficulties in our development process. They form an integral part of the broader strategy of struggle against economic and social backwardness, and to eradicate underdevelopment and build a socialist society in our country.

The main aims defined for the short and medium term are: the fight against hunger and the struggle against armed bandits.

The Economic and Social Directives of the Fourth Congress aim:

- to overcome the most elementary signs of hunger;
- to defeat the armed and unarmed bandits and put an end to the black-market;
- to consolidate the basis for more rapid development in the second five-year period of the decade.

They were drawn up on the basis of economic and social development forecasts to 1985.

The internal difficulties we are experiencing and the instability of external factors affecting our growth have led us to use this period as the basis, as it also corresponds to our present planning capabilities.

The rates now proposed will lead to little meaningful growth in our country's gross national product by 1985.

However an appreciable rise in living standards in this period is possible through high levels of organisation, discipline, austerity and rationalisation of work.

This means that on top of the effort to reach the proposed targets, we shall have to demand a qualitative growth from ourselves. This qualitative growth must put us in effective

189

control of our own growth so that within a short while we can resume higher growth rates that will enable us to eliminate underdevelopment. If our basic economic battle now is to eliminate hunger, we must in this battle be able to establish conditions for a more rapid growth in our economy in the following five-year period.

As we have said the immediate aims of economic and social development centre on the fight against hunger and on the country's defence. Priority is given to rapid growth in agricultural production with the aim of raising levels of supply to the people and saving foreign exchange on imported consumer goods. Priority also goes to strengthening the defence capability of the country for the fight against armed bandits and in defence of our country's territorial integrity.

At the same time we must pursue the achievement of fundamental actions in the economic plan which will lead to radical changes in the structure of our economy, and strengthen and develop the bases of a socialist economy.

Steps towards the establishment of a heavy industry sector come into this framework, since, as the Long-term Plan (PPI) forecasts, only with an engineering and chemical industrial base shall we be able to build the foundations of a socialist economy and work radical changes in the structure of our economy.

To put into effect the basic aims laid down for economic and social development to 1985, we must increase the gross national product by 10 to 12 per cent with special emphasis on improved agricultural production.

The Economic and Social Directives lay down the principal tasks for branches and sectors and the expected growth in the period from 1982 to 1985.

In the *agricultural sector*, the objective is to reach higher production levels, using available resources more intensively and effectively, in such a way as to permit increased yields per hectare and increased productivity of agricultural workers and peasants. It is also important to reduce imported inputs, particularly fuel, agro-chemicals and animal feed.

Within agricultural production, priority attention must be given to grain, cassava, sweet potatoes, beans, groundnuts, cotton, cashew nuts, tea, sunflower seeds, citrus fruit, tobacco, mafurra oil seeds and copra.

Agricultural production for market must increase by 30–35 per cent.
In order for it to do so, we must attain the following levels of marketed production in the 1984–1985 agricultural campaign:

Cotton—75,000 to 80,000 tonnes with an average national yield in the state sector of between 1.2 and 1.4 tonnes per hectare. Priority action must be concentrated in Nampula, Cabo Delgado, Niassa and Zambézia. Purchases from the family sector must reach about 36,000 tonnes.

Maize—155,000 to 165,000 tonnes, with an average national yield in the state sector of 2.5 to 2.8 tonnes per hectare. Purchases from the family sector must reach between 55,000 and 60,000 tonnes. Main efforts must be concentrated in the provinces of Zambézia, Manica, Tete, Niassa and Cabo Delgado.

Rice—60,000 to 65,000 tonnes, with the state sector reaching an average national yield of 2.7 to 3.0 tonnes per hectare. To do this, we must concentrate action in the Limpopo-Incomati and encourage the family sector, especially in Zambézia and Nampula.

Green leaf tea—at least 111,000 tonnes, with an average yield in the state sector of about 7 tonnes per hectare. We must proceed with the rehabilitation programme already in progress.

Cashew nuts—60,000 to 70,000 tonnes.

Beans—20,000 to 25,000 tonnes with priority actions in the family sector in the provinces of Zambézia, Nampula and Niassa.

Copra—45,000 to 49,000 tonnes, with actions concentrated in Zambézia and Inhambane.

Purchases of agricultural surplus from the family sector must grow by 40 to 45 per cent in the period from 1982 to 1985.

In livestock, we must increase production of meat and eggs, with minimal use of imported resources. Within this context, we must ensure more dynamic action in pig and small animal breeding, and encourage game hunting, thus minimising meat shortages.

Marketed livestock production must increase by 35 to 40 per cent. In order to do this, the following action must be taken:

Beef—centre the main efforts in purchases from the family sector, organising a network of animal treatment stations and creating permanent centres close to the peasants. Give priority to the provinces of Maputo, Gaza, Inhambane and Tete. We must place 9,000 tonnes on the market throughout the country in 1985, with 2,500 tonnes from the family sector.

Chicken meat and eggs—produce at least 6,000 tonnes of chicken meat and 55 to 60 million eggs, giving poultry priority in animal feed.

Pork—at least double the volume of pork sales to the people, minimising imported inputs especially feed, maximising the use of left-overs and by-products for fattening sucklings. The state sector must concentrate on producing breeding stock and fattening sucklings up to three months old. It must provide veterinary services to producers who specialise in fattening sucklings and must buy a part of their production.

We must adopt concrete measures to guarantee the correct structure management, planning and control of agricultural marketing at national, provincial, district and local levels, and do so in such a way as to make marketing policy a factor in stimulating production.

Special attention must be given by local authorities to the renovation of cattle dips and water troughs as a means of raising the yield per animal.

In the sphere of agricultural and livestock production, we must pursue and accelerate actions to establish national production of seeds and breeding stock. We must create varieties and breeds adapted to the diverse agro-ecological regions. They must also be adapted to the technological levels of the different social sectors in our country.

In forestry, we must ensure a growth in production of at least 70 per cent. To do this, we must make efficient use of investments already made in this field. We must maximise exports without disrupting the domestic market.

Special attention must be given to the organisation and development of agricultural research throughout the country, guaranteeing the publication and application of research results. We will thus contribute towards an increase in production and productivity, as well as towards a rational and economic use of resources and a minimisation of imports.

Research and extension centres must be set up in the rural areas where practical demonstrations should be given to peasants of the advantages of applying appropriate farming methods, leading to increased revenue and work efficiency.

The main short- and medium-term objectives for *industry* are:

a.   In the production sphere concentrate efforts in developing the production strategic goods for consumption and for import substitution, using local raw materials; promote production of export goods; give priority to goods related to defence needs; promote the production of essential consumer goods for agricultural marketing; guarantee the production of building materials; increase the capacity for repair and local production of spare parts.

b.   In the investment sphere, develop small-scale projects based on local resources, with a view to short-term solutions for the people's needs such as small-scale food processing, small flour mills, fishing, production of cooking oil and soap, clothing, shoes, building materials, farm tools and domestic utensils; guarantee that new capacity will be installed and start operations; carry out actions related to large-scale projects, finalising the studies on the basis of which decisions will be taken.

Industrial production must increase by 12 to 15 per cent, ensuring a minimisation of import costs.

In *energy* we must ensure production to satisfy the country's needs. To do this, we must continue to install the national energy grid and intensify the use of hydro-electric resources in the country.

In *coal*, we must ensure that the geological work under way at Moatize, Minjova and Mucanha-Vuzi is carried out, and adjust the levels of production to available transport capacity.

With respect to prospecting for and use of *hydrocarbons*, we must by the end of 1985 make an evaluation of the reserves in the areas of Pande and Temane and begin oil prospecting with foreign companies.

In the *mining industry*, we must give priority to the production of tantalite and increase export products. We must advance on studies and prospecting for precious stones and metallic minerals especially pegmatites.

In *metallurgy*, we must produce from 14,000 to 16,000 tonnes of steel building rods by 1985, and step up the production of steel ingots as well as the production of sugar crushers and grinders for cement. We must also carry out studies of iron ore in Tete, Manica and Nampula and speed up the installation of the new furnace at Cifel.

In the field of *tool making*, the objective is to maximise production of hoes, machetes, spades, ploughs for animal traction and other agricultural equipment. Particular attention must be given to improvements in quality of hoes and machetes adapting them to peasant need in different parts of the country.

We must reactivate small production units in the provinces in order to solve local problems. We must speed up the construction of the Beira farm implements factory, so that it starts production in 1985.

In *light engineering*, we must develop production of essential goods for the people, particularly for the rural areas. To do this, we must give special attention to the production of fittings, cutlery, basins, buckets, watering cans, plates and pans, also developing production at local level. In this field we must ensure the production of packaging.

In the *electrical industry*, we must produce more batteries, and raise production to at least 20 million units by 1985. We must also develop repair capacity for electric motors, and ensure the production of radios and other products based on available raw materials.

In *cement production*, the volume must reach 350,000 to 370,000 tonnes by 1985. In order to do this, we must ensure that equipment is maintained.

In the *building materials* sector, we must increase production, particularly through small-scale projects which use local resources and substitute imports. We must give special attention to stone quarrying to ensure supplies to important building works in the various branches of the national economy. Improved use and preventive maintenance of equipment are necessary.

We must do prospecting for non-metallic minerals which ensure the development of the building materials industry.

We must guarantee glass containers essential for the various sectors of economic activity, and manufacture consumer goods, especially plates and cups. Collecting and recycling of glass must be encouraged as a way of reducing imports for this industry.

In the *textile industry*, we must recuperate production, particularly cotton textiles, blankets and sacking. Production must grow by 45 to 50 per cent by 1985. We must build the Mocuba textile mill by the end of 1985, and use the newly installed capacity correctly.

In *footwear* the production of canvas shoes, espadrilles and sandals is important, especially organised in small-scale industries based essentially on local resources. We must start production in the Nampula espadrille factory and extend this experience to other provinces.

The *sugar* sector is key for domestic consumption and export, and must have a programme to renovate installed capacity. We must guarantee rapid repairs of equipment, preparing the factories more adequately and increasing industrial yields. In 1985 they must produce 150,000 to 160,000 tonnes of sugar.

Cooking oils and soap production must grow by 24 to 27 per cent in comparison with that in 1982. We must continue the extraction of tallow from the slaughter houses and advance with the programme to install small industries producing cooking oil and soap at local level. In this context, we must improve the existing productive base in Manica and Zambézia and set up units in Niassa and Tete.

We must look for ways to substitute imports in the *drinks* industry, particularly concentrates, and increase production from 23 to 26 per cent by 1985.

In *transport* we must ensure rehabilitation of the existing fleet and adequate maintenance of equipment in order for it to function normally. We must make more effective use of transport resources; we must save fuel; we must combine and rationalise the use of various types of transport, in all sectors including by individual and private transport.

In the *rail traffic* we must give special attention to solving the problem of moving coal from Moatize to rehabilitating the Dondo-Moatize line and the Northern line, and to the Beira coal terminal. We must study and define solutions for rehabilitating the Marromeu branch line and the Muanza link. In the case of national rail traffic, priority must be given to fuel, cement, coal, limestone, stone, timber, sugar, molasses and equipment. It is also necessary to solve the problems of international traffic, with encouragement in the first place for traffic with Zimbabwe.

In 1985 we must achieve 19 per cent more tonne kilometres than in 1982, in freight traffic. The total of passengers carried should increase to 12,400,000 by 1985.

In the *port* sector we must increase the volume of cargo handled, strengthening organisation and productivity of labour and port equipment and improving the indices of the quality of port labour. In this context, we must ensure a minimum level of port productivity on coastal shipping wharves of 400 tonnes per ship day.

In *road* traffic we must coordinate work in the state and private sector, to ensure meeting transport needs for products, especially strategic goods and building materials. We must improve technical care for equipment, promote renovation of broken-down vehicles, and encourage domestic production of spare parts.

The total number of passengers carried on the road network must increase by 29 per cent by 1985.

In *shipping*, we must improve the use and organisation of sea freight in order to reduce the volume of charter. We must carry out a rehabilitation programme for necessary navigational aids and for improving access channels to the ports. It is necessary to encourage freight and passenger transport by river and lake increasing their use, particularly on the river Zambezi, and on Cahora Bassa lake and lake Niassa.

In *air* transport, we must limit foreign exchange expenditure incurred for international air traffic documents, by rationalising and minimising their use. We must improve our crop and pest spraying capacity to meet the needs of agriculture.

In *communications*, it is necessary to increase the efficiency and quality of services provided to the people and to the national economy. We must create conditions for establishing the first phase of the national telecommunications network and complete the establishment of the maritime transport network.

We must improve discipline in the area of *investment* and reduce the current dispersal of investment activity, in order to increase its efficacy on a national scale.

We must take maximum advantage of installed capacity, rehabilitating it where necessary.

Resources must be allocated with priority for small-scale projects that have an immediate effect on the people's living standards, on the country's defence and in making best use of installed capacity.

In *construction*, new building must be reduced and efforts concentrated on completing buildings in progress within shorter time-table.

In particular, we must guarantee the conclusion of the following building works within the time limits indicated:

- the Mocuba textile mill in 1985
- the farm implements factory, the first phase in 1985 and completion in 1986
- 1,700 hectares of irrigation in Nguri and Chipemba, by 1985
- the pumping station, water main, collection and water purification plant to increase water supplies for the city of Maputo, by 1985.
- the Mueda water supply in 1984
- the Nacala-Monapo-Nampula power line in 1983 and the Centre-North power line to Nampula and the Caia-Luabo-Marromeu link by 1985.

In *internal trade* the priority is to organise marketing correctly and dynamically on the rural areas, by ensuring the sale of the agricultural tools and the industrial consumer goods that are normally used in each area. We must give priority to this activity and take action to end the considerable losses that are now occurring in this process.

We must at the same time take steps to enlarge state control over wholesale trade, support and favour consumer cooperatives in retail trade and exercise strict supervision over private enterprise through control by the people and administrative, economic and financial measures. The private sector must be integrated into a single national commercial system, and must respect the concretising of FRELIMO Party decisions.

We must establish an efficient and rigorous system to control merchandise from the point of production to the consumer, to put an end to robbery and the diversion of goods onto the black-market.

By 1985 we must increase the stock of goods for sale by 20 to 23 per cent at constant prices.

The state must organise the necessary machinery to guarantee priority in supply to workers. In this way we shall be more effective in combating parasitism and we shall favour those who work.

In *foreign trade relations*, the principal aims to achieve by 1985 are:

- to ensure an increase in foreign exchange earnings by increasing exports, not only of the usual export products, but also through specific measures to stimulate the export of other potential export items
- to develop foreign trade relations with other countries on the basis of respect for economic sovereignty and the principle of mutual advantage and reciprocal benefits
- to ensure a policy of strict austerity in foreign expenditure.

A constant rise in *labour* productivity from each worker, each work collective and from the whole of society is one of the principal tasks in the present phase.

Increased productivity can be attained on the basis of the following factors:

- strengthened organisation of production and effectiveness of leadership; adoption of measures to stimulate production by linking pay to performance and quality; implementation of norms that lead to control over lost work time and iron discipline over production and labour;
- improvement of production technology, and correct and careful use of equipment, raw materials, spare parts, fuel and energy;
- training of the labour force and preparation of competent cadres in a spirit of patriotism and dedication to the revolution.

We must eliminate surplus manpower in companies and services, and avoid under-utilisation of manpower due to the partial or total stoppage of the company, reassigning the workers to other tasks and workplaces. We must reduce the excessive number of civil servants in the state apparatus.

Strict control over manpower and its correct use is a precondition for control over the wages bill, which must not grow by more than the growth in production.

We must take immediate steps for effective control over the wages bill, above all in the unproductive sector, and ensure that its increase is less than the increase in production, with priority for wage measures in the decisive sectors for the national economy.

Finance is an important instrument in the hands of the people's state to ensure practical implementation of the economic and social policy laid down by the Party.

The effects of low productivity, extravagance, indiscipline and other negative aspects of the functioning of the economy converge on the area of finance.

We must take strict measures to increase the rigour of financial control and management in the state apparatus and in the productive sector, and to punish infractions in an exemplary manner.

Spending by the state apparatus must be cut, especially on the wages front and in the consumption of imported material resources that are scarce in the national economy.

We must ensure that all available resources are concentrated in the state budget, including those provided by donations from the international community, in order to guarantee their correct use and control.

We must adopt coordinated measures with relation to finance, credit, prices, wages and employment to stimulate the increase of material production, ensure normal monetary circulation and guarantee a balanced income and expenditure for the population, and balanced finances for the state.

During 1983 we must implement the plan for business accounting, with a view to establishing economic and financial control over production.

The basic aim of *education* is to ensure successful implementation of the national education system by 1985, through application in practice of the principles and programme defined.

In *literacy and adult education,* it is necessary to match the teaching materials to the economic and social need of each region, promote the correct integration of and support to the monitors through close liaison with the community and production units, make a significant increase in the numbers of those learning literacy, and dramatically reduce the rate of drop-outs and failures.

In *general education,* we must ensure a correct social composition of the student population at each level and for each type of education.

We must also:

- raise the quality of education and reduce the number of failures and drop-outs
- strengthen the authority in schools, through the allocation of staff with pedagogical experience, and exercise adequate control of their operation through regular inspections.

In this field, we must in 1985 increase the number of admissions by some 17.5 per cent and at least double the number who graduate, in comparison with the 1982 total.

In *technical and professional education* it is necessary to:

- organise and stimulate technical and professional education for adults, developing professional training and upgrading for workers in schools and work centres;
- improve the quality, level and syllabus for the professional training of young people and workers, establishing direct links between schools and productive sectors.

In this sphere, in 1985 we must increase admissions by around 20 per cent and graduations by 9 per cent.

In *teacher training* we must graduate 6,000 to 7,000 new teachers during the next three years, representing an increase of 30 per cent in comparison with the national teaching staff in 1982.

In *higher education,* we must:

- ensure a change in the class composition of the student body at this level through holding accelerated courses for vanguard combatants and workers, and the organisation of night classes specifically designed for workers;
- consolidate the link between syllabus content and the practical reality of our country.

We must graduate 400 to 470 technicians with higher education during the next three years.

In *health* we must develop our capabilities in such a way as to be able to carry out the following tasks in 1985:

- vaccinate between 360,000 and 380,000 children against tuberculosis, covering 67 to 70 per cent of new births;
- vaccinate 66 to 70 per cent of all children between the ages of nine months and two years against measles;
- give triple and anti-poliomyelitis vaccinations to between 270,000 and 280,000 children thus covering 51 to 53 per cent of children under two years of age;
- vaccinate against tetanus between 65 and 70 per cent of all children entering the first year of primary school for the first time;
- ensure supervision and regular treatment of between 65 and 70 per cent of all notified cases of leprosy and tuberculosis;
- provide pre-natal care to between 330,000 and 350,000 pregnant women, covering 48 to 51 per cent of the estimated total;
- ensure that between 210,000 and 225,000 births take place in health units representing from 33 to 36 per cent of the estimated total of births;
- hold control clinic consultations for between 510,000 and 550,000 children from

zero to four years of age, covering from 20 to 22 per cent of the estimated number of children of this age;
- hold between 40,000 to 47,000 periodical medical examinations for workers exposed to various occupational hazards, covering 50 per cent of the workers affected;
- train 290 to 330 monitors in industrial health and safety;
- increase the number of doctors to about 490, so as to reach a ratio of the order of 28,400 inhabitants per doctor;
- extend the network of health units, giving priority to health posts, the number of which should be increased to between 1,250 and 1,350, and increase the number of hospital beds;
- equip between 220 and 240 health centres with small laboratories.

In the sphere of *information*, the mass media play a fundamental role in the development of the revolutionary process, as tools in mobilisation for the consolidation of national unity, the strengthening of the power of the worker-peasant alliance, the defence of our revolutionary conquests and the struggle against underdevelopment.

We must therefore increase the coverage of the country, disseminating national and international realities; promote the gathering and spreading of news in the new population centres; and contribute towards raising the citizens' cultural level. We must organise radio and television programmes for teaching methods and techniques that will stimulate agricultural production.

We must develop research and technical and scientific progress in every sector of activity, as a decisive contribution toward materialising the fundamental objectives defined for the national economy in these economic and social directives.

The directives for the areas of *culture* and *sport* are contained in the Report of the Central Committee. Their implementation is essential to the correct development of the Mozambican personality and the all-round training of workers and Mozambicans in general.

Activities that encourage and widen culture, physical education and sport must take place in every factory, field, school and office.

These are the most important elements in the proposed Economic and Social Directives laid before the Fourth Congress.

Now we must ask ourselves how we can make them a reality? What are the central aspects that must be emphasised in our short- and medium-term activity?

The aspects are as follows:

1. ways of solving the food problem in the countryside and the towns and of struggling against armed and unarmed bandits;
2. the role of social sectors in socio-economic development;
3. the place and tasks of provincial and district bodies in the direction and planning process;
4. man, the author and object of development.

Let us say a few words about each of these aspects.

First, the fight against hunger. It takes place, basically, through increased food production. However, this increase has different implications for the countryside and the towns. In the countryside short- and medium-term efforts are to increase production of food and in the family sector. This increase, combined with better agricultural marketing and more efficient rural procurement and supply, will allow us to combat hunger in the countryside more effectively.

In towns, short- and medium-term efforts are to increase food production in the green belts, through support to small- and medium-size holdings, whether individual, cooperative, private or state. This support must particularly focus on encouraging production of vegetables, fruit, small animals and fish.

The fight against hunger means a fight against the drought that is currently ravaging large areas of our country. The fight against drought demands firm action. What is needed, therefore, is:

- the opening of wells and boreholes for ground water;
- the storing of water in small earth and stone dams, artificial lakes, reservoirs and the like;
- the avoidance of water being wasted and the introduction of restrictions on water use;
- use of drought resistant crops such as cassava and millet, and small animals such as goats;
- strengthening of local authorities, as well as technical support and special supply to drought affected areas;
- mobilisation of internal and international support for the population of the most needy areas.

The fight against hunger is also intimately linked to the struggle against armed and unarmed bandits.

In addition to the more general activity of the Mozambican Armed Forces (FPLM) all our people and workers in particular must commit themselves:

- to the training of local defence forces, especially militias;
- to the defence and protection of economic and social targets with emphasis on the more important ones such as roads, bridges, factories, shops, communications networks, transport, cattle, farms, schools and hospitals.

We must pursue a strong fight against black-marketeers, particularly through:

- effective control over the trade circuits from the producer to the consumer;
- involvement of the people, the mass democratic organisations and local authorities in organisation and control of supply;
- special consideration for workers in all supply matters;
- increase of people's vigilance and of suppression of black-marketeers.

Achieving all these forms of combat will take us ahead in the struggle against the strategic enemy: economic and social backwardness of our country, or in brief, underdevelopment.

The second aspect requires that we make clear the role and tasks of various sectors so that each will clearly perceive the contribution it must make to the current fight.

The family sector is the one that seems to us fundamental, not so much because of the economic strength it represents to the country, but essentially because more than ten million Mozambicans live in the sector.

Their tasks are:

a. to raise subsistence production to supply their own food needs;
b. to raise production of a marketable surplus, especially of cashew, cotton and oilseeds.

The state institutions in relation to the family sector must promote:

a. effective implementation of agricultural marketing to ensure purchase of the surplus;
b. organisation of a supply network that will stimulate exchange, with due regard to the differing needs and consumer habits from place to place;
c. supply of work tools;
d. support in organisational techniques and methods.

In this whole process, the principal agents will have to be the local authorities and state enterprises based in the area.

The overall aim of these actions is the gradual transformation of the family sector into a cooperative sector.

The agricultural cooperative sector has the following tasks:

    a.   to combine collective production with family production in a correct manner in the first instance to solve food supply for peasants in the cooperative, and in the second instance to produce a surplus for direct sale to the population or for direct sale to the state sector;

    b.   put into effect democratic management of cooperatives, with the cooperative members taking on the role of owners rather than paid workers.

State institutions must support the cooperatives with emphasis on those already in existence, with the purpose of making them viable and genuinely more effective than the family sector. This means support through credit, marketing and cooperation with state enterprises.

The existing private sector in our country has the following tasks:

    a.   to raise production through the use of local raw materials and other resources;

    b.   to invest in projects that:
- increase food production;
- develop exports;
- reduce imports.

For this purpose, the state institutions must:

    a.   implement the system of contracts between private firms and state enterprises, and thus integrate private companies into the planning system;

    b.   use economic mechanisms, such as credit, prices and fiscal policy, to encourage investment in the rural areas, in green belts and in fisheries, so as to interest the private sector in production, and in the first instance in food production;

    c.   encourage foreign capital investments in sectors that increase exports, substitute imports, and train skilled workers and technicians.

The state sector has the following tasks:

    a.   to increase production, productivity in and return from existing enterprises, making them the leaders because they are more efficient and not merely because they are larger;

    b.   to become the centre of diffusion of skills to the cooperative and family sectors;

    c.   to develop its role in strategic sectors, through the new investments laid down in the Economic and Social Directives.

The third aspect to consider is the place of provinces and districts in the economic direction.

After winning power, we developed a battle in our country for genuine control of the economic instruments that would guarantee power of the worker-peasant state over the economy. Already through the central state apparatus and state enterprises we essentially dominate external trade, banking, most industry, transport, internal trade, building, [and] the education and health system. This battle entailed in the first instance establishing planning and centralised control of the principal means of production and a command of economic instruments such as the currency, credit, wages, prices and the budget. The predominance of socialist forms of production, in conjunction with the existence of a centralised plan and control over the chief economic instruments, ensures for us today the main bases and conditions for planned direction of the economy.

Despite the efforts we made in this direction, the inexperience of our cadres and the weakness of recently created structures for direction of the country have meant that we have been unable to involve local authorities and workers in this overall planning process effectively. So even today and for many of us planning ends in the Central State Plan and in the State Planning Commission.

This weakness has led us to make mistakes that were fully brought out in the Report of the Central Committee and which we must correct. Extending planning as far as the district, and making districts the main base are the struggles we must engage in for the short and medium term.

Achieving this aim presupposes equipping local bodies to direct and plan local development. In this way we shall encourage economic and social activity at province and district level, with local authorities taking responsibility to:

a.   encourage people to organise themselves in communal villages, with priority to those already in existence, especially pilot communal villages;

b.   ensure at all levels the correct integration, administration and control of the productive sector under local subordinations, especially the cooperative and family sector, in order to increase production for the market and improve the people's living conditions;

c.   rehabilitate and activate existing productive infrastructure and ensure optimum use of the human, material and financial resources available;

d.   take action in agriculture to ensure the best use of under-cultivated farmland, in a way that can raise production, ensure self-sufficiency and thus surpass planned production;

e.   give effective encouragement and support to all social sectors involved in production in the green belts round the main urban centres, and ensure that through correct use of local resources, supplies of basic commodities for the people are increased;

f.   develop small-scale industrial production at local level based on local experience and resources, primarily to increase the supplies of consumer goods and means of production for the people;

g.   build productive and social infrastructure, based on local experience and local building materials, so as to create more viable economic and social activity and solve the people's problems;

h.   ensure correct maintenance of infrastructure, such as roads, tracks, airstrips, small dams and communal services;

i.   ensure strict supervision over the circulation and distribution of goods, from the province to the locality and severely punish disregard for the guidelines laid down, with energetic measures to fight against the black-market; organise people's control of commerce.

As we advance on these lines and take concrete actions of this sort, we shall solve many of our present problems.

The fourth aspect is the need to keep in balance the essential factor, the Mozambican as he is today, his role as the author and object of development.

Comrade President Samora Moises Machel has on various occasions and in various places warned and instructed us on this point. We owe much to him for the clarity of our Party over the process of creating the New Man.

In the Theses for the Fourth Congress we returned to this fundamental principle. It is closely linked to the process of self-reliance and implementing small-scale projects. These in turn are linked to the creation of socialist relations of production.

We have today a knowledge of history and of the various forms in which the socialist revolution triumphed in different countries. We have also the reality of the existence of a socialist camp in the world, to which we already belong and which provides our strategic rearguard.

However, the creation of a socialist society today, as was our victory in the armed struggle yesterday, is the result of effort and qualitative growth in the Mozambican and of correct leadership of the revolutionary process.

Self-reliance is not a temporary policy or a last resort in the face of an absence of an easy means to enrich the country. It means above all our constant and correct working method.

Self-reliance expresses the need for us always to be ready to define ourselves and our destiny in a conscious manner; always to be in a condition to achieve a process of growth in constant equilibrium. It is a process we master, a process in which man dominates the reality around him.

This reality becomes particularly clear to us when we think, for example, of the tractor.

In our country there are Mozambicans who already handle a tractor, but it is not enough to handle a tractor. The tractor is a means of production we use to obtain economic results efficiently. For us to take advantage of this equipment presupposes the existence of material and technical conditions that ensure its good use and the obtaining of good results. Handling a tractor must mean that we master the tractor, must mean that we know about the tractor, must mean that we understand that in the history of agriculture, the tractor is the result of a long process: from the hoe one went to the harrow, then to the plough and finally to the tractor.

Thus the growth of the Mozambican is on the one hand the result of the work process and constant thinking about it. On the other hand it is the result of schooling and gradual and continuous training.

In this context, introducing the tractor without bringing negative unbalance to the process of growth means ensuring that our tractor driver is able to understand the machine and keep it in operation.

This means that the problem does not lie in introducing new and more advanced technologies into our cultural reality. The problem is how to introduce these technologies in such a way that they can be taken up, understood and made effective.

Where we neglected this consideration is where today we find the machine stopped, the lorry seized up and the tractor misused.

It is for this reason that small-scale projects are not merely a necessity arising from a scarcity of resources for large-scale development. They are a constant method of achieving our growth, on the basis of a broad mobilisation of our people and with resort to locally available capabilities.

Our small-scale projects, therefore, are totally distinct from light industrialisation dependent on external raw materials, technologies and finance, such as many countries have developed and are still developing.

Small-scale projects are not importing feed for small animals in the family sector; they are not importing small fleets of lorries for each locality; they are not importing typewriters for small offices in the districts. This way of thinking maintains and makes more acute our vulnerability to external factors, maintains and perpetuates the consumer mentality and a taste for comfort, isolates the masses from our institutions of power.

For small-scale projects to be established correctly, our local authorities, provincial governments particularly, must be involved effectively in the process of their direction, implementation and control.

In brief, the aspect to bring out is that we must act to make planning better and better, broader and broader, more and more efficient, and more and more internalised by workers and our entire people.

These are the main points we wanted to stress in presenting the Economic and Social Directives.

It is our Party's task to lead effectively the development process and to ensure that the Economic Directives are implemented by state bodies.

In the next few years class struggle in our country will become more acute. We must be quite clear that our advances will provoke the reactions of the enemy. We shall have to be more and more implacable against the enemy, in the economic sphere as well.

Defence of our country and the fight against hunger are the chief aspects of our development policy.

The victory is ours, we represent the future.

It falls to us, as militants of the FRELIMO Party, to mobilise the people to face up to the problems, make the sacrifices, defeat the difficulties, wipe out underdevelopment and build socialism.

THE REVOLUTION WILL WIN!

SOCIALISM WILL TRIUMPH!

THE STRUGGLE CONTINUES!

Notes

A.H.M.	Arquivo Histórico de Moçambique (Maputo)
A.H.U.	Arquivo Histórico Ultramarino (Lisbon)
A.I.A.	Arquivo de Instituto de Algodão (Maputo)
A.I.M.	Agência de Informação de Moçambique
A.N.T.T.	Arquivo Nacional de Torre de Tombo (Lisbon)
D.T.I.	Departamento de Trabalho Ideológico de FRELIMO
J.E.A.C.	Junta de Exportação de Algodão Colonial
M.A.G.I.C.	Mozambique, Angola, Guinea Information Centre
Z.N.A.	Zimbabwe National Archives (Harare)

CHAPTER 1. INTRODUCTION

1. See, for example, Business International, *Mozambique: On the Road to Reconstruction and Development* (Geneva, 1980), for a discussion of Mozambique's economic potential in general and mineral potential in particular. For a more negative assessment, which nevertheless confirms the country's mineral wealth, see Business Environment Risk Information, *Force Report on Mozambique* (Washington, D.C., 1981).

2. Cahora Bassa produced 2,075 megawatts annually in the early 1980s. With the construction during the 1980s of a new generating station on the northern bank of the Zambesi River, production will almost double. After independence the new government changed the name of the dam from "Cabora Bassa" to "Cahora Bassa."

3. Interview with Samora Machel, president of Mozambique, on May 7, 1979.

4. The most recent census, completed in 1980, makes no reference to ethnic group, race, or religion. Estimates derived from the 1970 census, which is not considered very reliable, give the following ethnic breakdown:

Makonde	175,000	Peoples of the Lower Zam-	900,000
Yao	170,000	besi (Sena, Tonga, etc.)	
Makua-Lomwe	3,000,000	Shona	765,000
Ngoni	35,000	Thonga	1,850,000
Malawi	250,000	Chope and Tonga	450,000

Cited in Thomas Henriksen, *Mozambique: A History* (London, 1978), p. 247.

5. Interview with Maria Teresa Veloso, Ministry of Education, on August 24, 1977.

6. United States, Agency for International Development, *Development Needs and Opportunities for Cooperation in Southern Africa* (Washington, D.C., 1979), p. 36.

CHAPTER 2. THE PRECOLONIAL PERIOD, 1500–1880

1. These hunters and gatherers, the earliest known inhabitants of the country, were referred to in the indigenous languages as Anões, Akafula, and San. Elaborate rock paintings and passing references in Bantu oral traditions are all that is left of their history.

2. The land chiefs distributed rights of usufruct, which enabled the recipient to farm the land, pick the fruit from the trees, and hunt and gather within his designated area. Neither he nor his heirs could sell the land, and when they vacated it, it reverted to the land chief for future distribution.

3. Inequality took many forms. In addition to the privileged position of the chiefs, elders commonly appropriated labor and scarce resources from junior kinsmen, and women, despite their important contributions, were often reduced to units of production and reproduction. For a general summary of the role of women in precolonial Mozambique, see Barbara Isaacman and June Stephen, *Mozambique: Women, the Law and Agrarian Reform* (Addis Ababa, 1980), pp. 7–10.

4. The Muenemutapa was not only the spiritual link with the deceased ancestors, but he himself became a national ancestor spirit (*mhondoro*) upon his death. On the appropriate religious holidays, such as the first-fruit ceremony, and in times of national crises only the Muenemutapa and the royal spirit mediums, themselves closely aligned with the ruler, had access to the deceased kings and through them to the Supreme Deity, Mwari. For a general discussion of the kingdom of the Muenemutapa see David Beach, *The Shona and Zimbabwe, 900–1850* (London, 1980); and W.G.L. Randles, *The Empire of Monomotapa from the Fifteenth to the Nineteenth Centuries* (Gwelo, 1981).

5. One seventeenth-century observer estimated that there were between 60,000 and 90,000 miners. Although undoubtedly an exaggeration, this figure does suggest the scale of the operation. Biblioteca Pública de Ajuda, 51-VIII-43: "Sobre os Rios de Cuama" (1683).

6. In a recent article, Newitt has suggested that the Maravi (Malawi) state was formed at a somewhat later period, between the late sixteenth century and the middle of the seventeenth century. M.D.D. Newitt, "The Early History of the Maravi," *Journal of African History* 23 (1982):145–162. For detailed studies of the Maravi see H. Langworthy, "A History of Undi's Kingdom to 1890: Aspects of Chewa History in East Central Africa" (Ph.D. dissertation, Boston University, 1969); and K. Phiri, "Chewa History in Central Malawi and the Use of Oral Traditions, 1600–1920" (Ph.D. dissertation, University of Wisconsin, 1975).

7. Edward A. Alpers, *Ivory and Slaves in East Central Africa* (Berkeley, Calif., 1975), p. 266. Alpers and others maintain that the roots of Mozambique's underdeveloped and distorted economy lie in this period.

8. For a contemporary description of the 1569–1572 invasion see Padre Monclaro, "Relação de Viagem Q Fizerão os pes da Companhia de Jesus com Franco Barretto na conquista de Monomotapa no anno de 1569," in *Records of South East Africa*, G. M. Theal, ed. (Capetown, 1899), 3:186–201. For a discussion of this tradition of insurgency see Allen Isaacman (in collaboration with Barbara Isaacman), *The Tradition of Resistance in Mozambique* (Berkeley, Calif., 1976).

9. Eric Axelson, *Portuguese in South-East Africa, 1600–1700* (Witwatersrand, 1960), p. 33.

10. Alpers, *Ivory and Slaves*, p. 266; Newitt, "Early History of the Maravi," p. 160.

11. For a discussion of the prazos see Allen Isaacman, *Mozambique: The Africanization of a European Institution, The Zambesi Prazos 1750–1902* (Madison, Wisc., 1972); and M.D.D. Newitt, *Portuguese Settlement on the Zambesi* (New York, 1973).

12. Frei António Conceição, "Tratados dos rios de Cuama," in *O chronista de tissuary periódico*, J. H. da Cunha Rivara, ed. (Nova Goa, 1867), 2:64–65; Beach, *Shona and Zimbabwe*, pp. 230–235.

13. Arquivo Nacional da Torre do Tombo (A.N.T.T.), Ministério do Reino, Maço 604: Inácio Caetano Xavier to governor-general, December 26, 1758.

14. For a discussion of the rise of Indian merchant capital in Mozambique see Alpers, *Ivory and Slaves*, pp. 84–94.

15. The major demand for ivory was for the manufacture of marriage bangles, which were an important part of Hindu and Indian Muslim wedding ceremonies.

16. Philip D. Curtin, *The Atlantic Slave Trade: A Census* (Madison, Wisc., 1969), pp. 241, 247.

17. Lt. R. N. Barnard, *Three Years Cruise in the Mozambique Channel* (London, 1848), p. 37. As the slave trade continued unabated throughout the nineteenth century and the fragmentary accounts of the legal trade indicate average exports of more than 10,000 per year, this figure may actually be on the conservative side.

18. For a discussion of the nineteenth-century slave trade, see Alpers, *Ivory and Slaves;* James Duffy, *A Question of Slavery* (Oxford, 1967); Nancy Hafkin, "Trade, Society and Politics in Northern Mozambique, c. 1753–1913" (Ph.D. dissertation, Boston University, 1975); Isaacman, *Mozambique;* M.D.D. Newitt, "Angoche, The Slave Trade and the Portuguese, c. 1844–1910," *Journal of African History* 13 (1972):659–672; H. Leroy Vail and Landeg White, *Capitalism and Colonialism in Mozambique* (Minneapolis, 1980), pp. 7–41.

19. Edward Alpers, "Trade, State and Society Among the Yao in the Nineteenth Century," *Journal of African History* 10 (1969):411–412; Patrick Harries, "Slavery, Social Incorporation and Surplus Extraction," *Journal of African History* 22 (1981):309–330; and Isaacman, *Tradition of Resistance,* pp. 22–49.

20. Quoted in Eric Axelson, *Portugal and the Scramble for Africa* (Johannesburg, 1967), p. 14.

21. Arquivo Histórico Ultramarino (A.H.U.), Moçambique, Maço 25: Joaquim Mendes de Vasconcelos e Cirne to Paulo José Miguel de Brito, March 6, 1830.

22. David Livingston, *Missionary Travels and Research in South Africa* (London, 1857), p. 637.

23. For a discussion of these early conflicts see Axelson, *Portugal and the Scramble;* Isaacman, *Tradition of Resistance;* Newitt, "Angoche, the Slave Trade and the Portuguese"; and José Justino Texeira Botelho, *História militar e política dos portugueses em Moçambique,* 2 vols. (Lisbon, 1934–1936).

24. For a discussion of British economic penetration in southern Mozambique see Jeanne Penvenne, "Forced Labor and the Origin of an African Working Class: Lourenço Marques, 1870–1962" (Boston University, African Studies Center, Working Paper No. 13, 1979).

25. Lisbon suffered humiliating defeats at the hands of the Yao in 1891, of the sultanate of Angoche in 1893, and of the Makua in 1896. Botelho, *História militar e política,* 2:230–231; João de Azevedo Coutinho, *As duas conquistas de Angoche* (Lisbon, 1935), p. 32; Hafkin, "Trade and Society," pp. 367–373.

26. For a discussion of the wars of independence in northern Mozambique see Hafkin, "Trade and Society," pp. 359–403; and Newitt, "Angoche, the Slave Trade and the Portuguese."

27. Augusto de Castilho, *Relatório de guerra da Zambézia em 1888* (Lisbon, 1891), p. 37.

28. João de Azevedo Coutinho, *A campanha do Barue* (Lisbon, 1904), pp. 36–37. Interview with Chief Makosa on July 12, 1972; interview with Sande Nyandoro on August 1, 1972; interview with Stephen Mugumedza on July 19, 1972; and interview with Blacken Makombe on August 2, 1972. For a discussion of the Barue war see Coutinho, *A campanha do Barue,* and Isaacman, *Tradition of Resistance.*

29. For a detailed account of the actual military campaign see António Enes, *A guerra de Africa* (Porto, 1945); and Botelho, *História militar e política,* 2:419–504. On the Maguiguane uprising see J. Mousinho de Albuquerque, *A campanha contra o Maguiguana nos territórios da Gaza, 1897* (Lourenço Marques, n.d.).

30. Isaacman, *Tradition of Resistance,* pp. 37–38.

31. Douglas Wheeler, "Gungunyane the Negotiator," *Journal of African History* 9 (1968):587–602.

32. Hafkin, "Trade and Society," pp. 359–403; Isaacman, *Tradition of Resistance,* pp. 23–55; and Newitt, *Portuguese Settlement,* pp. 234–351.

CHAPTER 3. THE COLONIAL PERIOD, 1900-1962

1. In 1907 the principal districts were Lourenço Marques (including the region of Gaza), Inhambane, Tete, Moçambique, and Quelimane. The districts were restructured in

1947 into ten provinces—Lourenço Marques, Gaza, Inhambane, Sofala, Manica, Tete, Zambézia, Moçambique, Niassa, and Cabo Delgado—with the holdings of the defunct concessionary companies incorporated into this administrative system.

2. Europeans, primarily Portuguese living in the two cities, participated in international commerce or local trade or worked as artisans. A small number were involved in manufacturing beer, cement, charcoal, and other consumer goods. Beyond these two urban centers, Portuguese and Asian merchants were scattered throughout the interior, and small European farming communities were located in the fertile southern river valley, Inhambane, the Manica highlands, and north of the Zambesi River. Along the coast, Europeans of several nationalities organized sisal, copra, and sugar plantations.

3. Carlos Weise, "Zambesia—A Labour Question em Nossa Casa," *Boletim da Sociedade de Geografia de Lisboa* 25 (1907):244.

4. See Jorge Dias, *Os Macondes de Moçambique* (Lisbon, 1964).

5. Zimbabwe National Archives (Z.N.A.), N3/26/2/6/8: Statement of Shongorisho as recorded by H. A. Taberer, May 7, 1917.

6. For a general discussion of the administrative and legal system see Great Britain, Admiralty, *A Manual of Portuguese East Africa* (London, 1921), pp. 139–148.

7. Jeanne Penvenne, "Forced Labor and the Origin of an African Working Class: Lourenço Marques, 1870–1962" (Boston University, African Studies Center, Working Paper No. 13, 1979), pp. 3–4.

8. Quoted in J. M. da Silva Cunha, *O trabalho indígena: Estudo do direito colonial* (Lisbon, 1949), p. 144.

9. In nominally controlled parts of the colony tax laws date back at least to 1878 (Arquivo Histórico de Moçambique [A.H.M.], Fundo do Século XIX, Governo Geral, Cx. 1: Governador de Quelimane to Secretário Geral do Governador, February 4, 1886).

10. See, for example, H. Leroy Vail and Landeg White, *Capitalism and Colonialism in Mozambique* (Minneapolis, 1980), pp. 136–137; Allen Isaacman, *Mozambique: The Africanization of a European Institution, The Zambesi Prazos 1750–1902* (Madison, Wisc., 1972), pp. 161–182.

11. See, for example, J. Mouzinho de Albuquerque, *Moçambique 1896–1898* (Lisbon, 1913), p. 298; A. Rita Ferreira, *O movimento migratório de trabalhadores entre Moçambique e Africa do Sul* (Lisbon, 1963); Penvenne, "Forced Labor"; Ruth First et al., *The Mozambican Miner* (Maputo, 1977); David Webster, "The Origins of Migrant Labour, Colonialism and Underdevelopment in Southern Mozambique," in *Working Papers in Southern African Studies, 1977*, P. Bonner, ed. (Witwatersrand, 1979); Patrick Harries, "Labour Migration from the Delagoa Bay Hinterland to South Africa," in *The Societies of Southern Africa in the Nineteenth and Twentieth Centuries*, University of London, Institute of Commonwealth Studies, ed. (London, 1977), 7:61–76.

12. Quoted in Cunha, *O trabalho indígena*, p. 151.

13. Joint interview with Makwate Simba, Xavier Jossene, Mondwal Muene, and Amelia Macuacua on February 13, 1979; interview with Benjamin Mavunga on February 12, 1979; and interview with Nhacatala on July 28, 1979. See also Edward Alsworth Ross, *Report on Employment of Native Labor in Portuguese Africa* (New York, 1925), pp. 40–60.

14. Ross, *Report on Employment*, p. 40.

15. Ibid., pp. 40–60; Penvenne, "Forced Labor," p. 10.

16. *L. M. Guardian* (Lourenço Marques), May 1919; *O Africano* (Lourenço Marques), May 7, 1919.

17. For a general discussion of the agreement, see James Duffy, *A Question of Slavery* (Oxford, 1967), pp. 137–188.

18. Ibid., p. 158; P. R. Warhurst, "The Tete Agreement," *Rhodesian History* 7 (1970): 32–42.

19. The Zambesi Company's relationship to the state was somewhat different, as it did not receive a charter to administer its territory. Rather, it absorbed and leased out the *prazos* to estateholders who assumed de facto political authority over the indigenous population residing on their land.

20. Arquivo do Instituto de Algodão (A.I.A.), Junta de Exportação de Algodão Colonial (J.E.A.C.): "Província de Manica e Sofala," João Contreiras, O Inspector de JEAC, May 1945.

For a discussion of the Mozambique Company, see Barry Neil-Tomlinson, "The Growth of a Colonial Economy and the Development of African Labour: Manica and Sofala and the Mozambique Chartered Company, 1892–1954," in *Mozambique* (Proceedings of a Seminar at the Center of African Studies, University of Edinburgh, 1979); Leroy Vail, "Mozambique's Chartered Companies: The Rule of the Feeble," *Journal of African History*, 17 (1976):389–416.

21. Quoted in Vail, "Mozambique's Chartered Companies," p. 401.

22. Ibid., p. 400.

23. For a discussion of the Zambesi Company see Thomas Henriksen, *Mozambique: A History* (London, 1978), pp. 104–107; and Vail and White, *Capitalism and Colonialism in Mozambique*.

24. Between 1918 and 1920, for example, the price of rice, beans, soap, potatoes, and other staples doubled. On the other hand, during the 1920s the price of Mozambique's major export crops—copra, tea, sisal, sugar, and cotton—plummeted. *O Brado Africano* (Lourenço Marques), June 19, 1920; C. F. Spence, *Mozambique, East African Province of Portugal* (Capetown, 1963), p. 89; Alan Smith, "Antonio Salazar and the Reversal of Portuguese Colonial Policy," *Journal of African History* 25 (1974):660–661; and Vail and White, *Capitalism and Colonialism in Mozambique*, pp. 229–231.

25. Quoted in Keith Middlemas, "Europeans in Mozambique," *Tarikh* 6 (1980):34.

26. Manuel Brito Camacho, *Moçambique* (Lisbon, 1926); Manuel Brito Camacho, *Política Colonial* (Lisbon, 1938); and Smith, "Antonio Salazar," pp. 656–660.

27. For a discussion of the factors leading to the coup as well as the policy of the military junta see Douglas Wheeler, *Republican Portugal* (Madison, Wisc., 1978), pp. 214–253.

28. Quoted in C. R. Boxer, *Race Relations in the Portuguese Colonial Empire* (Oxford, 1963), p. 1. For an excellent critique of Luso-tropicalism, see Gerald Bender, *Angola Under the Portuguese* (Berkeley, Calif., 1978).

29. Quoted in James Duffy, *Portuguese Africa* (Cambridge, 1961), p. 368.

30. *Codigo Administrativo da Colonia de Moçambique* (Lisbon, 1938); Diploma Legislativo No. 162, *Boletim Oficial de Moçambique*, 22, 1ª series, June 1, 1929. This legislation on the *indigenato* was modified in certain respects by the Estatuto dos Indigenas Portuguese das Províncias da Guinea, Angola e Moçambique, Decreto-Lei no. 39.666 (1954).

31. Armindo Monteiro, *Da governção de Angola* (Lisbon, 1935), pp. 108–109.

32. Rui Balthazar, "The Judiciary Machinery Under Colonialism," in *Principles of Revolutionary Justice*, A. Sachs, ed. (London, 1979), p. 9.

33. United States, Department of State, NEA-4: "The Labor Movement in Mozambique—Basic Report," Ralph W. Richardson, U.S. vice-consul in Mozambique, March 29, 1955.

34. Ibid.; and *Regulamento de trabalho dos indígenas na colonia de Moçambique* (Lourenço Marques, 1929).

35. José Tristão de Bettencourt, *Relatório do Governador Geral de Moçambique* (Lisbon, 1945), 2:86.

36. For a critique of Portuguese labor policy see Marvin Harris, *Portugal's African "Wards"* (New York, 1958).

37. John Gunther, *Inside Africa* (London, 1951), pp. 586–587.

38. Interview with Pruan Hassan on July 27, 1979.

39. Group interview in Alto Molocué on July 16 and 17, 1976. (This interview was collected by Judith Head and is on deposit at the African Studies Center, Eduardo Mondlane University.)

40. See United States Department of State, AE-5: "Annual Labor Report for 1960," William H. Taft, U.S. consul in Mozambique, May 11, 1961; and Harris, *Portugal's African "Wards."*

41. These production figures were extracted from Colonia de Moçambique, *Recenseamento agrícola de 1929–1930* (Lourenço Marques, 1934); and Portugal, Província de Moçambique, Direcção dos Serviços de Economia e Estatística Geral, *Estatística Agrícola*, Ano 20 (Lourenço Marques, 1959), pp. 184–185.

42. United States, Department of State, COM-10: "Economic Review," Donald W. Lamm, consul general in Mozambique, February 23, 1954. For a detailed discussion of Portuguese immigration see Bender, *Angola Under the Portuguese*.

43. Until 1961 peasants were forced to cultivate and sell their rice to concessionary companies at fixed prices imposed by the state. The companies then milled the rice and sold it to the government.

44. The official figure is slightly less than 700,000, but it does not include the large number of minors and elders who also worked in their assigned family cotton fields.

45. For a discussion of the cotton regime see Nelson Saraiva Bravo, *A cultura algodoeira na economia do norte de Moçambique* (Lisbon, 1963); Allen Isaacman, Michael Stephen, et al., "Cotton Is the Mother of Poverty—Peasant Resistance to Forced Cotton Production in Mozambique, 1938–1961," *International Journal of African Historical Studies* 13 (1980):581–615.

46. Quoted in Eduardo Mondlane, *The Struggle for Mozambique* (Baltimore, 1969), p. 85.

47. Quoted in George Houser and Herb Shore, *Mozambique: Dream the Size of Freedom* (New York, 1975), p. 11.

48. United Nations, General Assembly, A/AC.109/1.388/Add. 2: "Territories Under Portuguese Control," April 21, 1967, p. 21.

49. Ibid., p. 9.

50. United States, Department of State, AE-5: "Annual Labor Report for 1960," William H. Taft, U.S. consul in Mozambique, May 11, 1960.

51. See Diploma Legislativo No. 238, Governador Geral, José Cabral, May 17, 1930, reprinted in *O ensino indígena na colonia de Moçambique* (Lourenço Marques, 1930), p. 6.

52. Mouzinho de Albuquerque, *Moçambique*, p. 508.

53. Quoted in Henriksen, *Mozambique*, pp. 144–145.

54. Quoted in Governo do Território da Companhia de Moçambique, "Relatório sobre a instrucção pública e projecto da sua reforma" (typed report, 1930).

55. Eduardo Sousa Ferreira, *Portuguese Colonialism in Africa: The End of an Era* (Paris, 1974), pp. 66–73.

56. Ibid.; Mondlane, *Struggle for Mozambique*, pp. 62–64; interview with Sarifi Amati on August 22, 1977; and interview with Francisco Sumaila on August 22, 1977.

57. Quoted in Mondlane, *Struggle for Mozambique*, p. 72.

58. "Interview with Dr. Helder Martins," *World Medicine*, 12 (January 26, 1977):22.

59. Hilary Flegg Mitchell, "Aspects of Urbanization and Age Structure in Lourenço Marques (Maputo), 1957," (University of Zambia, Institute for African Studies, 1975), p. 22.

60. Interview with Dr. Aires Fernandes, August 27, 1977.

61. A.I.A., J.E.A.C., Zona Algodoeira Inhambane (Jangomo), Confidencial 1947: Dias de Deus, Regente Agrícola, October 1947.

62. A.I.A., J.E.A.C., Papeis Diversos, 1941; J. Anachoreta, Chefe da Sub-Delegação do Sul de Save, September 1941.

63. Barbara Isaacman and June Stephen, *Mozambique: Women, the Law and Agrarian Reform* (Addis Ababa, 1980), pp. 11–12; group interview, Communal Village 7 de Abril, on June 6, 1979; group interview, Communal Village Paulo Samuel Kankhombe, on June 7, 1979.

64. A.I.A., J.E.A.C., Papeis Diversos, 1941; J. Anachoreta, Chefe da Sub-Delegação do Sul de Save, September 1941.

65. Jacques May and Donna L. McLellan, *The Ecology of Malnutrition in Seven Countries of Southern Africa and in Portuguese Guinea* (New York, 1971), p. 263.

66. A.I.A., J.E.A.C., Confidencial 1957–1959; Gastino de Mello Furtado to Presidente de J.E.A.C., September 1959.

67. May and McLellan, *Ecology of Malnutrition*, p. 275; R. Morgaod, "Main Food Areas and Nutritional Diseases in Mozambique," *Comptes-Rendus du Troisième Congres de l'Association Scientifique des Pays de Ocean Indian* (Tananarive, 1957), pp. 59–61.

68. United States, Department of State, COM-12: "Economic Review, 1955," March 6, 1956.

69. Moçambique, *Anuário Estatístico, 1966* (Lourenço Marques, 1967), pp. 284–285.

70. See Allen Isaacman, "The Mozambican Cotton Cooperative: An Alternative to Forced Commodity Production," *African Studies Review*, 24 (1982):5–25.

71. Isaacman and Stephen, *Mozambique: Women*, pp. 12–13.

72. See Jeanne Marie Penvenne, "A History of African Labor in Lourenço Marques, 1877 to 1950" (Ph.D. dissertation, Boston University, 1982), pp. 277–282.

73. Mitchell, "Aspects of Urbanization," p. 4.

74. Penvenne, "History of African Labor," pp. 269–276.

75. United States, Department of State, COM-12: William H. Taft III, U.S. consul general in Mozambique, March 12, 1961.

76. Mondlane, *Struggle for Mozambique*, p. 44.
77. A.H.M., Fundo do Governo do Distrito de L.M., Cx. 358: Júlio dos Santos Peixe to Secretário Geral, April 5, 1958.
78. José Capela, *O Vinho Para o Preto* (Porto, 1973), p. 166.
79. Isaacman and Stephen, *Mozambique: Women*, pp. 12–13.

CHAPTER 4. POPULAR OPPOSITION TO COLONIAL RULE, 1900-1962

1. Interview with Anjate on June 8, 1979.
2. Alfredo Augusto Caldas Xavier, *Estudos coloniães* (Nova Goa, 1889), pp. 25–26; and Joaquim Nunes, "Apontamentos para o estudo da questão da mão d'obra no Districto de Inhambane," *Boletim da Sociedade de Geografia de Lisboa* 46 (1928):116.
3. Arquivo de Tete, Documentos Diversos, Circumscrição Civil da Marávia: "Relatório da Administração referente ao anno do 1928, documento no. 8, Manoel Arnaldo Ribeiro to Administrador Manoel Alves Viana."
4. Nunes, "Apontamentos," p. 116.
5. Xavier, *Estudos coloniães*, pp. 25–26.
6. Carlos Wiese, "Zambézia—A Labour Question em Nossa Casa," *Boletim da Sociedade de Geografia de Lisboa* 25 (1907):241–243; Leroy Vail, "Mozambique's Chartered Companies: The Rule of the Feeble," *Journal of African History* 18 (1976):402.
7. Z.N.A., L5/5/28: General Letter No. A259: Assistant Native Commissioner, North Mazoe, "Report for the month ended 30 September 1904."
8. Vail, "Mozambique's Chartered Companies," p. 400.
9. Districto de Inhambane, *Relatório do Governador 1902-1909* (Lourenço Marques, 1909), p. 67.
10. Vail, "Mozambique's Chartered Companies," p. 402.
11. H. Leroy Vail and Landeg White, *Capitalism and Colonialism in Mozambique* (Minneapolis, 1980), p. 367.
12. A.I.A., J.E.A.C., Papeis Diversos: Despacho, J. Anachoreta, Chefe do Sub-delegado do Sul de Save, June 12, 1942.
13. This is a conservative estimate. In addition to the 380,000 Mozambicans in Nyasaland, there were thought to be 200,000 who clandestinely emigrated to South Africa and Southern Rhodesia. Mondlane estimated that there were more than 100,000 permanently residing in Tanganyika, Zanzibar, and Kenya, plus a smaller number in Northern Rhodesia. Panaf Great Lives, *Eduardo Mondlane* (London, 1972), p. 154.
14. Interview with Pruan Hassan on July 20, 1979.
15. Z.N.A., N3/17/7: W. H. Milton to general officer commanding Rhodesian field forces, July 20, 1900.
16. Quoted in T. O. Ranger, "The Last Days of the Empire of the Muenemutapa" (unpublished paper presented at the Central African History People's Conference, Lusaka, 1963), p. 16.
17. Allen Isaacman, "Social Banditry in Zimbabwe (Rhodesia) and Mozambique 1884–1907: An Expression of Early Peasant Protest," *Journal of Southern African Studies* 4 (1977):1–30. A number of other social bandits operated in the Zambesi Valley and adjacent regions. Dambakushamba, Mapondera's successor, struck repeatedly at government holdings and European concessionary companies from 1903 to 1907 and enjoyed the support of peasants throughout the Changara-Chioco region. They provided food, shelter, and strategic information that enabled Dambakushamba's forces to avoid detection. Ibid.
18. Edward Alsworth Ross, *Report on Employment of Native Labor in Portuguese Africa* (New York, 1925), p. 50.
19. Districto de Inhambane, *Relatório do Governador 1913-1915* (Lourenço Marques, 1916), p. 41.
20. A.I.A., J.E.A.C., Confidencial: October 28, 1939.
21. Group interview at Muide compound on November 14, 1976; and interveiw with Manuel Sabo on November 16, 1976. (Both of these interviews were collected by Judith Head.)

22. A.I.A., J.E.A.C., Confidencial 1947; Sub-delegado J.E.A.C., Beira, António Mira Mendes to Chefe da Delegação da J.E.A.C., December 20, 1947.

23. See, for example, Allen Isaacman, Michael Stephen et al., "Cotton Is the Mother of Poverty—Peasant Resistance to Forced Cotton Production in Mozambique, 1938–1961," *International Journal of African Historical Studies* 13 (1980):581–615.

24. A.H.U., Moçambique, Repartição Militar 1914–1917, fol. 85; Chiutica to Chefe de Gabinete, January 27, 1918.

25. See Allen Isaacman (in collaboration with Barbara Isaacman), *The Tradition of Resistance in Mozambique* (Berkeley, Calif., 1976), pp. 156–185.

26. José Alberto Gomes de Melo Branquinho, *Prospecção das forças tradicionais* (Nampula, 1966), pp. 81–82, 108, 114, 193.

27. For Boyte and Evans, "free social space" represents the "collective terrain, a part of a group's everyday life . . . that nonetheless retain[s] an important measure of insulation from elite cultural, organizational, and political domination. Politicized in a new way by specific historical developments, free social spaces begin to function as centers for a group's consciousness of insurgent democratic values, skills, and ideals." Sara M. Evans and Harry C. Boyte, "Schools for Action: Radical Uses of Social Space," *Democracy* 2 (Fall 1982):58.

28. Quoted in Eduardo Mondlane, *The Struggle for Mozambique* (Baltimore, 1969), p. 103.

29. For a discussion of these songs of protest see Vail and White, *Capitalism and Colonialism in Mozambique*, pp. 339–358.

30. The best collection of these carvings is to be found in the Nampula Museum in the city of Nampula.

31. For an important examination of the contradictory role of the white labor movement see José Capela, *O Movimento Operário em Lourenço Marques, 1910–1927* (forthcoming).

32. *Os Simples* (Lourenço Marques), June 24, 1911.

33. Jeanne Penvenne, "Preliminary Chronology of Labor Resistance in Lourenço Marques" (unpublished ms., n.d.), pp. 1–3. For the definitive study of the urban working class in Lourenço Marques and its struggles see Jeanne Marie Penvenne, "A History of African Labor in Lorenço Marques, Mozambique, 1877 to 1950" (Ph.D. dissertation, Boston University, 1982).

34. Jeanne Penvenne, "The Streetcorner Press: Worker Intelligence Networks in Lourenço Marques, 1906–1924" (Boston University African Studies Center, Working Paper No. 26, 1980), pp. 8–9.

35. See Penvenne, "History of African Labor," pp. 334–390.

36. Quoted in Jeanne Penvenne, "Labor Struggles at the Port of Lourenço Marques, Mozambique, 1900–1933" (unpublished paper, n.d.), p. 20.

37. *Herald Tribune* (New York), November 26, 1952, p. 16; Mondlane, *Struggle for Mozambique,* pp. 115–116; and interviews with Mussone Mulane, Manuel Cossa, and Marrulane Mondjane on March 2, 1978.

38. Mondlane, *Struggle for Mozambique,* pp. 115–116.

39. See Charles Van Onselen, *Chibaro* (London, 1976); A.H.M., Negócios Indígenas, Cx. 59, Processo 21: J. Serrão de Azevedo, Curado, to Intendente dos Negócios Indígenas e Emigração, July 29, 1913; and John Iliffe, "A History of the Dockworkers of Dar es Salaam," *Tanzania Notes and Records* 71 (1970):119–148.

40. Gregory Pirio, "The Role of Garveyism in the Making of the Southern African Working Classes and Namibian Nationalism" (unpublished paper presented at the Social Science Research Council–sponsored Conference on South Africa and the Comparative Study of Race, Class and Nationalism, New York, September 1982), pp. 21–22.

41. Branquinho, *Prospecção,* p. 77.

42. Ibid., pp. 73–80.

43. Ibid.; Eduardo Moreira, *Portuguese East Africa: A Study of Its Religious Needs* (London, 1936), pp. 38–39; H. Ivan Ferraz de Freitas, *Seitas religiosas gentílicas,* 3 vols. (Lourenço Marques, 1956–1957).

44. Freitas, *Seitas religiosas gentílicas,* 2:32–35.

45. Ibid., 2:134.

46. M.D.D. Newitt, *Portugal in Africa* (Essex, 1981), p. 131; Branquinho, *Prospecção,* pp. 56, 81, 108.

47. *O Brado Africano* (Lourenço Marques), December 24, 1926.

48. Ibid., February 28, 1925.

49. Ibid., February 28, 1925; December 13, 1924; and July 30, 1927; Jeanne Penvenne, "The Impact of Forced Labor on the Development of an African Working Class: Lourenço Marques, 1870–1972" (unpublished paper presented at the meeting of the African Studies Association, 1978), p. 10.

50. Quoted in Jeanne Penvenne, "Attitudes Toward Race and Work in Mozambique: Lourenço Marques, 1900–1974" (Boston University, African Studies Center, Working Paper No. 16, 1979), p. 10.

51. *O Brado Africano*, February 27, 1931. The English translation is taken from James Duffy, *Portuguese Africa* (Cambridge, 1959), p. 305.

52. Interview with Luís Bernado Honwana, October 3 and 4, 1981; and Russell Hamilton, *Voices from an Empire* (Minneapolis, 1975), pp. 164–167. For an alternative explanation of *O Brado Africano's* demise, see Elaine A. Friedland, "Mozambican Nationalist Resistance," *Afrika Zamani* 8-9 (1978):165–168.

During this period a small number of Mozambican intellectuals living in Portugal helped to form organizatións that were linked to the larger Pan-African movement. The most important were the Liga Africana and the Partido Nacional Africano. Liga Africana maintained close ties with W.E.B. DuBois's Pan-African Congress; Partido Nacional Africano sympathized more with Garveyism. Neither, however, had any substantial following in the colony.

Consider the career of João Albasini, an editor of both *O Africano* and *O Brado Africano*. The son of a well-to-do Italian merchant and a Ronga woman related to an important indigenous royal family, he was one of a small number of mulattoes with access to higher education and became part of the inner circle of Grémio Africano, a literary and cultural organization. Although he quickly gained a reputation as the champion of the downtrodden, he had no difficulty reconciling his moral opposition to the abuses of forced labor with his state position as overseer of African labor recruiters at the Lourenço Marques port. According to Penvenne, who interviewed numerous dockworkers, Albasini is remembered as a brutal man who "earned money by selling people" and "who taught the Portuguese *chibalo*." Her conclusion that Albasini "subscribed to the proposition that idle, ignorant African peasants must be forced to build a more prosperous Mozambique but that the government should properly house, feed and transport these workers and pay them" suggests the fundamental antagonism separating the embryonic African and mulatto bourgeoisie from the masses of African workers and peasants. See Penvenne, "Impact of Forced Labor," p. 21.

53. Throughout the remainder of the colonial period, *O Brado Africano* continued to publish, although it was totally divorced from insurgent literary activities. It was reduced to a state-sponsored journal highlighting Portugal's commitment to multiracialism and emphasizing the material and social advances of the leading families. As one contemporàry noted in 1960, "Although this paper is still in circulation today and is still the only Mozambican African paper, it has been thoroughly emasculated by the fascist government of Salazar so that it no longer says anything meaningful." Eduardo Mondlane, "The Development of Nationalism in Mozambique," in *Emerging Nationalism in Portuguese Africa*, Ronald Chilcote, ed. (Stanford, 1972), pp. 396–397.

54. Translated and reproduced in Luís Bernardo Honwana, "The Role of Poetry in the Mozambican Revolution," *Lotus: Afro-Asian Writings* 8 (1971):153.

55. Translated and reproduced in Margaret Dickinson, ed., *When Bullets Begin to Flower* (Nairobi, 1972), pp. 75–76.

56. Ibid., p. 69.

57. Translated and reproduced in Mondlane, *Struggle for Mozambique*, p. 110.

58. Ibid., pp. 70–74.

59. Interview with Luís Bernardo Honwana on October 3, 1981.

60. Mondlane, *Struggle for Mozambique*, p. 113.

61. Interview with Luís Bernardo Honwana, March 11, 1979; interview with Esperança Abiatar Muthemba, April 15, 1979; interview with Albino Magaia on June 7, 1979; and interview with Aquino de Bragança on June 7, 1979. (All but the first interview were conducted by Isabel Maria Casimiro as part of a senior seminar on popular resistance at Eduardo Mondlane University.)

62. Ibid.

CHAPTER 5. THE STRUGGLE FOR
INDEPENDENCE, 1962-1975

1. For an outline of these nationalist organizations see Ronald Chilcote, *Emerging Nationalism in Portuguese Africa* (Stanford, Calif., 1972), pp. 383-445; and Thomas Henriksen, *Mozambique: A History* (London, 1978), pp. 169-172.

2. Interviews with Justino João Benifácio on August 2, 1979; Cornélio João Mandande on July 30, 1979; and Zacarias Vanomba on August 2, 1979.

3. Quoted in Eduardo Mondlane, *The Struggle for Mozambique* (Baltimore, 1969), p. 118.

4. Quoted in Chilcote, *Emerging Nationalism*, p. 427.

5. For biographical accounts see Panaf Great Lives, *Eduardo Mondlane* (London, 1972); Thomas Henriksen, "The Revolutionary Thought of Eduardo Mondlane," *Genève-Afrique* 12 (1973):377-399; H. Kitchen, "Conversation with Eduardo Mondlane," *Africa Report* 12, 8 (1967):31-32, 49-51; Ronald Chilcote, "Eduardo Mondlane and the Mozambique Struggle," *Africa Today* 12 (1965):4-8.

6. Interview with Luís Bernardo Honwana on October 3, 1981.

7. Editorial, "25th of June, The Starting Point," *Mozambique Revolution* 51 (1972):1.

8. Ibid.

9. Aquino de Bragança, "A lutte de classes et l'émergence du marxisme au Mozambique" (unpublished paper, n.d.), pp. 1-7; Edward Alpers, "The Struggle for Socialism in Mozambique, 1960-1972," in *Socialism in Sub-Saharan Africa*, Carl G. Rosberg and Thomas A. Callaghy, eds. (Berkeley, Calif., 1979), pp. 267-277. For some different interpretations of these splits see Walter C. Opello, Jr., "Pluralism and Elite Conflict in an Independent Movement: FRELIMO in the 1960's," *Journal of Southern African Studies* 2 (1976):65-82; and Barry Munslow, "Leadership in the Front for the Liberation of Mozambique," *Southern Africa Research in Progress* (proceedings of a seminar at York University, 1978), pp. 118-138.

10. Among the initial breakaway parties were a resurrected UDENAMO, Monomotapa, MANCO, FUNIPAMO, and MORECO. None commanded a sufficient following to challenge FRELIMO's preeminent position. Most of these organizations ended up in disarray, with surviving elements coalescing in 1965 into COREMO—Comité Revolucionário de Moçambique—based in Lusaka, Zambia. For a useful summary of these exile machinations see Henriksen, *Mozambique*, pp. 175-177.

11. Quoted in Barbara Cornwall, *The Bush Rebels* (London, 1973), pp. 56-67.

12. Interview with Caciano Salósio on July 23, 1979.

13. Interview with Amade Sique Ibraimo on July 30, 1979.

14. Quoted in Cornwall, *Bush Rebels*, p. 65.

15. Quoted in Mondlane, *Struggle for Mozambique*, p. 149.

16. H. Kitchen, "Conversation with Eduardo Mondlane," p. 50.

17. John Saul, "The Revolution in Portugal's African Colonies," in idem, *The State and Revolution in Eastern Africa* (New York, 1979), p. 38.

18. Published in *Daily Telegraph* (London), September 21, 1966. After an investigation in 1964 revealed that Milas was actually a black American named Leo Clinton Aldridge, he was expelled from FRELIMO.

19. For primary documentation on this ideological split see S. Machel, *A Nossa Luta* (Maputo, 1975); FRELIMO, *Documentos Base de FRELIMO* (Maputo, 1976).

20. Typed draft speech by Dr. Eduardo Mondlane at the Mediterranean Congress for Culture, Florence, July 25, 1964.

21. Quoted in Cornwall, *Bush Rebels*, pp. 53-54.

22. *Mozambique Revolution* 51 (1972):16.

23. Quoted in Alpers, "Struggle for Socialism," p. 277.

24. Reprinted in Departamento de Trabalho Ideológico de FRELIMO (D.T.I.), *O processo revolucionário da guerra popular de libertação* (Maputo 1977), p. 101.

25. Mondlane, *Struggle for Mozambique*, p. 149.

26. *Mozambique Revolution* 51(1972):18. Interview with Eduardo José Macore on August 19, 1980; interview with Jaime on August 19, 1980; and interview with Cocote Zimu on July 23, 1979.

27. Marcelino dos Santos, "FRELIMO Faces the Future," *African Communist* 55 (1973):28.

28. Sérgio Vieira, "Law in the Liberated Zones," in *Principles of Revolutionary Justice,* A. Sachs, ed. (London, 1979), p. 13.

29. See Barbara Isaacman and June Stephen, *Mozambique: Women, the Law and Agrarian Reform* (Addis Ababa, 1980), pp. 8–19.

30. Quoted in *Mozambique Revolution* 26 (1966):2.

31. Interviews with Juliana Lais, Hirondina Romas, and Marcelina Joaquim, members of the Women's Detachment, on April 25, 1979; interviews with Horténcia Tina Miguel, Joaquina Felix Tobias and Rosa Savid Chitungula, ex-members of the Women's Detachment, on April 28, 1979.

32. Quoted in Centro de Estudos Africanos, "Towards a History of the National Liberation Struggle in Mozambique: Problematics, Methodologies, Analyses" (unpublished paper presented at the UNESCO Conference on Southern Africa, Maputo, August 1982).

33. Quoted in Mondlane, *Struggle for Mozambique,* p. 186. Ex-guerrillas expressed similar sentiments in a number of interviews. Interviews with Juliana Lais, Hirondina Romas, and Marcelina Joaquim, members of the Women's Detachment, on April 25, 1979; interviews with Horténcia Tina Miguel, Joaquina Felix Tobias, Rosa Savid Chitungula, ex-members of the Women's Detachment, on April 28, 1979.

34. *Mozambique Revolution* 45 (1970):18–19; 52 (1972):11–12.

35. Cornwall, *Bush Rebels,* p. 93.

36. Slowly a new political network was built in which these elected representatives of *circulos* went to district meetings at which, in turn, members were elected to provincial councils that had strong links to the FRELIMO National Congress. Although additional research is necessary on the actual operation of these legislative bodies, it is clear that both these councils and the embryonic legal system were critical aspects of a state-in-the-making. (For a discussion of the legal system see Barbara Isaacman and Allen Isaacman, "A Socialist Legal System in the Making: Mozambique Before and After Independence," in *The Politics of Informal Justice,* Richard Abel, ed. [New York, 1982] 2:281–323.)

37. Mondlane, *Struggle for Mozambique,* p. 175.

38. Interview with Maria Teresa Veloso, Ministry of Education, on August 24, 1977; and *Mozambique Revolution* 51 (1972):21–22.

39. Ibid.

40. "Interview with Dr. Helder Martins," *World Medicine* 2 (January 26, 1977):22.

41. *Mozambique Revolution* 51 (1972):25.

42. Interview with Cocote Zamu on July 23, 1979; interview with Cornélio João Mondande on July 30, 1979; group interview with Tanga Karingade Tangadiea et al. on July 31, 1979; and Vieira, "Law," p. 13.

43. Vieira, "Law," p. 13.

44. Interview with Armando Baradas on August 30, 1977; Mondlane *Struggle for Mozambique,* pp. 172–178; *Daily News* (Dar es Salaam), April 4, 1972.

45. Quoted in Samora Machel, *Mozambique: Sowing the Seeds of Revolution* (London, 1974), pp. 172–174.

46. Quoted in Cornwall, *Bush Rebels,* pp. 68–69.

47. Interview with Cornélio João Mondande; on July 30, 1979; FRELIMO, *Documentos Base de FRELIMO,* pp. 92–149. D.T.I., *O processo revolucionário da guerra de libertação,* pp. 118–120.

48. The position paper of the Mozambican students is reprinted and translated in *African Historical Studies* 3 (1970):169–180; see also Munslow, "Leadership."

49. Uria T. Simango, "Gloomy Situation in Mozambique" (unpublished document, November 1969).

50. In an interview shortly before his assassination in 1969, Mondlane noted, "The very circumstances of our struggle have led us to formulate a Marxist-Leninist type of doctrine. The rich theoretical experience of Marxism-Leninism, the political, economic, and social development of the socialist countries during the past fifty years, including their errors, has been a source of inspiration for us." Quoted in Bragança, *A lutte de classes,* p. 17.

51. Quoted in Alpers, "Struggle for Socialism," p. 287.

52. Opello, "Pluralism and Elite Conflict," p. 77.

53. Simango, "Gloomy Situation in FRELIMO."

54. This biographical sketch comes from Agência de Informação de Moçambique

(A.I.M.), "Biography of President Samora Moises Machel"; Iain Christie, "Portrait of a President," *Africa Report* 21 (May-June 1976):15–16.

55. Quoted in Basil Davidson, "The Revolution in Mozambique," *People's Power* 32 (1980):77–78.

56. Interview with Samora Machel, president of Mozambique, on May 3, 1979.

57. Quoted in United Nations, General Assembly, A/9621: "Report of the Commission of Inquiry on the Reported Massacres in Mozambique," 1974, p. 15.

58. Ibid.

59. Ibid.

60. Ibid.

61. These figures are drawn from the following sources: Brenden F. Jundanian, "Resettlement Programs: Counterinsurgency in Mozambique" (paper presented at the meeting of the African Studies Association, Syracuse, N.Y., 1973), p. 6; United Nations, General Assembly: A/AC.109/L.388/2, "Territories Under Portuguese Administration," April 21, 1967: and United Nations, General Assembly, A/AC.109/1.919: "Mozambique," February 8, 1974.

62. J. De Sidro, "Whys and Wherefores of the War in Mozambique," *Portugal: An Informative Review* 19 (1972):10.

63. *New York Times*, February 12, 1972, p. 10.

64. Jundanian, "Resettlement Programs," pp. 12–20.

65. Quoted in Edward Alpers, "Ethnicity, Politics and History," *Africa Today* 21 (1974):42. See also Henriksen, *Mozambique*, pp. 196–197.

66. *Mozambique Revolution* 51 (1972):18.

67. Quoted in Mondlane, *Struggle for Mozambique*, p. 149.

68. For a discussion of the expansion and Africanization of the colonial army see United Nations, General Assembly, A/9621: "Report of the Commission of Inquiry on the Reported Massacres in Mozambique," 1974; United Nations, General Assembly, A/AC. 109/ L.919, February 8, 1974; Henriksen, *Mozambique*, pp. 197–198; and F. X. Maier, *Revolution and Terrorism* (New York, 1974), pp. 28–30.

69. Ibid.

70. United Nations, General Assembly, A/AC.109/L.919: February 8, 1974, p. 12. See also United Nations, General Assembly, A/9621: "Report on the Commission of Inquiry on the Reported Massacres in Mozambique," 1974; and Henriksen, *Mozambique*, pp. 209–210.

71. Interview with Arihdhi Mahanda on July 23, 1979.

72. Franco Nogueira, *The Third World* (London, 1967), p. 22.

73. George Kennan, "Hazardous Course in Southern Africa," *Foreign Affairs* 49 (1971):230.

74. For a discussion of increased Western investment see William Minter, *Portuguese Africa and the West* (New York, 1972), pp. 114–143.

75. For an analysis of the Cahora Bassa project see Keith Middlemas, *Cabora Bassa: Engineering and Politics in Southern Africa* (London, 1975).

76. For a discussion of U.S. and NATO military support for Portugal see S. J. Bosgra and Chr van Krimpen, *Portugal and NATO* (Amsterdam, 1972); Allen Isaacman and Jennifer Davis, "U.S. Policy Towards Mozambique, 1946–1976: The Defense of Colonialism and Regional Stability," in *American Policy in Southern Africa*, Rene LeMarchand, ed., (Washington, D.C., 1981), pp. 17–62.

77. Isaacman and Davis, "U.S. Policy," pp. 23–29.

78. Minter, *Portuguese Africa and the West*, p. 144.

79. United Nations, General Assembly, A/AC.109/1.919: February 8, 1974.

80. United Nations, General Assembly, A/9621: "Report on the Commission of Inquiry on the Reported Massacres in Mozambique," 1974.

81. For a different analysis of the coup in Portugal see Kenneth Maxwell, "Portugal: A Neat Revolution," *New York Review of Books*, June 13, 1974, pp. 16–21; Paul M. Sweezy, "Class Struggle in Portugal," *Monthly Review* 27 (September 1975):1–26; James Mittelman, "Some Reflections on Portugal's Counter-Revolution," *Monthly Review* 28 (March 1977):8–64.

82. Some of these organizations, such as GUMO, were nothing but puppet groups created with the approval of the Caetano regime, while others, like PCN, consisted of former FRELIMO members, including Uria Simango and Mateus Gwenjere.

83. Interview with João Nduvane on August 20, 1977; joint interview with Vasco Cubai and Elias Cubai on August 22, 1977; interview with Christiano Tiago Teela on August

26, 1977; and interview with Marcelino dos Santos, minister of planning, on September 26, 1977.

CHAPTER 6. THE MAKING OF A MOZAMBICAN NATION AND A SOCIALIST POLITY

1. On this broad theoretical issue see Paul M. Sweezy and Charles Bettleheim, *On the Transition to Socialism* (New York, 1981). For an important theoretical statement with specific reference to Mozambique see John Saul, "The Politics of Mozambican Socialism," in *Southern Africa: Society, Economy and Liberation*, David Wiley and Allen Isaacman, eds. (East Lansing, Mich., 1981), pp. 145–169.

2. Albie Sachs, "Mozambican Legal System" (unpublished manuscript, n.d.).

3. Quoted in *Review of African Political Economy* 4 (1975):23.

4. The only organized opposition was an abortive military coup in December, 1975, which lacked popular support. See the *Sun* (Baltimore), December 19, 1975.

5. Quoted in Robin Wright, "White Faces in a Black Crowd: Will They Stay?" (Alicia Patterson Foundation, May 27, 1975).

6. Samora Machel, *Mozambique: Sowing the Seeds of Revolution* (London, n.d.), p. 24.

7. Constituição da República Popular de Moçambique, Article 18.

8. For an analysis of the Nationalities Law and the government's stated objective of preventing Mozambican women married to Portuguese men, who according to the Portuguese nationality law were Portuguese citizens, from exploiting the advantages of dual citizenship, see Barbara Isaacman and June Stephen, *Mozambique: Women, the Law and Agrarian Reform* (Addis Ababa, 1980), pp. 29 and 40.

9. Samora Machel, "Education in Revolution," in *The Task Ahead: Selected Speeches of Samora Machel* (New York, 1975). For an important statement by Machel on the role of revolutionary culture in Mozambique see *Tempo* 431 (1979):1–16.

10. Interview with Acácio Soares on August 30, 1977.

11. Matéus Lampião, "Mozambique," in *Beyond the Skin*, Chris Searle, ed. (London, 1979), p. 7.

12. Interview with Armando Manuel Machay on August 21, 1977.

13. Interview with João Nduvane on August 20, 1977.

14. Interview with Marcelino dos Santos, minister of planning, on September 22, 1977.

15. Joint interview with Vasco Cubai and Elias Cubai on August 22, 1977.

16. Group interview at Vidreira glass factory on August 16, 1977.

17. Barry Munslow, "FRELIMO and the Socialist Transition in Mozambique, 1975–1982" (unpublished paper, 1982), p. 6.

18. *New York Times*, November 14, 1977.

19. See Allen Isaacman, *A Luta Continua: Creating a New Society in Mozambique* (Binghamton, N.Y., 1978), pp. 67–84.

20. *Tempo* 326 (1977):38–53; David Ottaway and Marina Ottaway, *Afrocommunism* (New York, 1981), p. 76.

21. Agência de Informação de Moçambique (A.I.M.), *Information Bulletin* 9-10 (1977):6.

22. Ibid, p. 11.

23. Ibid.

24. Mozambique, Angola, Guinea Information Centre (M.A.G.I.C.), *Central Committee Report to the Third Congress of FRELIMO* (London, 1978), p. 35.

25. Ibid., p. 43.

26. Interview with Alves Gomes on September 12, 1982.

27. Ibid.

28. In some cases, such as Communal Village Chicuedo in Niassa, participants acknowledged that the discussions were perfunctory and all the candidates were accepted. Group interview, Communal Village Chicuedo, on August 17, 1980.

29. Quoted in Peter Sketchley, "Forging the New Society: Steel-Making in Mozambique," *Southern Africa*, 13 (October 1980):4.

30. *Tempo* 413 (1978):27–29.

31. *Notícias* (Maputo), June 25, 1982.

32. "A Summary of the Work of the Central Committee of FRELIMO, Elected by the 3rd Congress, Maputo, August 7–16, 1978," A.I.M., *Information Bulletin Supplement* 32 (1978): Supplement, p. 3.

33. *Notícias*, September 12, 1982.

34. The incident involving the president's sister-in-law appeared as a leading item in both the country's newspapers.

35. A.I.M., *Information Bulletin* 47 (1980):17.

36. Ibid. 49 (1980):1.

37. Many Western observers incorrectly assumed that their removal from senior state positions was an indication of a diminished commitment to Marxism, as both have figured prominently in defining FRELIMO'S ideological stance.

38. Barry Munslow, "FRELIMO and the Socialist Transition in Mozambique" (unpublished paper, n.d., pp. 26–29).

39. Quoted in *Notícias*, June 7, 1981.

40. Quoted in Iain Christie and Joseph Hanlon, "Mozambique," *Africa Contemporary Record, 1982* (London, forthcoming).

41. Ibid.

42. See Isaacman and Stephen, *Mozambique: Women*, pp. 67–77.

43. Interview with Manuel Armando Machay on August 21, 1977.

44. See Isaacman and Stephen, *Mozambique: Women*.

45. Interview with Zacarias Kupela, secretary general of the Mozambique Youth Movement, on August 20, 1980.

46. *Notícias*, November 6, 1976.

47. *Tempo* 378 (1978):52.

48. *New York Times*, November 12, 1977.

49. Barbara Barnes, "Elections in Mozambique," *Southern Africa* 10 (April 1977):5–6.

50. Ibid.

51. Ibid., p. 4; *Tempo* 378 (1978):18.

52. *Tempo* 378 (1978):54.

53. Ibid.

54. Interview with Carlos Candido Laisse, national director of literacy education, on August 11, 1980.

55. This was obviously a cumbersome process that often caused long delays, as in the case of the proposed family code, which, after more than five years, is still being debated.

56. Interview with José Forjaz, deputy to the Popular Assembly, on December 11, 1978; and interview with Fernando Vaz, deputy to the Popular Assembly, on December 12, 1978.

57. See Decreto Lei 12/78, December 12, 1978.

58. Interview with Teodato Hunguana, minister of justice, on August 12, 1980; interview with Aires de Amaral, Senior Judge of the Maputo Provincial Court, on August 8, 1980; A.I.M., *Information Bulletin* 63 (1981):16.

59. Interview with Teodato Hunguana on August 12, 1980.

60. Tribunal Popular da Aldeia Communal de Muaria, "Registos de Actas" (unpublished, 1979).

61. Interview with Aires de Amaral on August 8, 1980.

62. These rights are guaranteed in Article 35 of the Constitution.

63. Interview with Aires de Amaral on August 8, 1980.

64. Interview with Mário Fumo Bartolomeu Mangage, national inspector for prison services, on August 22, 1980.

65. For a discussion of the reeducation camps see Barbara Isaacman and Allen Isaacman, "A Socialist Legal System in the Making: Mozambique Before and After Independence," *The Politics of Informal Justice*, Richard Abel, ed. (New York, 1980), 2:307–310.

66. *Tempo* 625 (1982):18.

67. See World Health Organization and United Nations Children's Fund, *National Decision Making for Primary Health Care* (Geneva, 1981).

68. Alexandre Goncalves, "Priorité a la médecine préventive," *Afrique-Asie* 217 (July 1980):47.

69. Isaacman, *A Luta Continua*, pp. 78–81.

70. Graça Machel, "The National System of Education," A.I.M., *Information Bulletin* 66 (1981):Supplement, p. 13.

71. The "barefoot doctors," or *agentes polivalentes elementares*, were chosen by their communities to get training in simple preventive and therapeutic skills and then to return home to teach the peasants how to protect themselves from the most common diseases. The system seems to have failed because no provisions were made to compensate the paramedics, other than the vaguely defined notion that the community would support them. The low level of collective production often made this impossible, and the paramedics either ceased their activity or departed.

72. Assemblia Popular, *Resolução Sobre a Ofensiva Política e Organizacional e o Trabalho das Assemblias de Povo e dos Deputados* (Maputo, July 1980).

73. Ibid.

74. For an excellent account and analysis of the offensive see Bertil Egero, *The Political Offensive, 1980–81, in Mozambique* (Stockholm, 1981).

75. Quoted in Christie and Hanlon, "Mozambique."

76. *Guardian* (Manchester), November 11, 1981.

77. Quoted in Christie and Hanlon, "Mozambique."

78. Quoted in *Southern Africa* 13 (June 1980):17.

CHAPTER 7. TRANSFORMING THE ECONOMY

1. For a discussion of the European flight see Allen Isaacman, *A Luta Continua: Creating a New Society in Mozambique* (Binghamton, N.Y., 1978), pp. 25–29.

2. Unpublished opening address by President Samora Machel to a Business International-sponsored conference on February 26, 1980, in Maputo.

3. These statistics were provided in an interview with Prakash Ratilal, vice-governor of the Bank of Mozambique, on September 8, 1979. Ratilal has subsequently been appointed minister and governor of the bank.

4. The United Nations provided some assistance for the Zimbabwean refugees. Nevertheless, the Mozambican government had to divert badly needed foodstuffs to the refugee camps. See United Nations, General Assembly, A/AC.109/1.388/Add. 3,17; United Nations, Economic and Social Council, E/5812: "Assistance to Mozambique," 22–24; and United Nations, Security Council, S/PV 1980, 18.

5. M.A.G.I.C., *Central Committee Report to the Third Congress of FRELIMO* (London, 1978), pp. 43–44.

6. At the time of the congress knowledge about the economy was extremely scanty. Production, distribution, trading, and employment statistics were lacking both for the last years of the colonial period and the immediate postindependence period. See Bertile Egero, *The Political Offensive, 1980–81, in Mozambique* (Stockholm, 1981), p. 5.

7. Moçambique, *Linhas fundamentais do plano prospectivo indicativo para 1981–1990* (Maputo, 1982), p. 6.

8. Samora Machel, "Our Plan Is the Key to Economic Victory," A.I.M., *Information Bulletin* 64 (1981): Supplement, p. 3.

9. Interview with Mário Machungo, minister of agriculture, on August 23, 1980.

10. This shortage also reflected the changing food habits of Africans, especially those living in urban centers, who began to consume potatoes, bread, and other commodities formerly eaten exclusively by the Europeans.

11. United States, Agency for International Development, *Development Needs and Opportunities for Cooperation in Southern Africa, Annex B, Agriculture* (Washington, D.C., March 1979), p. 3.

12. David Ottaway and Marina Ottaway, *Afrocommunism* (New York, 1981), p. 87.

13. *Daily News* (Dar es Salaam), December 31, 1981; *Africa Economic Digest* 3 (January 15, 1982):20.

14. Mozambique, *Linhas fundamentais do plano prospectivo.*

15. United Nations, General Assembly, A/36/267/S/14627: "Assistance to Mozambique," p. 3.

16. Mozambique, *Linhas fundamentais do plano prospectivo*, p. 8.

17. Interview with Mário Machungo on August 23, 1980; interview with Arnaldo Ribeiro on August 23, 1980; group interview, Inhassune state farm, on August 6, 1980; and group interview, Matama state farm, on August 20, 1980.

18. Mozambique, *Linhas fundamentais do plano prospectivo*, p. 18.

19. M.A.G.I.C., *Central Committee Report to the Third Congress of FRELIMO*, p. 46:

The legal underpinnings of the reorganization of the rural areas are found in the Constitution and in the Land Law and the Cooperative Law passed at the Fourth Session of the People's Assembly. Article 8 of the Constitution provides that "the land and the natural resources of the soil and sub-soil . . . are the property of the State," and Article 11 speaks of the State's support for the decision of peasants and workers to organize themselves in collective forms of production. These principles form the foundation for the Law which recognizes the inalienable character of the State's ownership of land and encourages the replacement of isolated family farming with agricultural cooperatives. The Law also recognizes the right of all Mozambicans to live on the land, work it and remove its riches so long as this is done for their consumption without the use of salaried workers. Agricultural cooperatives, which are the economic foundations on which communal villages are supposed to be built, are one of the types of cooperatives regulated by the Law of Cooperatives.

20. Interview with João Nduvane on August 20, 1977; interview with Francis Sumali on August 22, 1977; interview with Manuel Armando Machay on August 21, 1977; interview with Aurélio Manave, governor of Niassa, on August 21, 1980; and Barbara Isaacman and June Stephen, *Mozambique: Women, the Law, and Agrarian Reform* (Addis Ababa, 1980), p. 72.

21. Interview with João Nduvane on August 20, 1977; and *Tempo* 341 (1977):36.

22. *Notícias* (Maputo), June 9, 1977.

23. Inteview with Francis Sumoli on August 22, 1977; interview with Manuel Armando Machay on August 21, 1977; interview with António Fernando on August 5, 1980; and Isaacman and Stephen, *Mozambique: Women*, p. 72.

24. For accounts of the organization of early communal villages see *Tempo* 283 (1975):16-23; 284 (1975):46-55.

25. Other figures place the number at approximately 1,200,000 (*Notícias* [Maputo], August 28, 1982). Whatever the correct figure, however, the absence of coercion is the most salient feature of the move to communal villages, unlike state-organized collectivization programs in a number of other countries. Undoubtedly, there were some overzealous state officials and dynamizing group members who intimidated the local population, but this was in direct contravention of government policy, and guilty officials were publicly chastised.

26. A.I.M., *Information Bulletin* 64 (1981):1.

27. Gabinete de Organização e Desenvolvimento das Cooperativas Agrícolas, "Documento Final," August 15, 1980.

28. Joseph Hanlon, "Does Modernization Equal Mechanization?" *New Scientist* 79 (1978):562.

29. Similar sentiments were echoed by cooperative members with whom we spoke in Cabo Delgado, Gaza, Niassa, and Inhambane provinces.

30. A.I.M., *Information Bulletin* 64 (1981):1.

31. Laurence Harris, "Agricultural Cooperatives and Development Policy in Mozambique," *Journal of Peasant Studies* 7 (1980):343.

32. Group interview at Communal Village Chicuedo on August 7, 1980.

33. António Johala, "Mozambique," *Africa Guide* (London, forthcoming).

34. The decrease in available consumer goods occurred as a result of the increasing balance-of-payments problem, which prevented the importation of many basic commodities.

35. Interview with Tomás Salomão on September 14, 1982.

36. *Notícias*, August 12, 1977; *Tempo* 348 (1977):60-61; and interview with Custódio Machava on August 22, 1977.

37. See Isaacman, *A Luta Continua*, pp. 79-84.

38. *Notícias*, June 4, 1982.

39. Interview with António Hama Thai, governor of Greater Maputo, on September 13, 1982.

40. Acts of sabotage ranged from dismantling heavy equipment and smuggling it out of the country to falsifying bills of lading so that the government would authorize the transfer of hard currency for nonexistent overseas purchases. For a discussion of the acts of sabotage see *Africa* 78 (February 1978):16–17.

41. This summary of the Sena Sugar episode is based on discussions with officials at the Central Bank as well as on the contents of documents they provided for our perusal.

42. Egero, *Political Offensive*, p. 18.

43. Quoted in Allen Isaacman, "Les difficiles chemins d'une restructuration totale," *Afrique-Asie* 217 (July 1980):31–32. See also *Africa Report* 24 (1979):39–40.

44. Ibid.

45. Interview with Samora Machel, president of Mozambique, on May 6, 1979; and interview with Prakash Ratilal, vice-governor of the Bank of Mozambique, on August 12, 1980. It is also anticipated that all major agreements will be joint ventures, with the state retaining a significant, though not necessarily majority, presence.

46. Unpublished transcript of Machel's opening comments on February 26, 1980. For a broad discussion of the meeting, see *Tempo* 480 (1980):44–47.

47. *Notícias*, November 6, 1976.

48. Interview with Augusto Macamo, chair of the National Commission for the Implementation of Production Councils, on August 12, 1980; interview with Rodrigues Mondlana on August 21, 1977; interview with Tony Butcha on August 23, 1977; and Peter Sketchley and Frances Moore-Lappe, *Casting New Molds* (San Francisco, 1980), pp. 14–23.

49. Ibid.

50. Interview with Estevo Mabumo, member of the National Commission for the Implementation of Production Councils, on September 6, 1982.

51. Interview with Augusto Macamo on August 12, 1980.

52. Quoted in *Tempo* 359 (1977):35–36.

53. Quoted in Business International, *Mozambique: On the Road to Reconstruction and Development* (Geneva, 1980), p. 50.

54. Group interview at Companhia Industrial de Matola, on July 31, 1980. At a Maputo food-processing plant, for example, the private owners refused even to meet with the production council, which remained moribund until the newly formed party cell and the newly appointed state administrator encouraged it to assume its mandate.

55. Peter Sketchley, "Problems of the Transformation of Social Relations of Production in Post-Independence Mozambique" (unpublished paper, n.d.), p. 5. See also Sketchley and Moore-Lappe, *Casting New Molds*.

56. United Nations General Assembly, A/35/297/S/14007, June 30, 1981; United Nations, Assembly, A/36/267/S/14627, August 21, 1981; and *Africa Economic Digest* 3 (January 15, 1982):20.

57. Business International, *Mozambique*, pp. 50–51.

58. Interview with António Branco, minister of industry and energy, on September 13, 1982.

59. Mozambique, *Linhas fundamentais do plano perspectivo*, p. 6.

60. Ibid., p. 7.

61. *Notícias*, June 14, 1981.

62. Ibid.

63. In the last year before independence, Mozambique earned approximately $150 million from the remittances of approximately 100,000 miners. By 1978 the number of Mozambicans working in the mines had decreased to 30,000, and in that year the South African government abrogated the colonial sales agreement, which stipulated that 60 percent of each worker's salary be paid directly to the Portuguese authorities in Mozambique in gold at a low fixed exchange rate. The Portuguese paid the miners in escudos and then sold the gold on the international market at much higher prevailing rates, thus generating a substantial source of invisible income. This was one of the main ways in which South Africa propped up the sickly Portuguese economy.

64. Interview with António Branco on September 13, 1982.

65. Business International, *Mozambique*, p. 38.
66. António Johala, "Mozambique."

CHAPTER 8. INDEPENDENT MOZAMBIQUE IN THE WIDER WORLD

1. Interview with Marcelino dos Santos, minister of planning, on September 2, 1977.
2. Quoted in Marina Ottaway, "The Theory and Practice of Marxism-Leninism in Mozambique and Ethiopia," in *Communism in Africa*, David E. Albright, ed. (Bloomington, Ind., 1980), p. 141.
3. M.A.G.I.C., *The Central Committee Report to the Third Congress of FRELIMO* (London, 1978), pp. 29–31.
4. At a historic meeting with Zimbabwe guerrilla chiefs in 1970, Machel candidly acknowledged the interconnected nature of their struggle. "Some of us, when we look at the situation in Mozambique, realize if we liberate Mozambique tomorrow, that will not be the end, since the liberation of Mozambique without the liberation of Zimbabwe is meaningless." Quoted in David Martin and Phyllis Johnson, *The Struggle for Zimbabwe* (London, 1981), p. 17.
5. For an excellent account of Mozambique's complex relations with ZANU and ZAPU see Martin and Johnson, *Struggle for Zimbabwe*.
6. For an assessment of the economic effects on Mozambique of the boycott see United Nations, General Assembly A/32/96, June 9, 1977; United Nations, General Assembly, A/33/173, July 12, 1978; United Nations, General Assembly, A/34/377, August 16, 1979; and United Nations, General Assembly, A/35/297/S/14007, June 30, 1977.
7. On December 19, 1981, the Zimbabwean president paid an official state visit to Mozambique and signed a formal treaty of friendship that called for strengthening military and economic ties and reaffirmed their common commitment to the liberation of South Africa and Namibia. A.I.M., *Information Bulletin* 66 (1981): 18–19.
8. *New York Times*, August 13, 1981. South Africa, most experts agree, already has nuclear capability.
9. *Notícias* (Maputo), August 24, 1982.
10. Interview with Marcelino dos Santos on September 2, 1977.
11. Interview with Joaquim Chissano, Mozambican foreign minister, on October 15, 1982. In late 1974 President Machel met with ANC representatives and indicated that the war experience, in which ANC guerrillas based in Tete unsuccessfully tried to infiltrate into South Africa, had demonstrated the difficulty of using external bases from which to launch attacks and made it clear that Mozambique would not be in a position to provide such bases.
12. *Guardian* (Manchester), June 25, 1981.
13. A.I.M., *Information Bulletin* 69 (1982):6–8.
14. Interview with Joaquim Chissano on October 15, 1982.
15. The government in Maputo has gone out of its way to assist Lesotho and Swaziland and to defuse tensions with Malawi—all pro-Western nations with fundamentally different economic orientations. The opening of a permanent Malawian embassy in Maputo in June 1982 signaled a further improvement in relations between the two countries. *Tempo* 614 (1982):5.
16. A.I.M., *Information Bulletin* 53 (1980):1–11. It should be noted, however, that the $650 million pledged to SADCC is appreciably less than the $1.9 billion that the member states estimate they require for transportation and communications needs alone.
17. Interview with Luís Maria Alcántara Santos, minister of ports and surface transport, on September 6, 1982.
Interregional coordination of investment projects or trade is much more problematic, as Mozambique and Angola reject "market forces" in favor of socialist central planning and most of the other SADCC countries are committed to a capitalist economy. The positions of Zimbabwe and Tanzania are somewhat ambiguous.
18. Mozambique, Ministério de Portos e Transportes, Departamento Estatística, *Informação Estatística* 4 (1981):3.
19. Interview with Luís Maria Alcántara Santos on September 6, 1982.

20. Pretoria's strategy includes organizing guerrillas to attack the railroad lines, pressuring Zimbabwean firms (many of which are, in fact, controlled by South African capital), and trying to seduce Swaziland by offering the kingdom the Kangwane Bantustan and the Igwavuma strip.

21. See United Nations, General Assembly, A/32/96, June 9, 1977; United Nations, General Assembly, A/33/173, July 12, 1978; United Nations, General Assembly, A/34/377, August 16, 1979; and United Nations, General Assembly, A/35/297/S/14007, June 30, 1977.

22. *Africa Confidential* 23 (July 21, 1981):1. For a slightly different account of the MNR's origin see Gordon Winter, *Inside Boss* (New York, 1981), p. 545.

23. Ibid.; *Sunday Times* (London), January 26, 1975; and *Domingo* (Maputo), January 10, 1982.

24. Resistência Nacional de Moçambique (MNR), "Comando Geral," Afonso Macacho Marceta Dhlakama, Supreme Commander, November 28, 1980.

25. MNR, "Relatório Referente a Sessão do Trabalho de R.N.M.E. do Representativo do Governo Sul Africano," Afonso Macacho Marceta Dhlakama, October 25, 1980.

26. Ibid.

27. Increased South African economic pressure on Angola and assistance given to insurgent UNITA forces there that enable them to disrupt the Benguela railroad, a major transportation network linking the copper belt of Zambia and Zaire to international markets, support this interpretation.

28. Group interview, Army General Staff, Maputo, on September 13, 1982; A.I.M., *Information Bulletin* 72 (1982):5; *Guardian* (Manchester), December 16, 1980; and Luís Lemos, "Mabote 2: The People Fight Back," Mozambique News Agency Feature (Maputo, 1982), pp. 3–4.

29. Ibid.; *Guardian*, August 20, 1982.

30. Group interview, Army General Staff, Maputo, on September 13, 1982; and interview with António Hama Thai, governor of Greater Maputo, on September 13, 1982.

31. Samora Machel, "The Path Ahead for the O.A.U.," A.I.M., *Information Bulletin* 25 (1979): Supplement, p. 6.

32. Samora Machel, speech at the Sixth Conference of Heads of State and Government of the Non-Aligned Countries, Havana, Cuba, September 4, 1979, A.I.M., *Information Bulletin* 39 (1979): Supplement, p. 6.

33. Samora Machel, "The Primary Task: The Liberation of Africa," A.I.M., *Information Bulletin* 49 (1980): Supplement p. 5.

34. Interview with Joaquim Chissano on October 15, 1982.

35. This interpretation was denied explicitly by the Mozambican foreign minister, Joaquim Chissano.

36. Interview with Prakash Ratilal, vice-governor of the Bank of Mozambique, on August 12, 1980; and A.I.M., *Information Bulletin* 70 (1982):2.

37. Mozambique has a permanent ambassadorial-level delegation in Portugal as well. In addition, since independence, there has been a permanent Mozambican representative to the United Nations.

38. Mozambican officials have privately expressed anger when comparing the types of weapons Moscow provided Ethiopia, South Yemen, Angola, and even ZAPU with the weapons Mozambique purchases. All these countries have received MiG-21s or MiG-23s, and ZAPU pilots were trained to fly both; Mozambique's air force has only Korean war–vintage MiG-17s. Moreover, the Soviet Union delayed sending spare parts for helicopters because Mozambique lacked the hard currency to pay for them. On the other hand, Mozambique has sources of arms other than the socialist countries, and other front-line nations have informed the Mozambicans that South Africa is able to find out what arms they have acquired from the West even before they arrive.

39. For a discussion of these military arrangements see Irving Kaplan, *Area Handbook for Mozambique* (Washington, D.C., 1977), pp. 201–206; George T. Yu, "Sino-Soviet Rivalry in Africa," in Albright, *Communism in Africa*, pp. 168–188; William M. LeoGrande, "Cuban-Soviet Relations and Cuban Policy in Africa," *Cuban Studies* 10 (1980):1–37; and *Notícias*, May 31, 1982. Information on the Cuban presence was provided in an interview with Foreign Minister Joaquim Chissano on October 15, 1982.

40. *Guardian,* February 22, 1980.

41. *Notícias,* May 29, 1982; and June 2, 1982.

42. The barter arrangements, primarily with East Germany, Bulgaria, and the USSR, are based on the principle of "mutual benefit." The Eastern European countries obtain a number of highly desirable raw materials without foreign exchange expenditures and Mozambique receives deliveries of badly needed manufactured goods, including machinery, trucks, agricultural equipment, canned foods, clothing, and household equipment. In short, both parties exchange desired commodities without foreign exchange expenditures.

Critics contend, however, that Mozambique is merely mortgaging its future in exchange for inferior products and that it would do better selling these commodities on the international market rather than working through socialist countries who often resell Mozambican products for substantial profits. For a detailed discussion of the barter arrangements see Wolfgang Schoeller, "Determinants of Economic Cooperation Between CME Countries and Underdeveloped Countries—Demonstrated in the Case of Mozambique," paper presented at the International Conference on Law and Economy in Africa, Ile-Ife, Nigeria, February 15–20, 1982.

43. Business International, *Mozambique, On tne Road to Reconstruction and Development* (Geneva, 1980), p. 38.

44. Ibid.; A.I.M., *Information Bulletin* 70 (1982):9; and Schoeller, "Determinants of Economic Cooperation," pp. 12–13.

45. Expatriates from the Warsaw countries, like those from the West, receive part of their salary in hard currency and part in local currency. The Cubans, on the other hand, receive their entire salary in meticais (Mozambican currency), thus permitting Mozambique to save badly needed hard currency.

46. *Guardian,* February 20, 1980.

47. Quoted in *Christian Science Monitor* (Boston), November 19, 1980.

48. Interview with Valeriano Ferrão, secretary of state for foreign affairs, on August 12, 1980.

49. *International Herald Tribune* (Paris), December 4, 1975; and James H. Mittelman, *Underdevelopment and the Transition to Socialism: Mozambique and Tanzania* (New York, 1981), p. 118.

50. Interview with Joaquim Chissano on October 15, 1982.

51. Quoted in David E. Albright, "Moscow's African Policy of the 1970s," in idem, *Communism in Africa,* p. 44.

52. Quoted in John Saul, "Mozambique: The New Phase," in idem, *The State and Revolution in Eastern Africa* (New York, 1979), p. 443.

53. For a discussion of tacit Soviet support for the 1977 insurrection led by Neto Alves and for Cuba's continued and explicit support of the government of President Neto, see LeoGrande, "Cuban-Soviet Relations," pp. 17–18. Almost immediately after the coup attempt Mozambique sent a high-level delegation to Angola to analyze the causes of the coup and the responses of various powers.

54. *Foreign Report* 1721 (March 25, 1982):6–7; and Schoeller, "Determinants of Economic Cooperation," pp. 14–17. Despite this reported decision, officials emphasized that "Mozambique is on the road to COMECON membership." *Guardian,* July 27, 1981.

55. *Foreign Report* 1721 (March 25, 1982):6–7.

56. "Extracts from the Report of the Standing Political Committee to the Fourth Session of the Central Committee of FRELIMO, Maputo, August 7–16, 1978," A.I.M., *Information Bulletin* 26 (1978): Supplement, p. 17.

57. Interview with Joaquim Chissano on October 15, 1982. The agreement enabled Mozambique to acquire badly needed agricultural implements and consumer goods to distribute to the peasantry.

58. Interview with Prakash Ratilal on August 12, 1980.

59. "Extracts from the Report of the Standing Political Committee," p. 14.

60. Interview with Samora Machel, president of Mozambique, *Africa Report* 24 (July-August 1979):43.

61. *Tempo* 385 (1978):21–22.

62. For information on the economic agreements with Western countries see Business

International, *Mozambique,* pp. 31–41; *Financial Times* (London), September 26, 1981; *Rand Daily Mail* (Johannesburg), January 30, 1981; *Notícias,* June 7, 1982; *Guardian,* May 25, 1981; and A.I.M., *Information Bulletin* 59 (1981):26–29, and 66 (1981):29. In addition to expressing concern about U.S. hostility, Mozambican officials emphasize West German efforts to block aid to Mozambique because until 1982 it refused to accept the "Berlin clause." See *African Business* 29 (1981):11–13; and *Guardian,* May 25, 1981.

    63. *Financial Times,* December 7, 1981; and *Tempo* 610 (1982):22–23.

    64. Quoted in *Tempo* 610 (1982):22–23.

    65. For a detailed Mozambican account of the CIA operations see Abel Mutemba, *Operação 6⁰ Anniversário: Como uma rede de CIA foi desmantelada em Moçambique* (Maputo, 1981).

    66. Interview with Joaquim Chissano on October 15, 1982.

    67. Interview with Prakash Ratilal on September 6, 1982.

    68. *African Business* 2 (1978):31; and *Guardian,* September 9, 1980.

    69. Interview with Joaquim Chissano on October 15, 1982.

Glossary

aldeamentos: Strategic hamlets organized by the Portuguese state as part of its counter-insurgency efforts against FRELIMO.

assimilados: Africans and mestizos whom the Portuguese state considered to have mastered the Portuguese culture and language.

Angoche: A Muslim sultanate and trading entrepôt located along the coast of northern Mozambique.

Barue: A Shona state located just south of the Zambesi River, long involved in anticolonial resistance.

Bonga: Afro-Goan warlord and owner of *prazo* Massangano.

Caetano, Marcello: Hand-picked successor of Portuguese dictator Antonio Salazar. He ruled from 1968 to 1974.

CAIL: The Limpopo Agro-Industrial Complex, located in Gaza Province in southern Mozambique.

chefes de posto: Local Portuguese adminstrators.

chibalo: Forced labor.

Chikunda: Originally warrior slaves on the Zambesi *prazos* and the conquest states that developed out of the *prazo* system. Many subsequently fled into the interior where they became a distinct ethnic group.

Chissano, Joaquim: Head of the transitional government (1974–1975) and currently foreign minister and member of the Standing Political Committee and Secretariat of FRELIMO. Ranked third on the Central Committee.

Chope: A southern Mozambique ethnic group that was conquered by the Gaza Nguni in the nineteenth century.

CONCP: An umbrella organization linking the nationalist organizations in Angola, Guinea-Bissau, and Mozambique.

EMOCHA: The state tea farm located in Zambesia Province, which employs 14,000 workers.

FRELIMO: The Mozambican liberation movement, which directed the armed struggle and is now the governing party in Mozambique.

Gaza Nguni: An immigrant group that fled from what is now South Africa into southern Mozambique and controlled much of the territory from the Lourenço Marques hinterland to the Zambesi River during much of the nineteenth century.

Gungunyane: The Gaza Nguni ruler at the end of the nineteenth century who led the fight against Portuguese imperialism in southern Mozambique.

indígenas: Unassimilated Africans and mulattoes as defined by the *indigenato* system.

indigenato: A legal system based on social and political inequality in which the African and mulatto population was divided into two juridical categories—*indígenas* and *assimilados.*

Lourenço Marques: The colonial capital of Mozambique located in the far south of the country. After independence its name was changed to Maputo.

MANU: An early nationalist movement that in 1962 became part of FRELIMO.

Machel, Samora Moises: First party secretary of FRELIMO, president of the People's Republic of Mozambique, and commander in chief of the army.

Makanhila: A Yao chief and slaver.

223

Makua: An ethnic group living in northern Mozambique. Makua chiefs and merchants were involved in the slave trade.

Malawi (Maravi) Confederation: A major political system in the seventeeth and eighteenth centuries located just north of the Zambesi River.

Mataka: A Yao chief and slaver.

Matakenya: An Afro-Goan warlord and slave trader who controlled a vast empire near Zumbo.

Mondlane, Eduardo: First president of FRELIMO. He was killed in 1969 by a Portuguese letter bomb.

Mossuril: A northern trading entrepôt located opposite Mozambique Island.

Muenemutapa: Personal title of the king of the Shona kingdom bearing that name. The kingdom, located south of the Zambesi River, was among the most powerful states in Mozambique during the sixteenth and seventeenth centuries.

NESAM: Mozambican student movement, which was organized in the late 1940s and became a center of early nationalist thought.

OJM: The Mozambique Youth Movement.

OMM: The Mozambique Women's Movement.

PIDE: The Portuguese secret police (the acronym was later changed to DGS).

prazos da coroa: Portuguese crown estates, located primarily in the Zambesi Valley.

prazeiros: Crown estate owners who progressively became Africanized.

Quelimane: A coastal port town just north of the Zambesi. In the nineteenth century it became a major slave-exporting entrepôt.

Rebelo, Jorge: FRELIMO party secretary for ideology and high-ranking member of the Central Committee, formerly minister of information.

Salazar, António: Portuguese dictator (1928–1968).

Santos, Marcelino dos: Founding member of FRELIMO and currently FRELIMO party secretary for economic planning and development; ranked second on the Central Committee.

Sofala: The first Portuguese administrative and trading center in Mozambique, located on the Indian Ocean not far from Beira.

Tonga: A common ethnic nomenclature in Mozambique. There are at least two different groups called Tonga. The Zambesi Tonga are a Shona-related people living between the towns of Sena and Tete. The southern Tonga live in the Inhambane hinterland and were incorporated into the Gaza Nguni empire.

sipais: African police in the service of the colonial state.

Soshangane: King of the Gaza Nguni.

UDENAMO: One of the first nationalist movements, which in 1962 became part of FRELIMO.

UNAMI: An early nationalist movement, which in 1962 became part of FRELIMO.

Yao: An ethnic group living in northern Mozambique. The Yao were renowned elephant hunters and traders who in the eighteenth and nineteenth centuries played an important part in the slave trade.

Abbreviations

ANC	African National Congress
APIE	State Housing Authority
CAIL	Limpopo Agro-industrial Complex
CIA	Central Intelligence Agency
COMECON	Council for Mutual Economic Assistance
CONCP	Conference of Nationalist Organizations of the Portuguese Colonies
EEC	European Economic Community
EPLF	Eritrean People's Liberation Front
FREITLIN	Front for the Independence of East Timor
FRELIMO	Front for the Liberation of Mozambique
GNP	gross national product
MANU	Mozambican-Makonde Union
MNR	Mozambique National Resistance
NATO	North Atlantic Treaty Organization
NESAM	Nucleus of African Secondary Students of Mozambique
OAU	Organization of African Unity
OJM	Mozambique Youth Movement
OMM	Mozambique Women's Movement
PIDE	Portuguese secret police
PLO	Palestine Liberation Organization
SADCC	Southern African Development Coordination Conference
SWAPO	South West African People's Organization
UDENAMO	National Democratic Union of Mozambique
UNAMI	National African Union of Independent Mozambique
WNLA	Witwatersrand Native Labour Association
ZANU	Zimbabwe African National Union
ZAPU	Zimbabwe African People's Union

Additional Readings

Listed below are a number of books and dissertations published in English. They are divided into chronological periods that roughly parallel the organization of this book. There are a number of journals that regularly publish articles on Mozambique, including the *International Journal of African Historical Studies*, the *Journal of African History*, the *Journal of Southern African Studies*, the *Review of African Political Economy*, and *Southern Africa*.

THE PRECOLONIAL PERIOD

Alpers, Edward A. *Ivory and Slaves in East Central Africa*. Berkeley, 1975.

Axelson, Eric. *Portugal and the Scramble for Africa*. Johannesburg, 1967.

Beach, David. *The Shona and Zimbabwe, 900–1850.*, New York, 1980.

Bhila, Hoyini. *Trade and Politics in a Shona Kingdom*. New York, 1982.

Gray, R., and Birmingham, D. *Pre-Colonial African Trade*. London, 1980.

Hafkin, Nancy. "Trade Society and Politics in Northern Mozambique, 1753–1913." Ph.D. dissertation, Boston University, 1973.

Isaacman, Allen. *Mozambique: The Africanization of a European Institution, The Zambesi Prazos 1750–1902*. Madison, 1972.

Langworthy, Harry. "A History of the Undi to 1890." Ph.D. dissertation, Boston University, 1969.

Mudenge, Stan. "The Rozvi Empire of the Feira of Zumbo." Ph.D. dissertation, University of London, School of Oriental and African Studies, 1972.

Newitt, M.D.D. *Portuguese Settlement on the Zambesi*. New York, 1973.

Phiri, King Mbacazwa. "Chewa History in Central Malawi and the Use of Oral Tradition, 1600–1920." Ph.D. dissertation, University of Wisconsin, 1975.

Randles, W.G.L. *The Empire of Monomotapa from the Fifteenth to the Nineteenth Centuries*. Gwelo, 1981.

Smith, Alan. "Trade and Politics in Southern Mozambique." Ph.D. dissertation, University of California, 1970.

Thompson, Leonard, ed. *African Societies in Southern Africa*. London, 1969.

THE COLONIAL PERIOD

Centro de Estudos Africanos. *The Mozambican Miner*. Maputo, 1977.

Duffy, James. *Portuguese Africa*. Cambridge, 1961.

———. *A Question of Slavery*. Oxford, 1967.

Hamilton, Russell. *Voices from an Empire*. Minneapolis, 1972.

Henriksen, Thomas. *Mozambique: A History*. London, 1978.

Isaacman, Allen (in collaboration with Barbara Isaacman). *The Tradition of Resistance in Mozambique*. Berkeley, 1976.

Middlemas, K. *Cabora Bassa: Engineering and Politics in Southern Africa*. London, 1975.

Minter, William. *Portugal and the West*. New York, 1972.

Palmer, R., and Parson, N. *The Roots of Rural Poverty in Central and Southern Africa.* London, 1977.
Penvenne, Jeanne Marie. "A History of African Labor in Lourenço Marques, Mozambique, 1877 to 1950." Ph.D. dissertation, Boston University, 1982.
Vail, H. Leroy, and White, Landeg. *Capitalism and Colonialism in Mozambique.* Minneapolis, 1980.

THE ARMED STRUGGLE

Cabral, Amilcar. *Return to the Source: Select Speeches of Amilcar Cabral.* New York, 1973.
Chilcote, Ronald, ed. *Emerging Nationalism in Portuguese Africa.* Stanford, 1972.
Cornwall, Barbara. *The Bush Rebels.* London, 1973.
Davidson, Basil, et al. *Southern Africa.* New York, 1976.
Dickinson, M., ed. *When Bullets Begin to Flower.* Nairobi, 1972.
First, Ruth. *Portugal's War in Africa.* London, 1971.
Friedland, Elaine Alice. "A Comparative Study of the Development of Revolutionary Nationalist Movements in Southern Africa—FRELIMO (Mozambique) and the African National Congress of South Africa." Ph.D. dissertation, City University of New York, 1980.
Hastings, A. *Wiriyamu.* London, 1974.
Machel, Samora. *Mozambique: Sowing the Seeds of Revolution.* London, 1974.
Mondlane, Eduardo. *The Struggle for Mozambique.* Baltimore, 1969.
Munslow, Barry. *Mozambique: The Revolution and Its Origin.* London, 1983.
Paul, J. *Memoirs of a Revolution.* London, 1975.
Panaf Great Lives. *Eduardo Mondlane.* London, 1972.
Saul, John. *The State and Revolution in Eastern Africa.* New York, 1979.

THE POSTINDEPENDENCE PERIOD

Isaacman, Allen. *A Luta Continua: Creating a New Society in Mozambique.* Binghamton, N.Y. 1978.
Isaacman, Barbara, and Stephen, June. *Mozambique: Women, the Law and Agrarian Reform.* Addis Ababa, 1980.
Machel, Samora. *Establishing People's Power to Serve the Masses.* Toronto, 1976.
Mittelman, James H. *Underdevelopment and the Transition to Socialism: Mozambique and Tanzania.* New York, 1981.
Saul, John, ed. *A Different Road? Socialism in Mozambique.* New York, 1983.
Thompson, Carol. *Challenge to Imperialism: The Frontline States in the Liberation of Zimbabwe.* Boulder, 1983.
Torp, J. E. *Industrial Planning and Development in Mozambique.* Copenhagen, 1978.

Index

About the Book and Authors

MOZAMBIQUE
From Colonialism to Revolution, 1900–1982
Allen Isaacman and Barbara Isaacman

Straddling the Indian Ocean and the volatile world of racially divided Southern Africa, Mozambique has assumed an increasingly strategic position. Its 2,000-mile coastline and three major ports of Maputo, Beira, and Nacala—all ideally suited for naval bases—have long been coveted by the superpowers. No less important is Mozambique's proximity to South Africa and Zimbabwe, which gained its independence in 1980 with substantial military and strategic assistance from Mozambique. The country's enormous mineral potential is another key factor.

Underdevelopment, oppression, and mass deprivation constitute recurring themes in Mozambican history; but so, too, does a long tradition of resistance. The country merits attention as well for its highly visible campaign against "tribalism" and racism—an unprecedented move on a continent marred by ethnic, religious, and regional conflict.

Drawing on oral interviews as well as written primary sources, the authors of this profile of Mozambique focus on the changing and complex Mozambican reality.

Dr. Allen Isaacman is professor of history at the University of Minnesota and has taught at the University Eduardo Mondlane in Mozambique. His study *Mozambique: The Africanization of a European Institution: The Zambasi Prazos, 1750–1902* (1973) won the Melville Herskovits Award in 1973 as the most distinguished book in African studies. His other works include *The Tradition of Resistance in Mozambique* (1976; in collaboration with Barbara Isaacman) and *A Luta Continua: Creating a New Society in Mozambique* (1978). **Barbara Isaacman,** a lawyer, has also taught at the University Eduardo Mondlane. She is coauthor of *Mozambique: Women, the Law and Agrarian Reform* (1980).